THE COLLEGE DEVALUATION CRISIS

THE COLLEGE DEVALUATION CRISIS

MARKET DISRUPTION, DIMINISHING ROI, AND AN ALTERNATIVE FUTURE OF LEARNING

Jason Wingard

STANFORD BUSINESS BOOKS
STANFORD UNIVERSITY PRESS
STANFORD, CALIFORNIA

Stanford University Press
Stanford, California

Special discounts for bulk quantities of Stanford Business Books are available to corporations, professional associations, and other organizations. For details and discount information, contact the special sales department of Stanford University Press. Tel: (650) 725-0820,
Fax: (650) 725-3457

Printed in the United States of America on acid-free, archival-quality paper

All figures are by Hanna Manninen, except as noted.

Library of Congress Cataloging-in-Publication Data

Names: Wingard, Jason, author.
Title: The college devaluation crisis : market disruption, diminishing ROI,
    and an alternative future of learning / Jason Wingard.
Description: Stanford, California : Stanford Business Books, an imprint of
    Stanford University Press, 2022. | Includes bibliographical references
    and index.
Identifiers: LCCN 2021056561 (print) | LCCN 2021056562 (ebook) | ISBN
    9781503627536 (cloth) | ISBN 9781503632219 (ebook)
Subjects: LCSH: Labor supply—Effect of education on—United States. |
    Employees—Training of—United States. | College
    graduates—Employment—United States. | Vocational
    qualifications—United States. | Education, Higher—Economic
    aspects—United States.
Classification: LCC HD5724 .W556 2022 (print) | LCC HD5724 (ebook) | DDC
    331.110973—dc23/eng/20220315
LC record available at https://lccn.loc.gov/2021056561
LC ebook record available at https://lccn.loc.gov/2021056562

Cover design: Tandem Design

To Gingi:
Partner-in-Charge.
Partner-in-Learning.
Partner-in-Life.

"Never let formal education get in the way of your learning."
—Mark Twain

CONTENTS

PREFACE

I am a fourth-generation descendant of slaves—slaves who toiled in the fields of Wingard Plantation in Wingard, Alabama—and I am the child of a family dedicated to, and beneficiaries of, education and professional development.

Although my paternal grandparents had only fourth- and eighth-grade educations, respectively, they nevertheless managed to instill in the minds of their six children the value of education. They saw it as a way that African-American families—*all* families—could rise up out of slavery, or poverty, or a systemic lack of access to benefits. For them, the very "saving" of America rested on getting an education, and they embodied the value of education as a prioritized and imminent pursuit. Five of those children earned college degrees, five earned master's degrees, and two, including my father, earned doctorates.

My father retired from a career in education with a final job as a public school superintendent. My mother retired from her position as head of human resources in the insurance industry. My sister earned her doctorate in English and is currently a college professor. I hold four academic degrees; my wife has two.

My extended family of aunts, uncles, and cousins holds jobs ranging from Wall Street executives and CEOs to college deans and prison wardens to judges and lawyers to colonels and entrepreneurs to physicians, nurses, and engineers.

Education degrees, in short, run rampant in my family.

My own twenty-five-year (as of 2021) professional career has focused on the education ecosystem—corporate, nonprofit, higher education, and K–12.

The educational degrees I have received were granted from Stanford, Emory, Harvard, and the University of Pennsylvania, while a selected sample of my job descriptions represent the aforementioned ecosystem diversity: president at Temple; dean at Columbia; chief learning officer at Goldman Sachs; vice dean at Wharton; executive director at Stanford; senior fellow at the Aspen Institute, and senior vice president at ePals and CEO of the ePals Foundation.

I value education. I have seen how it has advanced my family, and so many

Photo 1. Wingard Homestead Circa 1945. Credit: Dr. Edward L. Wingard.

other families, and I am aware of the benefits it has brought to my own career. To me, education is the best mechanism for inspiring talent, the best tool for measuring learning and achievement, the best foundational access to thought leadership at the highest level.

Three of my children are currently pursuing Columbia degrees. My wife and I certainly hope our other two children also attend college and earn degrees—to continue the legacy of opportunity for upward mobility that the degree has proven to be for our family over the last hundred years. To me, it remains an enabler of success and the basis of an individual's ability to rise to his or her rightful place in society and to a personally fulfilling life.

I first started to pay attention to the economic value of the degree in the summer of 2017. As a dean at Columbia, I oversaw not just a graduate school featuring sixteen master of science degrees, but also Columbia University's programs for high school students. That summer, I noticed a dramatic shift in the number of top employers recruiting directly from the pool of high school students in the summer program—and away from the pool of students in the undergraduate and graduate programs.

Something was up. The world's top companies recruiting directly from high schools for professional roles previously reserved for college graduates? What was going on? Did these young students know enough? What was the angle?

When I looked into it, the rationale I heard from the employers was that placement and performance data at the company level showed declining levels of job readiness and hiring satisfaction from college and graduate school hires. As a result, the hiring companies had to invest resources to train their newly trained college graduates in the skills needed to do the work. Since the college degree had ceased to be a guarantee that employers were going to get what they needed, why not hire younger and cheaper—right out of high school? Invest the time and money, instead, to train high school graduates and gain the likely benefit of retaining them longer.

I then embarked on a couple of years' worth of interviewing among recent college graduates at Columbia and around the country to try to learn how, in their eyes, their formal education had prepared them for their jobs. I also interviewed as many, if not more, employers on the same topic, with a special emphasis on interviews with senior leaders on-site at Fortune 500 companies. I held focus groups with lay people about their thoughts on the topic and about any experience with similar outcomes.

Overall, my research revealed that most Americans still believe a college degree is a pathway to professional success, and that most professional employers still selectively hire from colleges and universities for their junior talent. The value of the college degree still outpaces all other forms of professional preparation. But my research definitely leads me to believe that the sonic boom has been heard, and that a seismic shift is under way. The value of the college degree, in my estimation, has reached its peak and is on the wane, thanks to a host of factors stretching from cost and affordability to curriculum relevance to rapidly evolving skill needs to advances in automation and technology—and including the disruption in the workforce due to the COVID-19 pandemic.

As president of Temple University, and professor of human resource development and organizational leadership, I aggressively challenge students, faculty, employers, and policymakers to proactively and continually scan the marketplace, plan scenarios, and predetermine changes in job contexts and market dynamics. By my own advice, it looks to me like the industry in which I work is at risk. Higher education is under fire. Higher education is losing its value. As of this writing, we may still be "winning," but I don't see the winning as permanent. Some educational institutions are, in fact, currently losing to the point of extinction, while alternative organizations to college are capturing more and more competitive market share. Why is that? How is it happening? What actions can reverse the new trends? Will the next generation of students be predestined for college, or does the future suggest another route to skilled readiness? Will higher education pivot and adapt to resume supreme relevance, or will it resist change and be replaced? These are questions for Temple. These are questions for our global industry peers.

In this book, I explore the plight in which the college degree now finds itself. I bring to this examination what I've learned through research, executive and operational management, leadership training, and executive coaching—all needed, I believe, to examine the complexities of both the current context and the likely future of learning. People have asked how, as a university president and professor, I can write a book that questions the value of the product I "sell"; how can I support my day job while profiling, or even championing, the successes of competitive alternatives?

Well, Readers and Friends, that is academic scholarship—and may the best solution win!

Dr. Jason Wingard
Philadelphia
October 11, 2021

ACKNOWLEDGMENTS

The process of writing a book requires a multistakeholder village replete with diverse, collaborative partnerships and a committed support network.

I have been blessed with a community of allies, advocates, collaborators, and champions who have allowed me to realize the goal of advancing this research project. I owe a debt of gratitude to the following:

G. My wife, Gingi, stands beside me . . . always.

J-Krew. My kids, Jaelyn, Jaia, Jazze, Joye, and Jaxen Wingard, motivate me to pursue personal and professional excellence with balance.

Nuclear. My parents, Marcellene and Dr. Levi Wingard, love me, unconditionally, and pray for me, constantly. My sister, Dr. Leslie Wingard, inspires me to never stop. . . .

Ansley & Big'm. My elders, Jesse L. Wingard, Alice Wingard, Grady Wingard, Edward Wingard, Gloria Wingard, Jesse R. Wingard, Marline Wingard, Lanette Wingard, Lela Wingard Hughes, Leon Hughes, Stella Wingard, Azalea Yarbrough, Leona Langford, Sherman Jones Sr., Hennade Jones, Sue Elster, Leona Langford, Elizabeth Mitchell, James Mitchell, Jackie Barnes-Newsome, Larry Newsome, and Sherman Jones Jr. decry, as an everlasting value, "Boy, you better learn!"

'Laws. My mother and father-in-law, Dr. Alice and Joseph Duff, model, for me, uncompromised commitment to the cause. My sister and brother-in-law, Dr. Laura Stephenson and Dr. Jason Stephenson, serve as reminders to teach.

Book'ers. My research and developmental editing team, Susanna Margolis, Katie Sievers, Dr. Michelle LaPointe, Bianca Swift, and Arthur Goldwag, represent best-in-class professionalism and quality scholarship; their collaboration with me was absolutely instrumental. My illustrator, Hanna Manninen, deftly used the power of graphic design to convey complex ideas. My publishing editor, Steve Catalano, supported me with patience, kindness, and broad subject-matter expertise. My literary agent, Susan Ginsburg, held me to the highest standard.

And my public relations firm, Goodman Media (Tom Goodman, John Lee, Emma Lowenstein), exposed my thought leadership to a global audience.

@Columbia. My colleagues, Dr. David Madigan, Dr. Alondra Nelson, Dr. Kathy Phillips, Dr. Linda Fried, Dr. Carol Becker, Dr. Brent Stockwell, Suzanne Goldberg, Dr. Dennis Mitchell, Dr. Christine Farrugia, Yurij Pawluk, Ariel Fleurimond, Josh Burgher, Ronald Mangiacapara, Vanessa Carrillo, Dr. Matthew Connelly, Dr. Geraldine Downey, Dr. Dan O'Flaherty, Dr. Sam Roberts, Dr. Josef Soret, Dr. Greg Wawro, Dr. Josh Whitford, Dr. David Hadju, Raquel Munoz, Francisco Pineda, Alex della Rocca, Amanda Nelson, Caroline Henley, Anne Thornton, Nikisha Alcindor, Dr. Stephanie Rowley, Dr. Larry Rowley, Dr. Lisa Rosen-Metsch, Amanda Vogel, Scott Rosner, Andy Atzert, Dr. Tatum Thomas, Dr. Erik Nelson, Solveig Nicklos, and Dr. Yvette Burton, inspired and influenced my research agenda. My board, Ram Vittal (JPMorgan), Troy Vincent (NFL), Umran Beba (Pepsico), Gayatri Devi (Park Avenue Neurology), Don Duet (Goldman Sachs), Randall Lane (Forbes), Lisa Lutoff-Perlo (Celebrity Cruises), Eric Haller (Experian), Bennie Johnson (AIGA), Mike Ulica (National Geographic), and Jorge Rodriguez (Claro Enterprises), challenged me to disrupt higher education. And my teaching associates, Dr. Kristine Kerr, Dr. Reshan Richards, and Sarah Daly-Padron, taught me how to be a better educator.

Peer Peeps. My fellow deans of schools of professional and continuing education, Hunt Lambert (Harvard), Dan Colman (Stanford), Jonathan Michie (Oxford), James Gazzard (Cambridge), Robert Bruce (Rice), Thomas Gibbons (Northwestern), Leah VanWey (Brown), Diana Wu (Berkeley), Nora Lewis (UPenn), Christopher Guymon (Chicago), Carola Weil (McGill), Aaron Brewer (Wisconsin), Nelson Baker (Georgia Tech), Kelly Otter (Georgetown), David Schejbal (Marquette), Mark Rollins (Washington, St. Louis), Stephen Walls (Texas), Sarah Thompson (Colorado), Rovy Branon (Washington), Susan Catron (UC Davis), Mary Walshok (UCSD), Betty Vandenbosch (Purdue), Maureen MacDonald (Toronto), Bob Stine (Minnesota), Richard Novak (Rutgers), Ann Brewer (Sydney, Australia), Gary Matkin (UC Irvine), and Bob Hansen (UPCEA) challenged me to review and analyze best practices between the new world of work and innovations in learning.

Experts. My interview subjects, Lisa Gevelber (Google), Jonathan Stull (Handshake), Wes Sonnenreich (Practera), John Katzman (Noodle), Marni Baker-Stein (Western Governors University), Trent Henry (Ernst & Young), Sundar Subramaniam, Chris Kaiser, and Paul Crockett (Authess), Chris McCarthy and Kelly Palmer (Degreed), Julia Pollak (ZipRecruiter), Jonathan

Finkelstein and Sara Bartlett (Credly), Rob Sentz (EMSI), Chris Miller (Foliotek), Amy Lloyd and Nancy Hoffman (JFF), Rachel Carlson and C. J. Jackson (Guild), Jennifer Carlson (Apprenti), Rahim Fazal (SV Academy), Jake Schwartz and Tom Ogletree (General Assembly), Betty Vandenbosch and Chandni Brunamonti (Coursera), Mordy Golding (LinkedIn Learning), Gardner Carrick (FAME), Gautam Tambay and Eva-Marie Costello (Springboard), and Shelley Osborne (Udemy) shared with me insights, perspective, and recommendations for the future of learning in the new market economy.

THE COLLEGE DEVALUATION CRISIS

PART I

THE EVOLUTION OF JOB READINESS AND CREDENTIALING IN THE UNITED STATES

THE COLLEGE DEGREE

False Panacea or Freighted Promise?

Modern-Day Dilemma

As Alicia updates her LinkedIn profile and resumé to reflect a new internship, she worries, again, about her job prospects. A magna cum laude graduate of Princeton, Alicia majored in economics and English, was the president of Princeton Latinos y Amigos, mentored students in a local middle school, and was a member of the varsity soccer team for two years. She applied herself at Princeton, and she excelled.

Focusing on her grades and on giving to the community, she did not work much while in school. During her summers, she joined her father at the Nabisco factory near their home in northern New Jersey, earning considerably more than she would have in internships or entry-level office work. But although she graduated with a degree from a prestigious university, Alicia is back home with her parents, immigrants from the Dominican Republic who have tried to give Alicia every advantage in the United States—and who are confused by her dilemma.

Everyone said that college was the path to the middle class, and Alicia remains determined to find a professional job soon. For one thing, the six-month grace period for repaying her sizeable student loans will soon expire. She hopes that her current unpaid internship—in the communications office at Nabisco / Mondelez's North American headquarters in East Hanover, New Jersey—will teach her some marketable job skills that can help put her in line for a professional position at Nabisco.

Degree-in-Question: A Hypothesis

For most of the history of the United States, a college degree held only a minimal relationship to the labor market, work, and jobs. That began to change—slowly—around 1900, during the first industrial revolution, and then shift, dramatically, after World War II. From that point on, the interrelationship between the degree and a job or career followed a steep upward trajectory of growth and associated relevance,[1] culminating in a "golden age" of peak connectedness from around 1990 until the Great Recession of 2008 (Figure 1.1).

But by the end of the recession, the value of the degree had plateaued, and it began a slow decline, prompting the emergence of an alternative education movement.[2] This alternative both complements and supports the deficiencies of the long-standing, traditional college or university model; at the same time, it threatens to capture significant market share and, ultimately, to displace that model.

This book addresses this hypothesis of the debunked degree and devalued college education that inspired the subsequent birth of the alternative education movement. It explores the hypothesis through research into and analysis of a variety of stakeholder lenses—those of employees, employers, and educational providers—by addressing a range of research questions:

- Throughout U.S. history, how has the relationship and interdependence between work and the college degree evolved?

- What are the cultural, economic, and labor forces that initially, and increasingly, made the degree so valuable for its constituencies?

- How have global market forces disrupted the traditional education model, thereby challenging and lessening its value? What has been the impact of these changes on students and employees, employers, and the education industry at large?

- What is the current value of college education to students and employees? What is the current value of a college education to employers?

- How are the competitive marketplace and the entrepreneurial business landscape responding to deficiencies in the degree's current value? What are leading examples of alternative solutions?

- What are the trending implications for the future of learning and the future of work as a result of the value shifts in the traditional college degree?

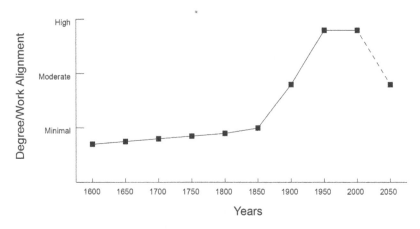

Figure 1.1. Arc of Education and Work Relationship: 1600–2050.

Rise in Relevance of the College Degree

Ask just about any American born in the twentieth century, or the early de-cades of the twenty-first, what it would have taken to achieve a successful life-time career, and the answer almost surely would have been: a college degree.

For some seventy years, from approximately 1950 to around 2020, that answer was reliably accurate. For employers, the degree was a logical cutoff point for recruitment in an economy that had become increasingly dependent on information technology to fuel corporate and organizational success, and higher education was the obvious provider of those information technology skills. Newly dubbed "the knowledge industry," colleges and universities answered the call.[3]

This nurtured an interdependence between the world of work and the institutions of higher learning that proved to be mutually beneficial and mutually profitable. Fueled by increased enrollment in an expanding number of educational institutions, and by growing public investment in higher education, this interdependence translated into a golden age for the college degree. Gaining one became not just a credential of achievement; it was a guarantee of value for both degree holders and the employers who sought them out.[4]

And, importantly, it paid off. College graduates received tangible recom-pense on their investment in higher education—the costs of tuition, books and materials, room and board—even if many had to go into debt to pay for the rising costs of it all. Upon graduation, they indeed obtained the gainful employment or "good jobs" reserved only for degree holders, jobs that typically led to steady upward promotion through the managerial and executive ranks and/or to recruitment from other organizations. Financial security made it possible for them to acquire the talismans of middle-class comfort: home ownership, family vacations, material possessions. The job and the security clothed college graduates in certain "supplemental" expectations as well—expectations held by others as well as by themselves: leadership, a role in the community, prominence. Sociologists and pollsters saw them as a distinctive class, "the college-educated"; they were profiled, appraised, listened to.[5]

As if all that weren't enough, when the COVID-19 pandemic began to ravage the nation's economy, college graduates performed distinctly better than most at holding on to their jobs and salaries: about six months into the pandemic's appearance in the United States, only 5.3 percent of college graduates age twenty-five years and older had lost their employment; for high school graduates, the figure was 8.9 percent[6]—60 percent more damaging a consequence than that suffered by degree holders. Instead, the latter simply stayed home and worked remotely while remaining salaried. In fact, data from the San Francisco Federal Reserve Bank show that "almost 65 percent of workers with a bachelor's degree or higher reported teleworking in response to COVID-19. In contrast, only 22 percent of workers with a high school diploma or less had teleworked due to the pandemic."[7] Value indeed.

The same was true on the other side of the equation—the colleges and universities dispensing the degrees and the employers relying on them as hiring tools. The former benefited from the prodigious surges in student enrollment, which in turn spurred surges in government grants as well as in endowments. The latter—employers—drew increased value not only from workers skilled in the knowledge and competencies the degree represented but also from graduates' comfort in working with others and indeed from the personal networking connections students had made in college—by-products of the college experience that proved useful.[8]

Thus, from all of these separate vantage points—of students, employers, and the educational establishment—the nearly iconic role of the college degree in the nation's culture and economy seemed to be a core value that bid fair to become permanent.

Shift in Market Needs: Unsatisfied Employers

But behind the apparent continuing value of the degree, the market was shifting. And in a capitalist economy, when the economic indicators move, so does the need for labor. The debunking and subsequent devaluation of the college degree is the result of the shift to a new world of work, one requiring a different set of skills that are not attainable during four years of college and that thus must be acquired in other ways. These are, primarily, applied skills related to advances in technology and increases in globalization and the "soft" human skills required of managers as they make the transition from being individual contributors to managing people, projects, and relationships in a continually unstable and changing work environment.

The first hard evidence came in a 2015 study, conducted by the Association of American Colleges and Universities, which found that many employers saw college graduates as falling short in their preparedness for work in several areas—including the ones employers tended to deem most important for workplace success.[9] By contrast, however, the college graduates themselves were notably more optimistic about their level of preparedness across those same seventeen outcomes, as shown in Figure 1.2.

What disappointed the employers were the college graduates' abilities to apply knowledge and skills in real-world settings, their critical thinking skills, and their written and oral communication skills—areas in which fewer than three in ten employers thought recent college graduates were well prepared, according to the AACU study. That's a pretty low assessment of skills that had once seemed to be assured by a college education.

What all this data suggests is that today's college students apply for, and invest in, a college education with the expectation that they will be well prepared for the workplace. Upon graduation, they believe that their hard work and demonstration of mastery, resulting in the credential of a degree, will translate to gainful employment and satisfactory performance. What we know, however, is that employers are actually dissatisfied with the level of preparedness of college graduates, particularly in the competency areas deemed most critical.[10] This draws into question the perceived and actual value of the degree.

Simply put, once employers realized that the college curriculum was not keeping pace with their needs for changes in products and services, the degree, as a threshold for hiring, lost its power and declined in value. At first, employers invested in training their newly "not-worth-it but educated employees." Corporate universities boomed in the late 1990s and early 2000s. But as the

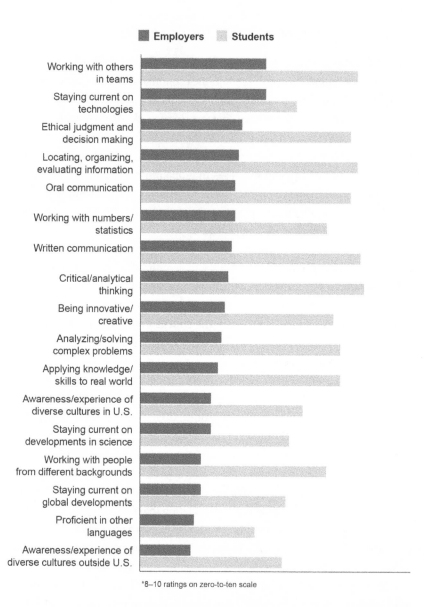

Employers **Students**

Working with others in teams

Staying current on technologies

Ethical judgment and decision making

Locating, organizing, evaluating information

Oral communication

Working with numbers/ statistics

Written communication

Critical/analytical thinking

Being innovative/ creative

Analyzing/solving complex problems

Applying knowledge/ skills to real world

Awareness/experience of diverse cultures in U.S.

Staying current on developments in science

Working with people from different backgrounds

Staying current on global developments

Proficient in other languages

Awareness/experience of diverse cultures outside U.S.

*8–10 ratings on zero-to-ten scale

Figure 1.2. Employer Versus Student Satisfaction with College Graduate Preparedness. Note: 8–10 ratings on zero-to-ten scale. Source: Selected findings from online surveys of employers and college students conducted on behalf of the Association of American Colleges & Universities by Hart Research Associates.

Students aren't getting what *they're* paying for;

and

Employers aren't getting what *they're* paying for.

higher education industry failed to catch up, employers moved on and out, seeking, as alternative learning, options that would not require their investment.[11]

There is nothing particularly unusual about this. Similar shifts have occurred across a variety of industries as the work environment changed and required "faster and better" skills. Consider the transportation industry when ships and trains gave way to trucks and planes, the postal industry dealing with the onslaught of mail, even the transition manufacturing had to undergo when wood was replaced by plastic—to name just a few examples. But the shift for both the world of work and the world of education is nevertheless profound.

Long-Term Value Proposition: What Is it Worth?

In truth, the efficacy of the college degree as a guarantee of value hit its peak circa 2010.[12] And as succeeding chapters will demonstrate, by 2030, a college education and the degree that assures it will be replaced as the dominant pathway for the kind of talent development that presages professional readiness and career success. As this book goes to press, a new world of work is aborning. It operates differently from the world of work for which most colleges and universities have previously prepared students. That shift requires a fresh set of skills, and the pathway to building and credentialing those skills does not go through the ivied gates of today's colleges and universities.

Where *does* it go? That is what *The College Devaluation Crisis* will analyze and explore. The answer will have profound implications for coming generations of students and for their lives as workers, for employers, and for the nation's educational institutions. For all these "constituencies," those implications will prove relatively disruptive. But the disruption itself—and the value shifts it produces—also suggest opportunities for new forms of talent development.

After all, as the next chapter will make clear, college was not always a prerequisite for success in the world of work. Indeed, the road to the "canonization" of the college degree as an employment tool was long and winding, and it began, effectively, in religion. From the colonial era through the Civil War, America's colleges were primarily seminaries representing varied Christian denominations; in them, young white men—exclusively—were trained to serve as pastors to a society grounded in an artisanal, agrarian economy.[13] The Civil War, due mostly to the impetus to improve weapons, gave a boost to mechanization and helped usher in an industrial age that ignited the need for mechanical and scientific competencies. Land-grant colleges in particular were established to answer this need, but, as in the colonial era, they remained exclusionary and privileged, while factory jobs, expanding at a swift pace, required little education at all—considered, at the time, a great boon to the economy.

It wasn't until what we now define as the Information Age that the kinds of competencies taught only in institutions of higher learning came to be valued by employers as essential for competitive advantage in a churning marketplace. We can date the start of that era to as long ago as the latter years of World War II, when technological developments not just in weaponry but in cryptography, intelligence-gathering, and analysis profoundly escalated and expanded the use of computers. The potential inherent in those developments became evident to all on July 20, 1969, when the Apollo 11 moonshot landed Neil Armstrong and Buzz Aldrin on the lunar surface. The landing, said then President John F. Kennedy, justified the vast expenditure his administration had committed to "information technology," and he pledged that the United States, at the time admittedly well behind the Russians in the race to outer space, would soon be able "by God, to pass them!"

The world of work the moonshot set in motion "moved the needle"—a favorite phrase of the time—on the kind of talent regarded as essential for economic growth; in turn, that meant scouting for new sources of the talent and finding new ways of approaching and securing candidates. In a sense, the Apollo 11 project "proved" the information technology potential projected by the likes of Alan Turing—namely, that the relentless gathering of technology resources and the proper mobilization of those resources could be transformative. In the minds of employers across a range of industries, that "moonshot mentality" elevated such skills as critical thinking, creativity, diversity of perspective, even the ability to effect disruption to be essential to success.[14] The place to look for such skills was higher education. And colleges and universities, eagerly supported by legislatures at all levels of government, responded with gusto, elevating the relationship between the world of work and the college degree to a new prominence and opening the door to the degree's golden age. Why and how the degree, and the education it testified to, has lost its value for the world of work is the first step toward defining what may be needed to rethink models, and both the why and the possible alternative paths represent the linked analyses at the heart of this book.

We can best understand why the value of the degree has diminished by analyzing how it gained such value in the first place. How did a certificate warranting that the bearer completed four-year college requirements earn such prominence in our cultural and economic life? And why is that prominence now threatened by alternative notions of skill-building and credentialing?

Alicia, the talented Princeton graduate highlighted at the beginning of this chapter, seemingly was well prepared for the job market after demonstrating success at one of the world's premier universities. But she attempted to enter the job market just as the golden age of the college degree began to wane. The degree *should* have meant an automatic hiring. It *should* have represented the most powerful credential for entry any professional could possess and demonstrate—but she experienced its descending value. Alicia and her parents were left wondering, "Why does the marketplace not value her degree? Doesn't the curricular foundation they invested in ensure readiness for an entry-level position?" The answers will be explored more fully in the coming chapters.

THE ARC TO THE "GOLDEN AGE"...
AND EMERGING DECLINE

For roughly the seventy-five-year period from 1945 to 2020, college has been perceived in the United States as the primary pathway into the middle class, despite the reality that a majority of jobs, across sectors (but excluding professional services), do not actually require a college degree in order to provide a living wage.[1] How did this perception arise, given the fact that, since colonial times, most people have learned the skills that facilitate their work outside of school? What forces made the degree so valuable? Why did the slow evolution of higher education in the United States coexist with a parallel rise in the perception of its value?

This chapter takes up those questions by examining a number of factors across four economic periods: the Agrarian Era, the Industrial Era, the Knowledge Era, and the current and looming Post-Recession/COVID Era. The factors we explore illustrate, quantitatively, qualitatively, and contextually, the key elements of the relationship between the degree and its shifting economic value. Among these factors are the nature of the economy in each period and the education and training required for available work; the level of education in the nation; the accessibility of education, including the number of colleges and universities in the United States; and who bears the financial burden of earning a degree. We then investigate the rapidly changing world of education, training, and employment in the twenty-first century.

Figure 2.1 describes the chronological relationship between education and work, over centuries, in the United States.

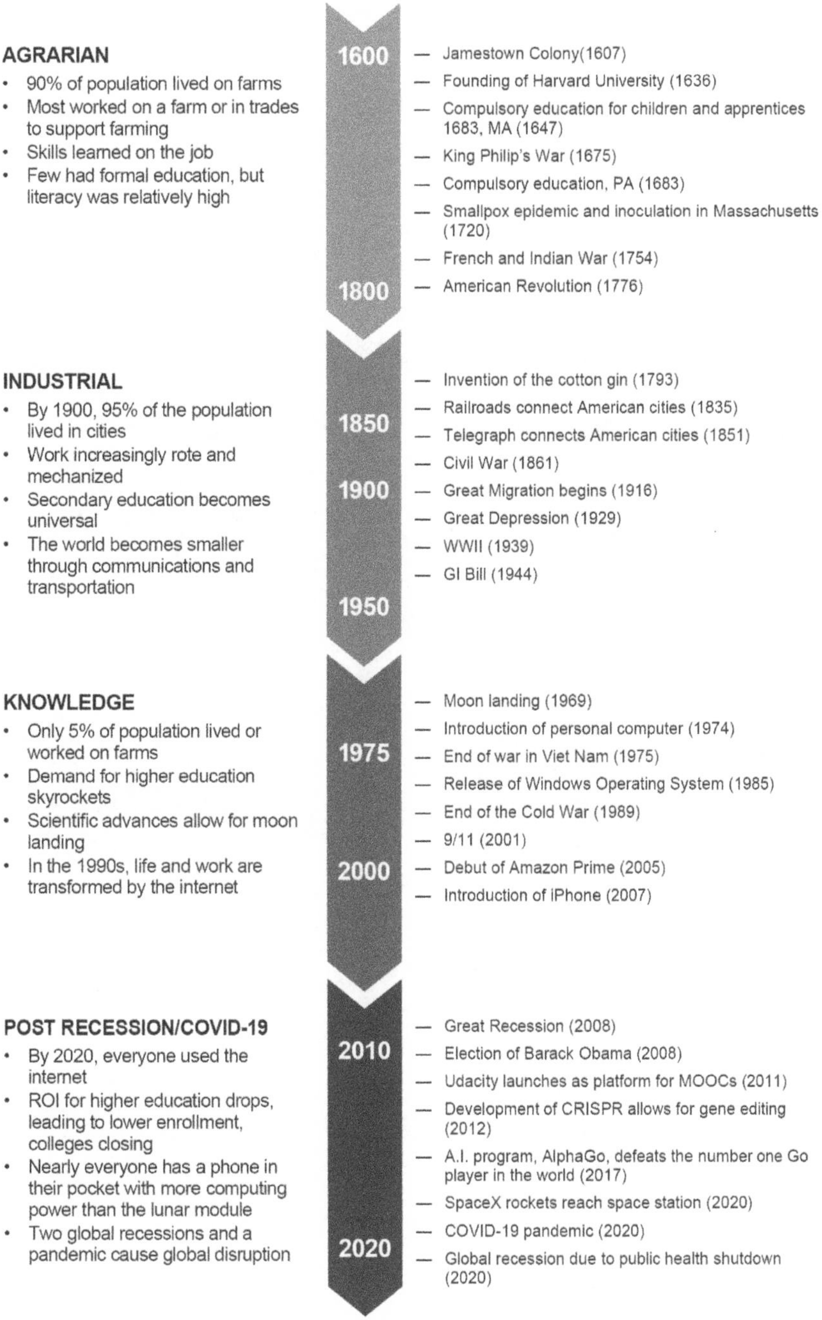

AGRARIAN

- 90% of population lived on farms
- Most worked on a farm or in trades to support farming
- Skills learned on the job
- Few had formal education, but literacy was relatively high

1600

1800

— Jamestown Colony (1607)
— Founding of Harvard University (1636)
— Compulsory education for children and apprentices 1683, MA (1647)
— King Philip's War (1675)
— Compulsory education, PA (1683)
— Smallpox epidemic and inoculation in Massachusetts (1720)
— French and Indian War (1754)
— American Revolution (1776)

INDUSTRIAL

- By 1900, 95% of the population lived in cities
- Work increasingly rote and mechanized
- Secondary education becomes universal
- The world becomes smaller through communications and transportation

1850

1900

1950

— Invention of the cotton gin (1793)
— Railroads connect American cities (1835)
— Telegraph connects American cities (1851)
— Civil War (1861)
— Great Migration begins (1916)
— Great Depression (1929)
— WWII (1939)
— GI Bill (1944)

KNOWLEDGE

- Only 5% of population lived or worked on farms
- Demand for higher education skyrockets
- Scientific advances allow for moon landing
- In the 1990s, life and work are transformed by the internet

1975

2000

— Moon landing (1969)
— Introduction of personal computer (1974)
— End of war in Viet Nam (1975)
— Release of Windows Operating System (1985)
— End of the Cold War (1989)
— 9/11 (2001)
— Debut of Amazon Prime (2005)
— Introduction of iPhone (2007)

POST RECESSION/COVID-19

- By 2020, everyone used the internet
- ROI for higher education drops, leading to lower enrollment, colleges closing
- Nearly everyone has a phone in their pocket with more computing power than the lunar module
- Two global recessions and a pandemic cause global disruption

2010

2020

— Great Recession (2008)
— Election of Barack Obama (2008)
— Udacity launches as platform for MOOCs (2011)
— Development of CRISPR allows for gene editing (2012)
— A.I. program, AlphaGo, defeats the number one Go player in the world (2017)
— SpaceX rockets reach space station (2020)
— COVID-19 pandemic (2020)
— Global recession due to public health shutdown (2020)

Figure 2.1. Chronology of Education and Work Relationship: 1600–2030.

Table 2.1. Analysis of Education and Work Relationship, 1600–2030.

	Agrarian Age (~1600–1800)	Industrial Age (~1800–1965)	Knowledge Economy (~1965–2007)	Post-Recession / COVID (~2008–2020+)
Types of Jobs or Skills	Semi-skilled, manual labor, or artisan	Early: semi-skilled Height: no skills Later: increasingly skilled	Highly skilled, formally educated	Highly skilled, evolving pathways for acquiring skills
Level of Education	Literacy rate 70%, but only a primary education	Secondary education increasingly common	College degree prized for entry to middle class	Skills prioritized over education
Number of Colleges	1776: 9	1900: 977 1950: 1,851	1990: 3,535 2000: 4,084	2015: 4,627 2020: 4,313
Cost of Higher Education	Tuition minimal or not charged; students mostly paid for room and board	Tuition generally in line with the ability of upper-middle-class families to pay out of pocket	Tuition and fees increasingly beyond the ability of a student or family to pay without significant scholarships or loans	Tuition and fees increase at most colleges and universities
Investments in Education	Education considered a private good; few if any public investments	In the 1800s and early 1900s, individuals paid tuition (some scholars were offered free attendance by institutions); federal funding was available via the Morrill Acts of 1862 and 1890. During the Great Depression, the federal government began backing student loans; after WWII, federal investments included the GI Bill, grants to institutions for scientific research. States heavily invested in their higher education systems.	Although states paid the bulk of the cost of a degree in the state higher ed system through the 1970s, by the 1980s, spiraling costs resulted in high student loan debts (both government-backed loans and private, for-profit loans).	The Great Recession cut already meager state investments in the higher education system.

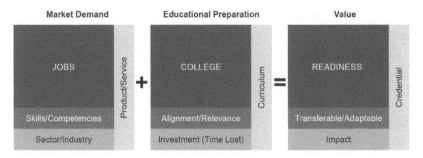

Figure 2.2. Valuation Framework for Education and Work.

As a complement to Figure 2.1, Table 2.1 maps the four primary histori-cal eras we're examining, representing the relevant variables and comparative historical data for each.

A Valuable Framework

The relationship between education and work can be assigned a general value based on a contextual framework. Figure 2.2 illustrates a concept that features the connected elements.

Work is constantly influenced by *market demands*, and jobs are created and evolve on the basis of unpredictable market dynamics. In order to perform the jobs effectively, workers must possess a mastery level of skills and competen-cies—aligned with the nuanced needs of the relative sector and industry. The quantity and quality of the product or service that an organization offers are dependent on, and directly attributable to, the abilities of the collective labor force.

Those members of the labor force require specialized *educational prepara-tion* to fortify them with a necessary foundation for work. In certain cases, a college degree is the appropriate credential for getting a job, keeping a job, and advancing in a job. Of course, a heavy investment, in the form of time and money, is required to acquire the college degree, but it is worth it if the cur-riculum design aligns instruction with the relevant skills and competencies that keep one competitive.

Ultimately, the metric for success in the workplace is *value*. Is the worker armed with the readiness profile to do the job? Are the worker's skills and competencies adaptable and transferable to the changing business environment? Does the credentialed worker make an impact against goals and objectives?

We will apply this framework to each of the historical eras to determine the generative value of the degree in each—noting the significance of its rise and predicted fall.

The Agrarian Era

An eleven-year-old orphan named Prudence had few assets or prospects. Before her parents died in the smallpox epidemic of 1721, she attended the Dame School taught by one of the mothers in her neighborhood in Lexington, Massachusetts, but her uncle could no longer pay the fees.

In addition to learning reading, writing, and arithmetic, however, girls in a Dame School also learned to sew. Prudence had fine needlework skills, so her uncle drew up an apprenticeship contract with a tailor in Cambridge. When Prudence turned twelve in the spring, she would live with the master tailor and work in his shop in exchange for learning the trade.

Alignment Review and Analysis

From the settling of the first English colony in Jamestown in 1607 until the early decades of the republic, America was an agrarian economy. It was a busy era of social and economic development that included the establishment of English colonies in North America, their struggles for dominance with both European powers and Native American tribes, a developing identity as Americans, and the slow shaping of a domestic economy. Most production in the Americas was focused on survival: agriculture, lumbering, and whatever families needed to make their own clothing. Luxury goods were imported from Europe. The bulk of the population—90 percent—lived in the countryside during this agrarian, colonial time, and most farmed their land, in which family wealth was rooted.

Whether farming or working at trades that supported farming, most work required on-the-job training but little formal education.[2] Even medical doctors learned their profession as apprentices and did not receive a formal education.[3] Opportunities for higher education were limited as there were only nine universities in the colonies. The majority of college graduates became ministers, but colleges also prepared affluent young white men for leadership roles in the colonies.[4] Future leaders typically spent a year or two studying and then began their careers without completing a degree.[5] Still, literacy levels for white men

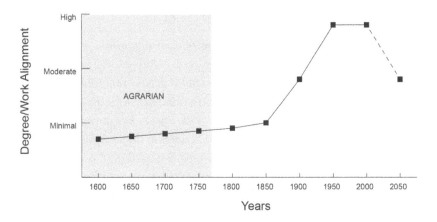

Figure 2.3. Arc of Education and Work Relationship: Agrarian Age.

hovered around 70 percent, and society seemed to value the general education required to read the Bible and do the books for a farm or small business.[6]

Valuation in Context

The market demands of the Agrarian Era were largely subsistence-based and were met by domestic labor in farming, lumbering, clothing, and care work. As a result, the jobs required skills that were mostly learned via apprenticeship; the competencies for those jobs lasted nearly a lifetime. Only a specialized few men in society were privileged to pursue higher education.

The value of a college degree during the Agrarian Era, therefore, was *minimal*.

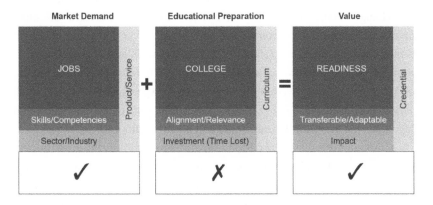

Figure 2.4. Valuation Framework for Education and Work: Agrarian Era.

The Industrial Era

Height of the Era: Worried about pogroms (violent riots aimed at an ethnic or religious group, particularly Jews) in other parts of Russia, Lev's family had undertaken a long journey to America. They landed in New York City in 1882 with plans to continue west and secure a farm. To raise money for the journey, however, they sought work in New York. Back in Russia, Lev had attended school full time and had begun learning about apprenticeships in the family's rural community. In New York, fifteen-year-old Lev got a job in a textile factory, standing at a single machine for twelve hours each day, repeating the same task over and over.

Waning Days of the Era: Robert served in the U.S. Army in World War II. Injured in the invasion of Sicily in 1943, he returned home to his family in Chicago to heal. Walking with a limp, Robert was able to join his brother on the line at U.S. Steel. But in 1944, with the passage of the GI Bill, Robert began to consider going to college, especially as his leg injury made it difficult for him to stand and a career on the factory floor seemed unlikely. He was thankful his family had come to Chicago in the 1930s; had they stayed in Alabama, Jim Crow laws would have prevented him from taking advantage of the state-administered GI Bill. Even in Illinois, it would be a challenge to find a university where he could enroll, but he was determined to explore other options for his life's career.

Alignment Review and Analysis

The Industrial Age began around 1800 and, after a slow start, lasted until the 1950s. It encompassed many key historical periods, highlighted by the Civil War, the emancipation of nearly 20 percent of the population, the westward expansion, the rise of cities and manufacturing work, and two world wars. Society also changed dramatically: the United States became more diverse, and more opportunities opened for women and African-Americans. The mid-twentieth century saw the largest migration in U.S. history, as millions of African-Americans left southern states and moved north for better jobs. In 1900, 90 percent of African-Americans lived in the rural South. By 1960, half lived in the north and 80 percent lived in urban areas—both north *and* south.[7] This migration highlights the overall shift away from rural life throughout the Industrial Age.

Although these historical periods have little in common, the economic era that spans the late eighteenth century to the mid-twentieth century is characterized by work that increasingly involved rote interactions with mechanized technology. Most jobs required skills readily learned on the job. The era is also characterized by increased access to developing technologies. By the end of the Industrial Age, transportation and communication technologies had made the world smaller.

The economy slowly made the transition from agrarian to industrialized in the early days of the republic. Early industrialization addressed labor shortages and developed ways to mechanize the refining of raw goods into useable materials. Mills, for example, were increasingly used to transform lumber into boards ready for building, while in 1793, the cotton gin transformed agriculture in the South and fed the textile mills in England. In addition, advances in transportation and communication allowed the young nation to expand geographically.[8] Although technology was changing daily work, the engineering required in this era did not require a college degree.

Such advances, however, gave the Union an advantage during the Civil War. The emerging technologies of the railroad and the telegraph were invaluable to the war effort,[9] while Union contracts spurred nascent factories to mass produce uniforms for the troops.[10] Following the war, factory work increased, requiring only semi-skilled labor at first. By the late 1800s, factories were seeing high turnover primarily from waves of immigrants, who often arrived in the United States with limited English. They often moved west to become pioneers or rapidly sought better-paying jobs as they acquired skills. To address this high turnover, factory managers deconstructed the work so that an employee often stood in front of one machine for twelve hours a day. These rote assignments required little skill or training.[11]

The era also saw the beginning of public investment in education. Education had long been viewed as a private good accessible to those who could afford it; there were virtually no public investments in colleges and universities. With the Morrill Act of 1862, however, the federal government began funding higher education, initially founding state institutions that focused on agricultural science and technology.[12] The second Morrill Act of 1890 increased federal investments in higher education, even creating colleges for African-Americans.[13] During the later 1800s, the level of education in the United States slowly advanced. Free, primary education became universal while secondary education become common.[14] As secondary schooling became more common, more people were prepared for higher education. By 1900, there were 977 colleges and universities and 160,000 students enrolled in higher education.[15]

With industrialization increasing, families were less likely to own a family farm or a trade that could be passed on to the next generation. Middle-class families began encouraging their sons to seek alternative professions that would maintain the family's standard of living.[16] At the same time, states began to demand and create professional standards—demonstrated baseline competency or mastery required to, for example, practice law, audit financials, medically treat patients, invest capital, or teach students; the professional careers they defined increasingly required higher education.[17]

College enrollment actually increased during the Great Depression,[18] likely due to the Roosevelt Administration's doubling of federal investments in education while also providing work study grants directly to students.[19] During this time, colleges and universities began partnering with businesses and employers to develop skills that would increase a graduate's chance of employment.[20]

It was just after World War II that the United States began the transition from an industrial, manufacturing economy to what became known as the Knowledge Economy. Even though most people continued to do manual labor or work in a factory, an increased premium was placed on the college education. The federal government played a large role in shifting that perception, both through direct investments in institutions and by paying tuition for veterans.[21] College was increasingly seen as the primary path into the middle class.

Valuation Assessment

The market demands of the Industrial Era saw a substantial shift toward manufacturing work. As a result, the repetitive and mechanized jobs required skills that were mostly learned on the job. While primary and secondary education became universally free, preparing more of the workforce for college, most competencies for the jobs of the era did not exceed high school preparation. The Great Depression, however, became a catalyst for enrolling more students than was necessary for the labor market, due to the lack of available work.

The value of a college degree during the Industrial Era, therefore, dramatically shifted from *Minimal* to *Moderate*.

The Knowledge Era

Tim was frustrated in his office job. A math major, he had hoped he would enjoy accounting and learn a new career. But it's been a slog and long days that took him from his bride. Newlyweds, Tim and Lucy had left the Peace Corps in India and settled near her parents in San Diego. They knew, as former Peace Corps vol-

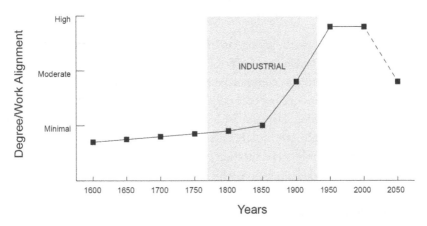

Figure 2.5. Arc of Education and Work Relationship: Industrial Era.

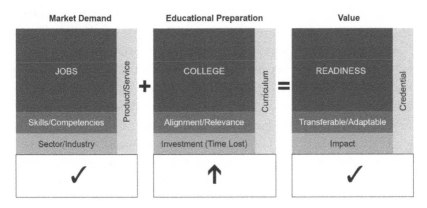

Figure 2.6. Valuation Framework for Education and Work: Industrial Era.

unteers, that they could get jobs with the federal government, but it would require a move to Washington, DC.

After a long week of tax season, Tim came home with news: he had quit his job. Lucy had her own news: they were having their first child in about eight months. Tim booked a flight to DC and within a week had a job.

A month into the job, Tim's boss announced they needed to train someone on the new computer system. It was 1975, and this would be the first computer system in the office. Tim jumped at the opportunity. He was excited at the chance to learn a novel skill and one that seemed likely to play an important role in this career over the next decades.

Alignment Review and Analysis

Roughly bounded by the moon landing in the late 1960s and the Great Recession of 2008, the Knowledge Era was primarily defined by the computer technologies that became common both on the job and in the home. Every sort of work required more computer skills, from manufacturing to office work to retail sales to teaching. Demand for higher education also increased, with the perception that high-tech work required a formal degree.

The demand for higher education was primed in part by increased federal investments in higher education, which had first escalated during World War II and continued to swell through the Cold War. In 1953, federal investment in higher education was $13 billion (in constant 2014 dollars). By 1967, it was $88 billion, and in 1990 it hit $104 billion, an increase of over 700 percent.[22] At the same time, states were recognizing higher education as a public good. In the 1970s, state funding covered, on average, 75 percent of the cost of a student's college degree at a public university.[23] Tuition remained low, and a college degree was widely accessible. The return on investment seemed high.

College enrollments skyrocketed in tandem with this public investment in higher education (Figure 2.7). It had begun with the GI Bill, passed in 1944, which expanded access to college to veterans from a variety of backgrounds.[24] From the late 1940s to the late 1950s, enrollment increased from 2.4 million to 3.6 million, then doubled in size by the late 1960s.[25] Between 1949 and 1979, college enrollment increased by almost 400 percent,[26] and it continued to creep up to a high of twenty-one million college students enrolled in 2010.[27] As demand for a degree increased, the number of colleges also increased (Figure 2.8). In 1950, there were 1,851 colleges and universities in the United States. That number increased to a high of 4,726 in 2013.[28]

But beginning in the 1980s, state investments in higher education dramatically declined. California, a state that had spent lavishly on public education, was forced by the "taxpayer revolt" of the late 1970s to cut back its educational investments. The state's per-student spending declined by 68 percent between 1960 and 2010.[29] Demand for college nevertheless continued to increase until the economy and career expectations began to change during the Great Recession.

Valuation Assessment

In the Knowledge Era, market demand required more technical skills and utility with computers across functions, sectors, and industries. During World War II, the U.S. government began significantly investing in and subsidizing

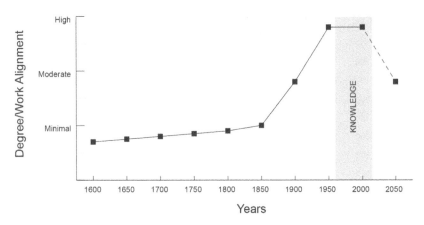

Figure 2.7. Arc of Education and Work Relationship: Knowledge Era.

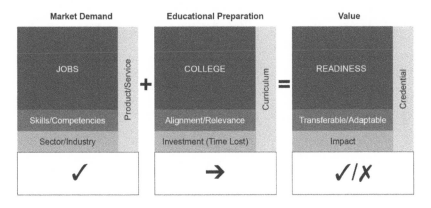

Figure 2.8. Valuation Framework for Education and Work: Knowledge Era.

higher education. More citizens than ever in the country's history took advantage of the opportunity to attend college and to leverage their new skills in the workforce.

The value of a college degree during the Knowledge Era, therefore, was *High* and "golden."

The Post-Recession/COVID-19 Era

Chelsea was struggling. In 2018, she and her young children were living in a homeless shelter. Chelsea was anxious to find a position that would enable her to support her family. She landed a job as an office manager at Goodwill In-

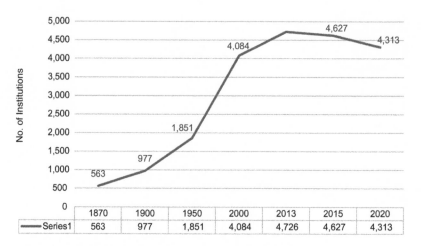

Figure 2.9. Historical Number of U.S. Colleges and Universities.

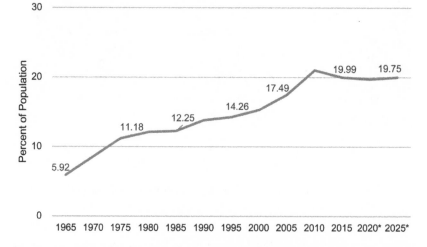

Figure 2.10. Percentage of U.S. Population Enrolled in Higher Education.

dustries, which offered her training to earn the Google IT Support Professional Certificate.

The certificate helped her get a job as a technician at Google's data center in Clarksville, Tennessee, where she makes sure the hardware and data servers run efficiently. She was able to triple her salary. These days, Chelsea can provide her family with security.

Alignment Review and Analysis

Since 2008, the United States has experienced a period of rapid change and major disruptions. Given the dramatic increases in technology and scientific advancements, this time could be a continuation of the Knowledge Economy. In 2007, for example, the iPhone was introduced; very quickly, nearly everyone had a smartphone—iPhone or Android. This meant, among other things, that people were literally carrying in their pocket more computer capacity than available on the lunar model of 1969. In 2012, the creation of CRISPR allowed for relatively easy gene editing, thereby spurring the development of vaccines to protect against COVID-19 in less than one year. In 2017, the AlphaGo AI software beat the top-ranked Go player in the world. While computers beating humans make great headlines, they also offer a glimpse into how artificial intelligence has begun to change the economy and the world of work.

Still, these advances were punctuated by dramatic shifts in the economy and society. In 2008, the world plunged into the Great Recession. The U.S. housing market collapsed. People began losing homes and jobs. It took twelve years of slow but steady economic recovery, at which point the world was hit with a deadly pandemic and, in an attempt to limit human interactions to stop the spread, generated another worldwide recession. The pandemic further advanced changes already under way. Given such dramatic shifts in the economy—resulting in a sharp reduction in family wealth and in difficult and lengthy job searches that leave many people unemployed for long periods—and given also the ever-present uncertainty of life, the high cost of tuition makes a college degree seem like less of an investment and more of a burden.[30]

For at least the final twenty years of the twentieth century and the first twenty years of the twenty-first, the perceived value of education increased, costs increased, but public funding for higher education investment dropped.[31] By 2017, as public investments declined in every state, public university students were responsible for 50 percent of the cost of their degree (up from 25 percent in the 1970s).[32] Federal investments in higher education continued to increase to a peak of $151 billion in 2010, at which point such investments began to decline.[33]

As a result, students and graduates, convinced of the necessity of a college degree, have borrowed to finance their education[34] and have been subsequently crushed by mounting student loans.[35] In November 2018, U.S. Education Secretary Betsy DeVos announced that the loan portfolio of Federal Student Aid, the agency managing the government's student loans, represented "10 percent of our nation's debt."[36] She added that "nearly 20 percent" of those loans were delinquent or in default. In 2019, 54 percent of college attendees had taken on debt to pay for their college careers,[37] and the total amount of student loans reached a new all-time high of $1.41 trillion.[38]

The first two decades of the twenty-first century were shaped by the Great Recession of 2008 and the COVID-19 pandemic that arose in 2020. The most stable jobs required technology skills and the ability to adapt to changing conditions. At the same time, careers increasingly came to be characterized by short-term jobs. Effective workers had the capacity to continuously upgrade their skills,[39] but given the increased cost of college, many began questioning the value of a degree that does not certify the acquisition of marketable skills. College enrollments slowed, then dropped even further. With a reduced demand for higher education, many smaller, private colleges cannot survive the drop in tuition income.[40] The bottom line is that the higher education landscape is shifting.

The decline in enrollment is likely to continue. The Strada Center for Consumer Insights found that in 2020, adults contemplating enrolling in higher education were considerably less likely than in 2019 to believe a college degree would be worth the cost *or* would get them a good job. Sixty-eight percent of those considering enrolling in additional education were more interested in nondegree pathways—up from 50 percent the previous year.[41]

Although a college degree has long been perceived as the pathway to the middle class, what does a degree tell employers about a job candidate? A degree is often a proxy for family background, access to high-quality secondary education, and persistence in completing a course of study. A college degree is only a small measure of whether a potential employee has the required knowledge and skills. In fact, as we have shown, surveys suggest that employers are generally dissatisfied with the skills of recent college graduates.[42] One report suggests corporations are spending $90 billion on employee training.[43]

During the golden age, a college degree simply meant someone had problem-solving and critical thinking skills that assured employers they could learn whatever skill or competency was needed—regardless of whether they had any actual work experience or not. But this simply no longer reflects the modern work landscape; the nature of jobs themselves has changed—most work now requires a level of technical ability beyond the "I can learn and achieve a goal" baseline the college degree was originally designed to satisfy.

How are companies and other organizations going to make up for these skills shortages? Who is going to do the persistent reskilling that these research reports and other experts insist are essential—the kind of reskilling or upskilling the experts say must be ongoing throughout the course of a career? Future economic growth on a global basis *and* future professional careers on a personal, individual basis are at stake. Where is the training to come from? Whose responsibility is it? And why isn't it happening now?

To an extent, it *is* happening now, as the case studies in the pages that follow make clear. Digital credentialing . . . online learning . . . gig skilling and last-mile training . . . public-private partnerships issuing *ad hoc* certification: these are just some of the responses to the ongoing need for new and different skills.

In addition, many institutions of higher education are themselves slowly evolving to "remain relevant." Some colleges are offering rebates to graduates who do not secure jobs within six months of graduation or are providing additional semesters at no cost to build marketable skills. Others are adding courses and departments to connect with real-world demand. Nationwide, educational institutions added 55,416 new programs in the five years from 2012 to 2017. These include four hundred schools offering credentials in cybersecurity, for which demand is growing three times faster than in other IT fields. Rice University partnered with Trilogy Education Services to add credentials in cybersecurity and has expanded the partnership to include credentialing in data analytics and financial technology.

These partnerships go both ways: Pace University has partnered with telecommunications companies to train employees as network technicians. L.L. Bean has contracted with nearby Husson University to provide education and training to their employees.[44] Perhaps the most comprehensive of these initiatives is the strategic plan of Southern New Hampshire University. Under the leadership of President Paul LeBlanc, SNHU began in 2015 to "reinvent what a university can be and needs to be for the digital age," in LeBlanc's words.[45] The plan sets out how to evolve from the current institutionally centered, one-size-fits-all model of learning to a learner-centered, more personalized experience in which the institution instead curates, assesses, and certifies learning—perhaps making the transition into becoming a lifetime learning platform, with students of every age slipping in and out as needed.

Valuation Assessment

The market demands of the Post-Recession/COVID-19 Era continued from the Knowledge Era, accelerating advances in technology and science with a particular explosion in the hi-tech industry. As a result, more jobs than ever before

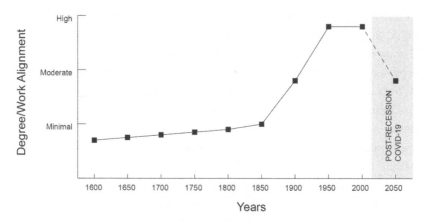

Figure 2.11. Arc of Education and Work Relationship: Post-Recession/COVID-19 Era.

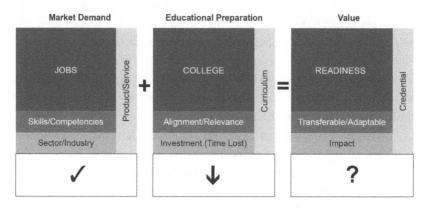

Figure 2.12. Valuation Framework for Education and Work: Post-Recession/COVID-19 Era.

required a college degree as an entry-level and qualifying credential. However, as the skill demands for jobs began to significantly increase in complexity and to evolve more rapidly, it became progressively clearer that the college education failed to prepare graduates to meet employer expectations.

The value of a college degree during the Post-Recession/COVID-19 Era, therefore, receded from *High* to *Moderate*. With enrollment, career placement, and employer satisfaction data *decreasing*, the next era indicates a *drop* in value.

Why is the value of the college degree *dropping*? And what is filling the void and taking its place?

The next chapter examines the traditional model of higher education and exposes its shortcomings with respect to market demand expectations. The subsequent chapters will highlight case studies of organizations putting forth new models to replace the degree and the ageing model of learning it represents.

Colleges and universities will ignore the findings from these studies at their peril. We need a new way of learning, of assessing learning, and of continually expanding skills. With the diminishing return on investment of the college degree, alternative models that can fulfill those needs will supplant what has for so long been the prized position of higher education in U.S. society.

PART II

INNOVATION AND THE RISE OF COMPETITIVE
HIGHER EDUCATION ALTERNATIVES

COMPETITIVE MODELS

Traditional Versus Alternative

The Reality: A Gap Exists

If it is incontrovertible that the value of the college degree is in decline and that a new world of work requires new skills—and it is the contention of this book that both statements are true—then it is equally certain that a fresh method of teaching and learning those skills is essential. How will the workers in this emerging reality obtain the expertise and capabilities—technical, interpersonal, cognitive—on which their futures and the progress of society as a whole will depend? The bulk of available jobs do not require a degree in order to obtain gainful employment, but they do require certain requisite skills. And for those professional services roles where standards are required or a degree facilitates advancement to the executive ranks, a more dynamic base of skills and competencies is needed to align with contemporary labor demands.

This chapter examines how and why the traditional model of education—the four-year college leading to a bachelor's degree—is no longer sufficient to achieve that goal. We probe the weaknesses of the model and appraise its strengths, often two sides of a single coin, to affirm the thesis of this book—namely, that the traditional way of preparing for the world of work has gone past its sell-by date. And we propose a new and fundamentally different model for achieving the shared goal of both learners and the employers in the new world of work: lifelong learning for continual upskilling to meet market needs and provide individuals with the financial wherewithal and personal fulfillment they seek in a career.

The Learning Process

What does not change, from model to model, is the teaching and learning *process*, the means by which knowledge or the mastery of a skill is transferred from expert to learner. From our most ancient ancestors passing on the arts of survival from mother to daughter and father to son, down the ages to Plato's Academy, then to the worker mastering the several steps of his or her task in a long assembly line, and to Commencement Day every June, there is a sameness in the way we impart and gain skills. Here's how it flows:

- The learner engages with whatever institutional structure is appropriate—tutor, university, master artisan or technician, book, video—to discover the skill deficiencies that need to be corrected or compensated.

- From there, one actor in the process, the institutional structure, whatever it may be, teaches or imparts, while the other, the learner, learns and absorbs.

- Both assess the results; if and when the results are deemed satisfactory, the institutional structure issues to the learner some form of credential that certifies his or her skills or qualifications.

That is the *modus operandi* of education. It is how understanding or proficiency is taught, learned, and recognized, and it will apply to education in the new world of work as potently as it did to the present model, the one that is now falling short of what the world of work needs and what workers must provide.

The necessary revision is not in the facts of this methodology—engagement into the educational "institution," discovery of what needs to be taught and learned, the teaching and learning, assessment of what has been taught and learned, recognition of the learner's preparedness through some form of credential. Rather, it is in the way the model is structured.

The Two Models Compared

Since we are suggesting that the existing model of learning for our time, the one leading to the college degree, needs to be revised if the skill needs of the future are to be met, we must first look at how the *traditional* model functions and where its strengths and weaknesses lie. We must also note that this traditional model remains the current model as of the writing of this book. The analysis of it can clarify the path to revision and the proposal of an *alternative* model to serve emerging skill needs. As a means of comparison, and to make

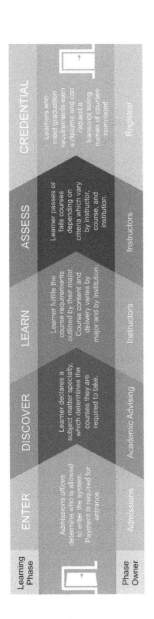

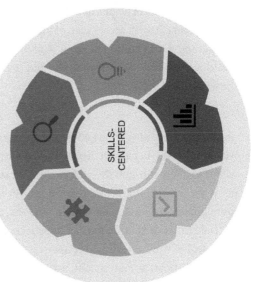

Figure 3.1. Traditional Learning Model Versus Alternative Learning Model.

the case for change, we will define the component characteristics of each and highlight their respective pros and cons.

The Traditional Model

The Model Defined

The traditional model—the college experience that many readers may have experienced for themselves—is a strictly linear progression of steps or phases, each phase "owned"—instigated and directed—by a separate and different entity. The progression begins at a single entry point, an open door at the front of the line—that is, with acceptance of the application and the learner showing up on opening day of freshman year—and it leads to a single destination, a door that closes behind the learner at the end of the line—namely, graduation and the granting of the degree.

Enter

The first phase, *Enter*, is owned by the college or university Admissions Office, which holds the key to the firmly locked entry door. It bases the decision on whom to allow through the college door on such criteria as high school grade point average, standardized tests (in recent years, of decreasing weight), and the applicant's essay, demographics, interests, and varied "recommendations."

The reality of this gatekeeper approach, however, is that colleges spend a great deal of time, effort, and resources marketing themselves to targeted cohorts of the population—specific secondary schools, for example, or particular individuals among student-athletes or superachievers—as part of burnishing their own reputations and "market value." The evaluation process, theoretically aimed at being able to predict which applicants will be most successful in life because they attend the particular college, has become instead a somewhat narrow choosing among already successful prospective students. Discovering those applicants for whom the college might be the hoist that lifts them beyond where they are today has taken second place to the goal of "yield"—the percentage of acceptances offered from among the number of applications received. One result is that the evaluation process too often validates students already part of a system of cumulative opportunities and experiences that suggest they will have no trouble doing well in the world of work, and this represents an inherent inequity in the admissions process.[1] Such inequity significantly undermines the traditional model's efficacy and its relevance to marketplace needs. It renders

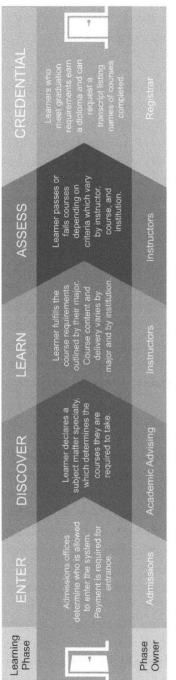

Learning Phase	ENTER	DISCOVER	LEARN	ASSESS	CREDENTIAL
	Admissions offices determine who is allowed to enter the system. Payment is required for entrance.	Learner declares a subject matter specialty, which determines the courses they are required to take.	Learner fulfills the course requirements outlined by their major. Course content and delivery varies by major and by institution.	Learner passes or fails courses depending on criteria which vary by instructor, course, and institution.	Learners who meet graduation requirements earn a diploma and can request a transcript listing names of courses completed
Phase Owner	Admissions	Academic Advising	Instructors	Instructors	Registrar

Figure 3.2. Traditional Learning Model.

Learning Phase	ENTER	DISCOVER	LEARN	ASSESS	CREDENTIAL
	Admissions offices determine who is allowed to enter the system. Payment is required for entrance.	Learner declares a subject matter specialty, which determines the courses they are required to take.	Learner fulfills the course requirements outlined by their major. Course content and delivery varies by major and by institution.	Learner passes or fails courses depending on criteria which vary by instructor, course, and institution.	Learners who meet graduation requirements earn a diploma and can request a transcript listing names of courses completed.
Phase Owner	Admissions	Academic Advising	Instructors	Instructors	Registrar

Figure 3.3. Traditional Learning Model: Enter.

suspect the claim to "blind" admission, and it thereby sabotages the model's productivity right from the start, at the first phase of the process.

Discover

Once admission has become acceptance and the student is indeed entered into the college, phase 2 of the traditional model, *Discover*, offers a period of exploration for the first-year learner, who typically "shops around" to determine which subject-matters to emphasize. It is a time of exposing oneself to different topics, to a range of viewpoints, and to fellow students as part of figuring out the learner's best road to success. Typically, he or she signs up for various "general education" courses and is likely to consult with an academic advisor. The aim is to declare a major course of study in which to specialize, and that declaration then determines the courses the learner will be required to take over the next few years.

Learn

The next phase, *Learn*, is the core step in the process—the actual nuts and bolts of gaining understanding and of acquiring skills through study and practice. On one level, this is a matter of fulfilling the requirements of the chosen major; more deeply, this is when the learner's base body of general knowledge is gained, when skills and competencies are shaped and sharpened, and when the foundation of a future career is laid down.

The learning process is mostly face-to-face with instructors who are typically tenured professors or on the tenure track and are experts in the field, holders of advanced degrees and/or with research experience. Naturally, the framing of the course content and the style of teaching will vary by instructor and by institution. Instructors, being people, bring their own preferences and learning theories into the classroom. This means that a course on Economics 101, to take just one example, might in one instance be lecture-based, in another textbook-based, in yet another project-based. It may be "delivered" by an instructor schooled in behaviorist learning theory, wrested from the students themselves by a constructivist, or evoked out of free-for-all discussions by a connectivist. The mode of delivery might be in-person, online, or mixed—a bit of each. Students can thus choose from among different modes of tuition, banking on such tools as course reviews and peer experience as they select courses or instructors that best fit their schedule and their likes and dislikes.

It is also in this phase of the process that students must represent what they have learned from assigned reading and research—and from their own think-

Figure 3.4 Traditional Learning Model: Discover.

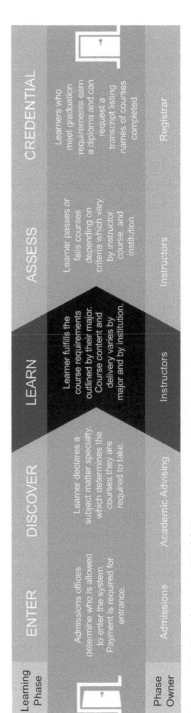

Figure 3.5 Traditional Learning Model: Learn.

ing—as they take on the challenges of quizzes and tests, and as they confront peers and instructors through classroom discussion and debate. In this way, they can measure the theory they have learned and fine-tune the ways they might apply it in the world of work.

Assess

To *Assess* in this traditional linear model is simply to gauge between pass and fail. The interim gradations of accomplishment rate the learner's achievement as excellent, good, less good, mediocre. Whatever the grade, passing the course is a metric that affirms that, at a minimum, the learner participated, performed all the assignments, took the exams, and learned the material in some substantive way.

Credential

The *Credential* that proves it all is the college degree. It assures whoever sees it that the learner has met the institution's requirements, has gone through the gauntlet of the previous four phases—admission, discovering what to study, studying it, and proving that it has been learned—and has passed muster. For the learner, after all, the degree was the purpose of attending the institution. Thus armed, he or she can proceed directly either to the labor market or to advanced studies in search of yet more degrees, any and all of which will typically be framed to be hung on the wall of the office the graduate will one day occupy.

For if admission to college is the most important element in this traditional linear model of learning, getting out of college is the second most important element. Getting out, after all, was the purpose. Getting out is when you get handed the prize esteemed by generations of Americans—the coveted, career-insuring, life-shaping Bachelor of Arts diploma.

This description is in no way meant to demean the degree or the learners who have striven year after year to obtain it. The traditional linear model served students, the institutions at which they studied, and the marketplace for a very long time. It has for generations represented a constant intention: to find the best and the brightest, put them through a particular learning process, and, when they do get through it, award them with a credential. It persisted in that intention consistently, without any fundamental alteration, for a period of some seventy years or more.

It can claim other achievements as well. The "college experience" included ample room for various lines of discovery through a range of "extracurricular" activities and projects. The collaboration with peers and the relationship-

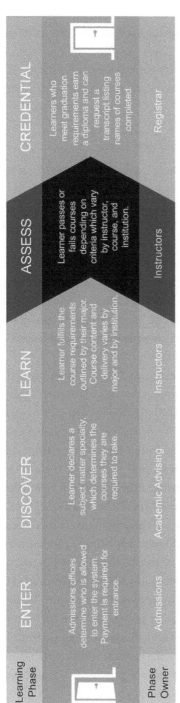

Figure 3.6. Traditional Learning Model: Assess.

Figure 3.7. Traditional Learning Model: Credential.

building it ignited created friendships and lifelong connections that could not but build social capital.

Perhaps above all, the diploma itself really did unlock opportunities. The degree truly was a sure-fire ticket to a fulfilling and successful lifetime career.

Until it wasn't.

Pros and Cons of the Traditional Model

Of course, the traditional linear model of learning had its weaknesses along with its strengths. Often, in fact, a weakness was the other side of one of its strengths. That is not unheard of: in education as in everything else, when you turn over an evident advantage, the flip side can often look less favorable for success than originally anticipated, which at best may diminish the advantage, at worst become an argument against it altogether.

Both the strengths and weaknesses—pros and cons—of the traditional model of learning provide clues to why it is proving to be insufficient for both learners and employers in the new world of work. Each "pro" of the model also contained an equal and opposite "con" threatening to cancel out the benefit of the pro—a proposition worthy of exploration.

Perhaps the greatest strength of the traditional, linear model was the very consistency of its structure and *modus operandi*. Enter, Discover, Learn, Assess, exit with Credential. The process moved step by step in a straight line from start to finish, which meant that both learner and the prospective employer in the marketplace knew precisely what they were getting. And indeed, for those seventy or so years from around 1950 to the time of this writing, colleges and universities barely changed their approach to students or to teaching them, tinkering around the edges of the traditional model in search of various improvements but never challenging its fundamental linear progression.[2] The result is that graduates are bringing to the marketplace today much the same caliber of strengths they offered in 1950— important strengths in many ways, but clearly less relevant than needed in a changing marketplace reality. Again, this approach worked for decades because the college degree provided adequate preparation for them to be qualified for the job demands of the time and, thus, imminently hirable. But the model no longer works, due, in part, to the technical-orientated and continuously and rapidly evolving skill needs not provided by traditional four-year institutions.

An assessment of the pros and cons of each phase of the traditional linear model shows why and how it is failing today's students and the emerging marketplace they will enter.

ENTER

The prevailing admissions process, based almost universally on standardized requirements, offers an excellent example of an advantage the traditional model delivered and thus constitutes a strong argument *for* the model. The argument holds that standardized admission requirements provide an objective metric for entry and are a proven predictor of a successful academic career. The bottom line of this argument has been that standardization leveled the playing field and that learners knew what they were looking for and got the education that met their expectations. Those expectations were for a wide and varied range of academic offerings—from liberal arts to the sciences, from technology to agriculture, from preparation for the major professions to preparation for further study—that would challenge the learner's mind and sharpen his or her critical thinking. A student could take a course on Kabuki theater, another on molecular biology, a third on medieval history while also studying Spanish and attending a seminar on the African Diaspora—all in a single semester. The courses and the classes would engender a rigor of mind that would serve the student well in whatever life path he or she might choose.

Standardized admission requirements, it was argued and believed, guaranteed that everyone entering college was equally well prepared to succeed in these offerings and would benefit equally from the value the degree would bestow.[3]

But the guarantee was undermined, as we observed earlier, by the fact that while the requirements for admission to a college's dazzling array of choices were standardized, they were geared to and primarily met by those privileged enough to access the means to meet the standards. In other words, with the right home life, the right school, the right tutors preparing you for standardized tests, the financial backing that enabled volunteer jobs "serving the community" during high school rather than jobs that paid wages, you were more than likely already bound to be successful, and the high-powered degree served as confirmation of the fact, not as the hoist that uplifts that the traditional model of education is supposed to be.[4]

In other words, the standardized admissions process, lauded as the key to college acceptance and therefore to what a student learns, is actually dependent on an applicant's access to external resources. Those resources, available only to a portion of the population, are the true preparers for, and predictors of, success, and this fundamental inequity in the ability to access those resources has long meant inequity in admissions. Figure 3.8 illustrates the dilemma—which leads to inequities in applications and admissions.

That inequity was the contra argument, the downside of the intended—and perceived—pro. In fact, despite changing laws and consistent renewal of standards over the years, this exclusionary impact proved immovable; no strategies successfully defeated it. The resulting exclusivity meant lost opportunities not only for those excluded but also for the institutions, which had to fall back on selecting from a narrow field from which many "best and brightest" were certainly excluded.

Also exclusionary in far too many cases was the cost of the traditional linear model. This is the clear explanation for the increasing frequency and the rising number of cases of students accepted for admission and deciding not to attend, or agreeing to attend but then failing to show up. As far back as 2015, the Hechinger Report estimated that "up to 40 percent of low-income students who are accepted to college in the spring never make it to the first day of class in the fall. They're stymied by tuition sticker shock."[5]

Many others start but do not finish, which puts them at a severe disadvantage in the eyes of employers. This calls into question the return on investment for economically disadvantaged students considering college.

Regrettably, efforts to undermine the inherent inequity of standardization have not worked, and an admissions model supposedly bent on finding and educating the best and the brightest and sending them on to successful lifetime careers has proven itself inadequate to the task.

DISCOVER

For those who do attend college or university and can pay the bill, the discovery phase of the learning process presents an enormously rich palette of choices along with a large selection of resources to help students contend with the process of exploration—surely a strength of the traditional linear model. Advisors, career counselors, mentors from the sophomore, junior, or senior classes . . . career path advice from alumni . . . internships . . . field trips . . . are all available to help freshmen sort through the choices. And then there are the "Majors Fairs," held on the lawn or in a large indoor space, in which each discipline sets up a table and struts its stuff, doing all it can to attract freshmen to declare it as their major.

The story is told of a Russian professor at one such fair held at one of what were once referred to as the Seven Sisters, the elite East Coast liberal arts colleges originally for women only. The Russian professor sat alone and lonely at

✓	College-Educated, Dual Parents ✗
✓	Educated and Resourceful Family and Friends Network ✗
✓	A-Rated Quality Schooling ✗
✓	Extracurricular Activities/Clubs (in school) ✗
✓	Extracurricular Activities/Clubs (out of school) ✗
✓	Academic Coaches/Standardized Test Tutors ✗
✓	Domestic and International Travel Experiences ✗
✓	College Counseling, Visits, and Application Resources ✗

Figure 3.8. Inequitable Applicant Profiles.

her table, watching with envy as starry-eyed freshmen gathered at the "storefronts" for the French department, Italian, even Latin. Finally, she could bear it no longer. Raising her arms and extending them as if for a group hug, she expostulated in her thick accent: "Come to me, my darlings. I have no subjunctive!" Whether this appeal worked or not, the storyteller did not know, but the professor's action surely constituted an early form of Majors Fair Marketing.

The flip side of this richness of possibilities, however—the con to its pro—is the rigor of course requirements, the no-excuses stipulations for the degree, scattered both within the chosen major and collegewide. Where the wide range of possible courses appeals to intellectual curiosity and passion, requirements speak more narrowly to time schedules and papers due. Some colleges and universities, for example—Columbia is one—insist on a core curriculum to ensure that every student has a grounding in the "great works" the university defines as essential to the educated mind. It is a rigorous requirement that consumes a good bit of each student's time in college.

But time is not the only issue. Increasingly, students in a widening number of institutions of higher learning are surprised, as they think about what to major in, that so few of their choices align with the needs of the market.[6] The "well-rounded," cross-disciplinary education that colleges and universities make possible—the range of subject-matters to pursue—can also operate like too many separate silos, with students feeling out of touch with their own learning and certainly with their own futures. Comparative literature is exciting and soulful, but will it help me into the career I seek as a software engineer, doctor, investment counselor, social worker, researcher? No small number of institutions have tried to address this issue but have found that long-established policies make it difficult to alter the structure of academic programming. This can put students at odds with tenured professors, for whom there are fewer accountability levers and who perhaps see no reason to undermine what has long been a successful set of courses taught.[7]

Once a major is chosen and students are embarked upon a course of study, the traditional linear model of learning shows its great strength, the teaching of content that is its central purpose. Vetted instructors who have reliably gone through a rigorous process are at the heart of high academic standards. These instructors typically have graduate degrees, yet as part of their tenure track process they are required continually to up the ante on their expertise and to demonstrate having done so by publishing books and articles. They are also encouraged or self-driven to polish their teaching *bona fides* through rankings by students and employer surveys by the institution. It means they must prove and prove again that they are at the top of their game and effective at transmitting their expertise.

Yet classroom learning is only the beginning of the richness of the possibilities the traditional linear model supports, possibilities limited only by a student's imagination and flexibility. Summer school, a year abroad, flexibility in fulfilling course requirements, being part of a cohort and collaborating with others on projects all expand learning possibilities. So too do the multitudinous activities available outside the classroom: lectures, sports, student government, clubs, organizations, arts performances; the opportunities can seem endless.

The downside of this largesse, however—the contra to this pro—is that both the content of a course and the quality of teaching vary from instructor to instructor, while the circumstance that so affects the learning varies from lecture-style instruction in an assembly hall to small seminar. Some instructors are better at research than at teaching; some engage brilliantly with students, others seem removed. Teaching is a tough job in itself, and the pressure of the tenure track only adds to it, while for some instructors, gaining tenure lowers the incentive to engage meaningfully with students.

All of this affects both the level and quality of the learning experience as well as the outcomes for students. This is true not only for the instruction delivered but for the support and advice on which so many students depend. It means that to the richness of the learning experience must be added its patchiness, from often exciting and enriching to what students can find dull, irrelevant, even a waste of time and effort.

ASSESS

The assessment process in the traditional linear model offers students the advantage of choosing a course of study in which they know they can excel—a big pro for this model of learning. The learner who freezes at the sight of a blank computer screen or piece of paper can simply avoid those courses that require long-form papers and exams with essay questions. Others concerned about how the transcript will read can rely on courses that instructors will grade on a curve, which can "correct "for less than stellar performance.

The downside of this is that the assessment is neither skill-based nor role-based. It does not provide the kinds of information an employer is looking for: information on what role the learner can play in an organization and/or how well equipped he or she might be to add value to the organization. It is an assessment of ability to think critically and understand broadly, but it is a theoretical judgment, not applied science—and not recognizably applicable to students' career preparation needs.

CREDENTIAL

And this brings us to the final phase of the traditional linear learning process, the credential known as the college degree. Its great strength—thus far, its unmatched strength—is that it carries a lot of weight in terms of serving as the universal and recognized standard for higher educational attainment. It delivers the widely accepted fact that the person holding it has faced and overcome some profound challenges: the challenge of admission into something not easy to get into and the challenge of succeeding at something difficult to do. Something expensive to boot. A degree holder has been "certified" as having learned a lot of as yet undefined knowledge, having access to a dynamic social network, and being worthy of respect.

But what the college degree does not tell anyone at all is what the degree holder knows how to do and is capable of achieving with that set of skills. This is just one result of the misalignment between market needs and the content of the college curriculum. That framed diploma that will adorn the office wall says nothing about the capabilities the learner has mastered, nothing about the types of assessments that confirm those capabilities, nothing about the content of the learner's achievements in the classroom or laboratory or even on the college campus. But for a long time, this emerging reality didn't matter to employers because the basic problem-solving and critical-thinking skills that a college degree guaranteed in a candidate implied they could do the job being offered—or were at least a trainable professional.

That is why, increasingly, the degree has become a validation of generally universal academic requirements. Upon review, a graduate's official transcript depicts topics studied and relative performance for each course of completed study. But it doesn't tell us enough. What specific, applicable skills is the graduate armed with? How well do those skills align with the needs of a particular job? Are the learnings predictive of performance success in a new job? Are the learnings based on a lifelong framework that allows for continued skill development? The answer is no; the degree is losing its power and, indeed, its efficacy as a credential.

Where does that leave students—both those who can afford four years of college and collect the credential and those who cannot and drop out? The latter are particularly badly off: they have spent money to no purpose; they lack a degree and must scramble for a place in the workforce. The former, however, have also not been well served. Their education, theoretically the engine of a successful life, has failed to align with what the marketplace needs. Laden with debt in many cases, they find themselves confronting a marketplace the needs of which they are ill equipped to handle. It does not bode well for them finding the successful life they sought.

Another reality suggests itself here: a college or university education may not be necessary—certainly not for everyone. Prohibitive cost for a credential that has lost its efficacy begins to sound like a senseless proposition.

All of these realities suggest the need for a different way of preparing individuals for a career that can be personally fulfilling and financially rewarding. It is time to revise the traditional, linear model of the learning process and replace it with one that is on-target relevant to the emerging world of work as it really is. The linear process no longer equips college graduates as viable job candidates because it is not meeting the needs of a market that dramatically shifted from what it was originally designed to achieve.

An Alternative Model

The Model Defined

The core of the alternative model is simple: a circle versus a straight line, an ongoing cycle versus a sequence of actions, each dependent on its precursor and therefore bound to a calendar. While the alternative model affirms the core elements of every learning process—enter, discover, learn, assess, credential— each of those elements operates differently in the cyclical model. Moreover,

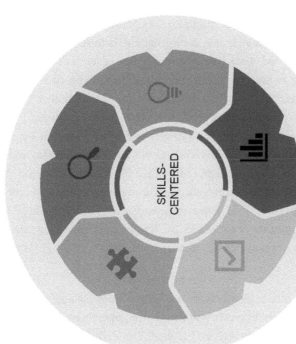

DISCOVER

Learners explore career pathways and competency mapping tools to understand where they are and where they need to be.

LEARN

Learners leverage a variety of educational resources to upskill and meet the needs of the current and future workforce.

ASSESS
Learners' abilities are assessed on the basis of demonstrated ability.

ENTER

Learners enter at various phases throughout their lifetimes.

CONNECT

Learners find or are recruited for jobs on the basis of validated skill data, ensuring that learners will be able to do what they are hired to do.

CREDENTIAL

Learners' abilities are recognized, validating skills in a transparent, contextualized, and standardized way.

Figure 3.9. Alternative Learning Model.

the alternative adds a fifth element to the learning process, evidenced in the graphic representation of the model as "Connect." As will be discussed in some detail, this denotes the interaction between the learner and the marketplace. More on that below.

First, how do the fundamental elements of the learning process work in the alternative model?

Enter

First and perhaps foremost, since the cycle has neither a beginning nor an end, the alternative model provides multiple entry points into the learning process throughout a lifetime. Simply put, the learner enters the learning process anywhere in the circle and at any time—time and time again, if needed or desired. There are no phases here, no distinct periods of time, no precursors that must be realized or overcome before the learner can move ahead. Rather, the circle is progressive, reflecting a learning process that is in essence continual.

This means also that there is no single "owner" of a student's entry into learning—no gatekeeper with a key who unlocks the door to learning and, when learners exit, closes it behind them. Entry might conceivably be generated at the instigation of an institutional structure or through an employer, but the circle is equally open to the learner acting independently in order to add or refresh or improve any number or type of skills. This situates learners at any age for lifelong learning: enter as needed, as often as needed.

Discover

Discover is the exercise in which the learner can examine and evaluate his or her own current skills, interests, and proclivities, map them to the competencies needed in the marketplace, and evaluate the learning needs that must be filled if he or she is either to advance in a current job, find another, or do something totally different.

Discover begins with a click or tap that triggers the immediate exploration of marketplace options and career pathways across all subject areas to meet whatever need impels the individual in the first place. Perhaps it is because the learner senses that the market is trending in a particular direction and believes that new kinds of skills will be useful to keep up with it. It could be a sudden, last-minute need: a new opportunity spotted or a new contract achieved or a flat-out need to make more money.

Whatever the impetus, the learner can peruse both the opportunities and the skill requirements for each subject area of interest and can thus plot the delta

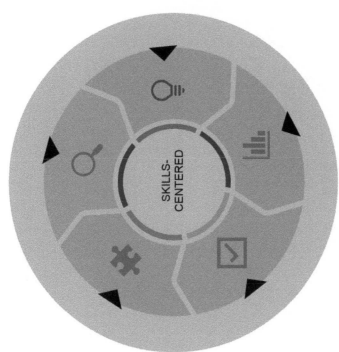

DISCOVER

Learners explore career pathways and competency mapping tools to understand where they are and where they need to be.

LEARN

Learners leverage a variety of educational resources to upskill and meet the needs of the current and future workforce.

ASSESS

Learners' abilities are assessed on the basis of demonstrated ability.

ENTER

Learners enter at various phases throughout their lifetimes.

CONNECT

Learners find or are recruited for jobs on the basis of validated skill data, ensuring that learners will be able to do what they are hired to do.

CREDENTIAL

Learners' abilities are recognized, validating skills in a transparent, contextualized, and standardized way.

Figure 3.10. Alternative Learning Model: Enter.

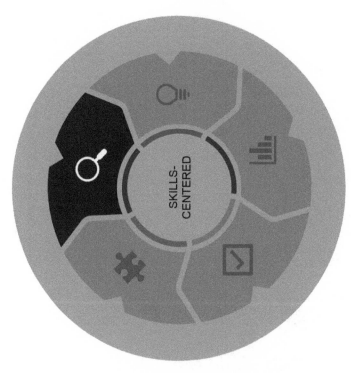

DISCOVER
Learners explore career pathways and competency mapping tools to understand where they are and where they need to be.

LEARN
Learners leverage a variety of educational resources to upskill and meet the needs of the current and future workforce.

ASSESS
Learners' abilities are assessed on the basis of demonstrated ability.

ENTER
Learners enter at various phases throughout their lifetimes.

CONNECT
Learners find or are recruited for jobs on the basis of validated skill data, ensuring that learners will be able to do what they are hired to do.

CREDENTIAL
Learners' abilities are recognized, validating skills in a transparent, contextualized, and standardized way.

Figure 3.11. Alternative Learning Model: Discover.

between the market's need and his or her qualifications. He or she can graze an ever-widening field of upskilling, reskilling, or *de novo* learning possibilities, not just matching skills to a job but also looking at potential new roles, or gig-work projects that might be of interest, or even a complete shift to an emerging area that seems more appealing.

Moreover, this discover process can be created as many times as the learner chooses—without limit. It empowers learners on their own to control their journey to growth and improvement.

Possible drivers of entry into the *Discover* part of the alternative learning model process include

- "I love to cook. Is there a way I can get paid to do it?"

- "I need a base salary of $70,000 per year to support my family. How can I earn that amount?"

- "My chosen field is moving toward obsolescence. What should I do to protect the viability of my career?"

Example: Charlotte has been furloughed from her job as an interior designer and staging engineer. Given a decrease in new housing construction starts due to a weakening economy, she decides to pivot to a new line of work. Her initial engagement with the educational platform provides her with recommended functional specialties matching her unique skill set.

Learn

Learning in the alternative model is goal-driven, whether the overarching aim is to refurbish old skills or gain new skills, and whether the intent is to move ahead or up in a current job, rise to the C-suite, pivot to a different field, or earn more compensation. Whatever skill, knowledge, or understanding learners seek, the alternative model empowers them to leverage a variety of educational resources—shaped by expert instructional designers—to advance it. And the forms of learning available—the options on the table today and those being introduced at a sometimes hectic pace—are virtually limitless, are incredibly diverse, and stretch across a multifaceted universe of delivery platforms.

Naturally, choosing the form will depend on the goal. If the need is to brush up on a skill learned a while ago so as to overcome an immediate obstacle or to support an immediate assignment, the learner might look to as-needed,

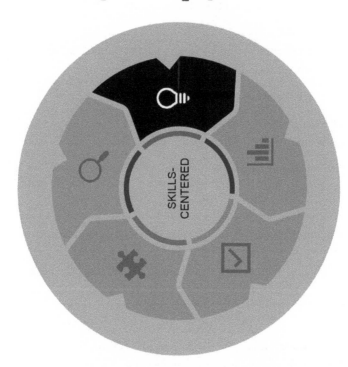

DISCOVER

Learners explore career pathways and competency mapping tools to understand where they are and where they need to be.

LEARN

Learners leverage a variety of educational resources to upskill and meet the needs of the current and future workforce.

ASSESS

Learners' abilities are assessed on the basis of demonstrated ability.

ENTER

Learners enter at various phases throughout their lifetimes.

CONNECT

Learners find or are recruited for jobs on the basis of validated skill data, ensuring that learners will be able to do what they are hired to do.

CREDENTIAL

Learners' abilities are recognized, validating skills in a transparent, contextualized, and standardized way.

Figure 3.12. Alternative Learning Model: Learn.

self-guided learning—perhaps a video tutorial that demonstrates the skill. If the need is to support new responsibilities, the learner would likely seek more guided experience—a classroom course or a bootcamp. In some cases, learning might mean returning to a formal university setting—or entering one for the first time, taking advantage of upskilling resources available through an employer, or pursuing learning opportunities independently.

The learner can read a book. Watch a video tutorial. Take a course, either online or in a classroom, possibly taught by a scholar-practitioner from the organization he or she hopes to join, or attend a bootcamp designed by that same organization and validated by its C-suite. In the learning process of the alternative model, there is ample room for learners to pursue whatever modality works for them in order to gain the needed skills. With no time restraints, multiple entry points, and myriad pathways into instruction, the alternative model ensures that there are no closed doors to acquiring content.

Possible drivers of entry into the *Learn* part of the alternative learning model process include

- Buy a digital textbook and application workbook on cybersecurity and data protection;

- Search for a tutorial video on how to replace an air conditioning condenser in a late model automobile;

- Dedicate three months to a coding bootcamp sponsored by an industry leader or potential employer.

Example: Tucker resigned from his job as an investment banker to pursue his dream job of running a nonprofit. In order to sustain part of his family's standard of living, he decided to earn supplemental income serving as an executive coach to junior bankers. He leveraged the alternative educational platform to learn foundational frameworks and secure a certification.

Assess

Since the acquisition of a skill is categorical, so is the assessment. The learner is able either to perform the skill or not, and the means of assessment are designed precisely to test that performance in a practical, applied demonstration. But because capability exists within a context, assessment in the alternative

DISCOVER

Learners explore career pathways and competency mapping tools to understand where they are and where they need to be.

LEARN

Learners leverage a variety of educational resources to upskill and meet the needs of the current and future workforce.

ASSESS

Learners' abilities are assessed on the basis of demonstrated ability.

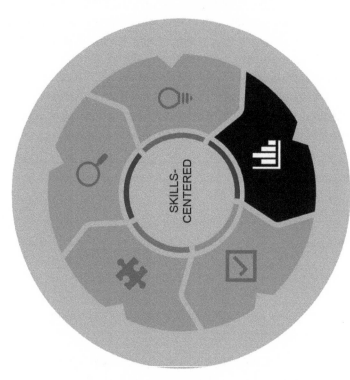

SKILLS-CENTERED

ENTER

Learners enter at various phases throughout their lifetimes.

CONNECT

Learners find or are recruited for jobs on the basis of validated skill data, ensuring that learners will be able to do what they are hired to do.

CREDENTIAL

Learners' abilities are recognized, validating skills in a transparent, contextualized, and standardized way.

Figure 3.13. Alternative Learning Model: Assess.

learning model actually provides learners a more holistic way to prove them-selves across different frameworks.

For example, the range that a demonstration covers may be on a project basis, on a portfolio basis, in an exam, or via a simulation. And because capabil-ity comes in different sizes, from mastery of micro skills to competency-based assessments of work a learner has performed for years to a learner proving his or her skill in a professional certification exam, the dimensions of the assess-ment will also differ.

Possible drivers of entry into the *Assess* part of the alternative learn-ing model process include

- Undergoing a competency-based assessment to show that you can do something you've been doing for years—but without getting formal rec-ognition for it;

- Taking a professional certification exam that doesn't require any formal training—except perhaps self-study;

- As a hiring manager, mapping the job description for a position you are hiring for to ensure optimum alignment with the desired skills you are seeking for the role.

Example: Kristine applied for a promotion as an accounting manager. Although selected as a finalist, she was not selected for the job. The rationale she was given was that she didn't have the requisite skills for governance auditing. Disagreeing, Kristine engaged with the platform provider to as-sess (and prove) her comprehensive skill level in the field.

CREDENTIAL

The credentialing part of the alternative learning process both recognizes and validates the learner's skills and achievements. Where the college degree of the traditional model is vacuous, providing the name of an institution, the gradu-ate's name, and the title of the degree earned, the credential created for an in-dividual in the new model of learning is totally contextualized. It tells not just what skill was demonstrated but also how it was validated, by whom, and in what kind of framework. Standardized in format and content, such a credential offers transparency and precision. It signals to an employer precisely what the learner is equipped to contribute, certifies that he or she will do so fully and

DISCOVER

Learners explore career pathways and competency mapping tools to understand where they are and where they need to be.

LEARN

Learners leverage a variety of educational resources to upskill and meet the needs of the current and future workforce.

ASSESS

Learners' abilities are assessed on the basis of demonstrated ability.

SKILLS-CENTERED

ENTER

Learners enter at various phases throughout their lifetimes.

CONNECT

Learners find or are recruited for jobs on the basis of validated skill data, ensuring that learners will be able to do what they are hired to do.

CREDENTIAL

Learners' abilities are recognized, validating skills in a transparent, contextualized, and standardized way.

Figure 3.14. Alternative Learning Model: Credential.

reliably, and transmits not just the fact that the skill was learned but also exactly how the learning was designed, the criteria for validation, and what went into assessing the learner's achievement.

And it is portable—for a lifetime. As the individual learner adds skills, so does the credential. It is transferable across an ecosystem of different employment needs because it validates applied skills, not familiarity with a body of knowledge. And it is inherently more trusted than a diploma from an institution because it is tied to the specific validator of a specific skill.

Clearly, entry into the credentialing element of the alternative learning process requires a partner doing the credentialing, as will be discussed in detail in the chapters that follow.

CONNECT

Another point of ongoing entry into the new model of learning is the connection that takes place when the credentialed learner and a prospective employer come together. The alternative learning model that this book is proposing both optimizes and at long last equalizes the exercise of making use of human capital.

Today's marketplace resounds with employer complaints about being "unable to find the skills we need!" At the root of these complaints, however, are hiring policies that still look to the diploma, which confirms only that the degree holder took courses in a broad-based subject and is entitled to write "BA" after his or her name. Indeed, a bachelor's degree indicates analytical, writing, and critical thinking skills that represent core value-added traits beneficial to any workplace. But in practice, such hiring policies perpetuate the inequality in the admissions process noted earlier—leaving a wasteland of directly skilled workers unable to find work and ever louder employer complaints about an inability to find employees with the "right capabilities." Relevant skills and abilities (coding, data analysis, financial modeling) are now the priority, supported by the aforementioned foundational traits (analytical, writing, critical thinking).

The alternative learning model can derail and ultimately defeat this inequality by connecting employers seeking precise skills with workers credentialed to perform those very skills (again, this is currently the domain where the majority of living wage jobs reside). In both directions, the process is data-based, unambiguous, and objective: the data defining the employer's need for a particular skill (and for nothing else) and the data validating the prospect's mastery of that skill. In the new model, this demand-response process achieves

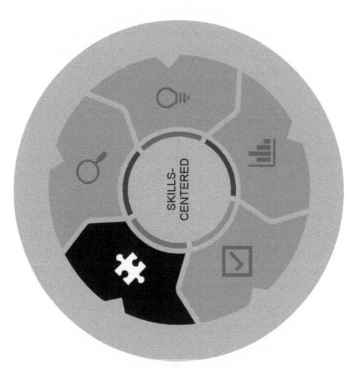

DISCOVER

Learners explore career pathways and competency mapping tools to understand where they are and where they need to be.

LEARN

Learners leverage a variety of educational resources to upskill and meet the needs of the current and future workforce.

ASSESS

Learners' abilities are assessed on the basis of demonstrated ability.

ENTER

Learners enter at various phases throughout their lifetimes.

CONNECT

Learners find or are recruited for jobs on the basis of validated skill data, ensuring that learners will be able to do what they are hired to do.

CREDENTIAL

Learners' abilities are recognized, validating skills in a transparent, contextualized, and standardized way.

Figure 3.15. Alternative Learning Model: Connect.

a level of exactitude unimaginable in the traditional learning model based on the college degree.

The employer's aim, after all, is not only to find the skills needed but to make sure that the person claiming the skills has been credibly validated and can perform the job successfully. Connecting with employee prospects in the new model of learning assures the employer that the candidate has the skills and that his or her mastery of those skills has been validated in a way the employer understands and can recognize. The emerging economic reality clearly must rely on such efficiency and relevancy to drive the hiring process.

The prospective employee also finds efficiency and relevancy in this part of the process. He or she submits an application, creating a profile that an algorithm will match to a job. If the employee falls short of gaining the job—perhaps there have been changes in the marketplace, not surprising in a quickly shifting economy—this can be a signal to him or her to reenter the Discover part of the learning process. Indeed, for the learner, reentry into discovery and ongoing learning as needed is a constant that the new alternative learning process enables and encourages. This is lifelong learning made real.

Pros and Cons of the Alternative Model

The fundamental underlying strength of the alternative this book advances is that it is learner-centric, answering the need for lifelong learning that is increasingly recognized as the way truly to serve employers of the future. Focusing on the individual learner, not on any single institution, is the obvious path to placing the right person in the job. And placing the right person in the job is essential both for achieving global growth in the emerging world of work and for ensuring maximization of human capital. The weakness of this alternative model is that right now there is no roadmap to making it happen.

Rather, as this book goes to press, scores of startup ventures are developing and attempting to validate scalable prototypes encompassing all elements of the alternative model we have put forth here. The change is under way, but there is no advisor meeting learners at the door and showing them the way. Instead, it is left to the individual learner to decipher the right entry point into the process and to figure out how to navigate once inside. It's their responsibility to (1) figure out which alternative learning provider is most appropriate, (2) identify employee-needed skills, and (3) determine how to equip themselves with said skills. Which path to follow, how to filter out what doesn't work from what does: right now, learners have to work that out for themselves (although we will have more to say on the subject in Chapter 8). True, the technology continues to advance at its usual rapid pace, especially as algorithms in machine learning become increasingly more effective, but as of this writing, the elements of the new alternative are more like automated products than a personal pathway.

In the matter of the learning itself, it is fair to say that the people delivering the content are not as well vetted as college professors. Who does the vetting of content providers and what the standards of worthiness might be are nowhere near the level of the requirements and peer review of instruction in college. Yes, it is true that a number of professors and of well-known corporate executives and consultants take part in the automated learning now on the market, which constitutes a good beginning, but it does not amount to a reliable set of standards for a critical examination of content providers.

In a number of instances, the assessment of learning by new alternative startups is misrepresented. A knowledge test might be passed off as a competency assessment, somehow fudging the difference between (1) answering a question correctly and applying a particular skill in context, or (2) foundational knowledge and mastery of an operational function. The ultimate solution for finding the right way to verify skills is probably to be found in a holistic design of the material and a holistic way to assess it. Such a solution is likely some way off, as it isn't clear as yet how to assess tasks that do not translate into objective tests, which—notably—stymie those learners who, by contrast, do very well at demonstrating skills in a wider context. It is time to come up with new ways, other than paper and pencil, to evaluate how humans learn skills.

The Connect experience represented in the alternative model can also be a weakness. In this part of the model, learners find jobs on the basis of connecting their validated skills with those needed by employers. But the way the skills are validated is by the learners earning badges and chips as they master competencies. Some employers, unfamiliar with this new engaged learning approach, may incorrectly assume that the learning is less comprehensive due to its "gamified" design.

Learners engaged in the alternative model may also have a negative perception due to the "skill for skill" nature of the job connection. As the gig economy grows and more contractors are being engaged, this hiring practice may seem biased toward the gig economy. Therefore, the process may feel like a transaction, and the question lingers, "Am I being hired for a job, or for a temporary project?"

What it all comes down to is there are a multitude of alternative learning platforms in silos—that is, designing and delivering curricula in unique and distinctly different ways. At present, there is no common language, such as an

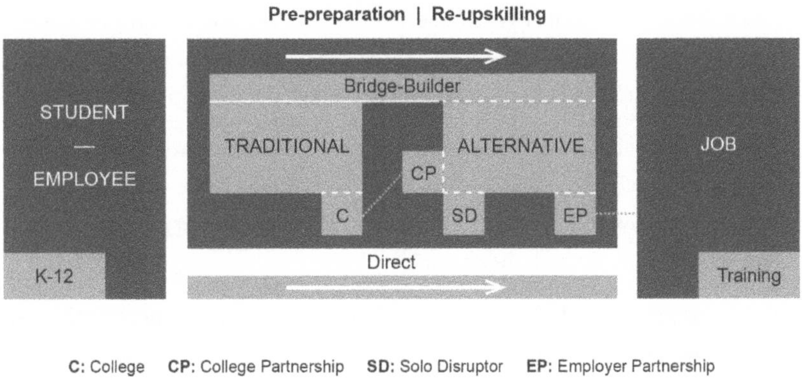

Pre-preparation | Re-upskilling

C: College   **CP**: College Partnership   **SD**: Solo Disruptor   **EP**: Employer Partnership

Figure 3.16. Career Pathway Model.

inventory of skills or taxonomy of competencies, to translate the learnings from those silos to relevant (and commercially valuable) products for their learners. Further, there is no single, defined technological infrastructure to create such a classification for a common skills language. The result is an ecosystem of inconsistent learning and risky hiring, which has the potential to undermine trust and thrust us back to the old standards of the old model, with all its biases and inadequacies of linear, misaligned learning.

So the new, alternative model of learner-centric, skill-based teaching and learning is still a startup. This book aims to change that, first by profiling and assessing the key players shaping the new alternative model, then by plotting a way forward toward the realization of the model—sooner rather than later.

Pathway Options

Current and future employees now have multiple pathways to engage in work: directly, following pre-preparation education, or after already working to reskill.

In this chapter, we have introduced two provider models: traditional learning and alternative learning. The traditional model is based on enrollment in a college or university. The alternative model may be undertaken in partnership with a college or university, in partnership with an employer, or directly through a solo disruptor provider (all three supported by bridge-builder organizations). These three pathways will be discussed, in greater detail, in the next four chapters.

Figure 3.16 demonstrates the pathway in detail:

- Path 1: Students or employees engage in the workforce directly from their K–12 experience. Once working, they have the opportunity to be trained by the employer and/or to engage in re- or upskilling through the alternative model.

- Path 2: Students or employees engage in pre-preparation through the traditional route of college or one of the alternative routes. Once working, they, once again, have the opportunity to be trained by the employer or to engage in re- or upskilling through the alternative model.

The Career Pathway Model shows that there is significantly more optionality by engaging in the multiple options that the alternative route provides versus the "one-and-done" option of the traditional route.

The Cases: Structured Methodology

The four chapters that follow explore startup organizations at the forefront of bringing into being an alternative learning process to serve the world of work that will drive the emerging global economy. Sixteen organizations are profiled, divided into four categories:

- Organizations in partnership with colleges

- Organizations in partnership with employers

- Solo (unpartnered) disruptors

- Bridge-builders providing infrastructure

The categories broadly correspond to the inflection points at which, in our alternative model, students enter, or reenter, the learning process—that is, as part of or in addition to traditional higher education, in response to an employer need, or for lifelong or career-long upskilling or reskilling. Bridge-builders provide the infrastructure to support all three approaches. Within each category, we'll look at how the company—and its partner approach, where warranted—improves on the traditional model, if it does, and assess where it goes from here.

We chose these specific organizations because they demonstrated proficiency in one or more elements of the alternative model this book puts forth and because all are reaping success greater than that of their peers, as measured by a number of yardsticks.

At the same time, the choices embody a representative cross-section of a rapidly expanding universe of alternative education providers and skills-based trainers.

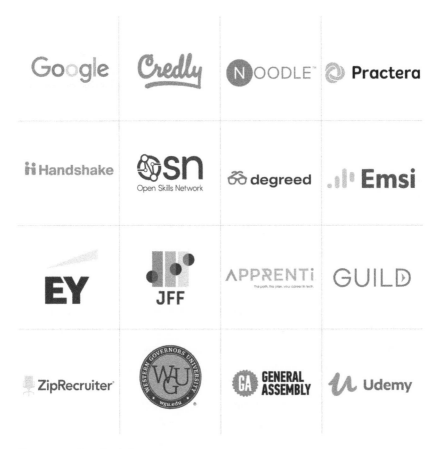

Figure 3.17. Case Study Logos.

Figure 3.17 highlights the organizations profiled.[8]

Two methodologies were relied upon to carry out the case studies: detailed written questionnaires followed by in-depth interviews with senior executives. In the first instance, therefore, organizations presented what they wanted to be heard about how they saw themselves and their mission; in the second instance, there was an effort to probe deeply into those self-assessments and discuss in detail current issues and future plans.

What follows are the findings, conclusions about those findings, and assessments of where alternative learning processes are headed and how they will shape the future.

$$\textbf{4}$$

COLLEGE PARTNERSHIPS

No one is predicting the end of the traditional college education as a viable pathway to success in career and life. Many students will continue to pursue the "college experience" for the usefulness and significance they believe it can provide. For these students, therefore—and there are a lot of them—the college degree still represents high value. So, it is not surprising to find organizations that partner with colleges to help them attract more applicants by lowering barriers of entry and raising the perceived value of their degrees. This chapter profiles three such organizations, while a fourth case study looks at a university that is pursuing the same goals internally.

Case Study 1: Noodle Partners

Learner's Experience

At noodle.com/signup, I created an account, clicked on the state where I live, selected "Undergrad College," declared that I'm a high school student researching my options for a four-year school, and admitted that I was feeling a bit anxious. To that I added that cost is an important factor—I need a school with low tuition, or one that will give me a big scholarship.

When I was asked what type of setting I'd like to pursue my degree in, I hovered my cursor over "Traditional" at first, because I want to attend classes on campus at a big university. But then I noticed that there were online options too, so, I clicked on "Not sure, want help deciding." That took me to a landing page where I clicked "Schools," which opened up a list topped by the Ivy League institutions affiliated with Noodle. I definitely can't afford any of them, so I started to filter by cost, type, campus setting. . . .

This was all starting to feel a bit daunting. So, I clicked on "Experts" to find someone who could help me through the process. That gave me a list of admissions counselors at a variety of undergraduate and graduate institutions, as well as some authors and other experts. I clicked on a counselor at a college that I was pretty sure is in my state.

By then it was after 10:00 p.m., and I was even more anxious than I was when I started. I found a link that let me schedule a free twenty-minute phone call with the counselor early the next morning. Between my large public high school's stretched resources and my busy schedule of extracurricular activities, I hadn't been able to schedule a meeting with my school's career center yet; this would be my first opportunity to talk with someone who can help me figure all this out. As I logged off my computer, I could feel my nervousness turning to hopeful anticipation.

About Noodle

"The industry was moving in a direction that was problematic . . . and rather than stand on the street corner and shake my fist, I thought I would just start Noodle. . . . We have a really simple mission, which is to help universities use technology to transform themselves to the digital age."
—John Katzman, founder and CEO

Noodle Partners is an online program management company that works with colleges and universities to not only help applicants manage the complexities of their admissions processes, but also "elevate campus-wide teaching and technology," in the words of a September, 2020 article in *Business Wire,* by providing students with a rich online learning experience once they are enrolled.[1] The company is the brainchild of John Katzman, who also founded the college admissions test prep juggernaut The Princeton Review and the educational technology company 2U.

In our interview, Katzman described Noodle as the "best friend of smart colleges and universities." By creating "really agile programs," he said, "we can lower the cost of higher ed by about a quarter without . . . in any way dumbing down" the educational experience. "Noodle's really simple mission," he said, is to "help universities use technology . . . to raise capacity, raise engagement, [and] improve outcomes."[2]

Problems Addressed

TRANSFORMING EDUCATION FOR THE DIGITAL AGE

Noodle generally uses its own in-house learning designers when developing courses for its partners, Katzman explained, but if a university prefers to create its own online content, Noodle will support that work. While the learning theory and focal competencies are determined by the university, the learning experience is based on Noodle's EPIIC framework—specifically EPIIC Rubric version 2—which enables a learning experience that is behaviorally, emotionally, and cognitively *Engaging*; *Personalized* (in keeping with Roger Schank's idea that "learning occurs when someone wants to learn" and not "when someone wants to teach"[3]); *Interactive*, in that it encourages a two-way flow between demonstrating learning and receiving feedback; *Intuitive*, because its seamless design allows students to focus on content and learning; and *Collaborative*, as it provides students with opportunities to learn from peers. Classes are run by university faculty via either synchronous or asynchronous online programs.

LOWERING THE COST OF EDUCATION

How does Noodle lower costs? In Katzman's words, if a school wants to take its net tuition down by a quarter, it must do two things. The first is to add capacity. For example, "if you're using the campus in the summer, or if you're sending students off for a semester in an internship married to two online courses so that they're staying on track for graduation, you can get 25 percent more undergraduate students without building another building." The second is to increase enrollment, by as much as 100 percent, by offering programs online. Online graduate school is a much more accessible option than full-time, in-person programs, because it does not conflict with students' jobs. The COVID pandemic provided a dramatic demonstration of the viability of online learning, Katzman added, and he predicted that the portion of online learners would never again dip below 50 percent.

At the same time, he cautioned, it is essential to ensure that prospective applicants understand what they will really pay. The cost pages on most school websites are incoherent, he said, adding that "universities are terrible marketers in terms of how they frame their financial aid." While airlines advertise their best rate, he said, "universities advertise their most expensive seat, which is the full tuition."

Noodle changes the equation. In addition to offering students free twenty-minute counseling sessions—a service with a 93 percent Net Promoter Score (a measure of customers' perceptions of brands)—Noodle also works directly with colleges to solve the problem at its root. The first step, as already noted, is to talk in terms of net rather than stated tuition. The second is to express the net tuition cost clearly and without jargon, and to explain that it is what the average student pays. Third, every potential applicant should be able to see what he or she specifically will pay. This is easy enough to do, Katzman explained, because there are algorithms that allow colleges to "ask you a bunch of questions and spit out an estimate of what you will pay." Fourth, applicants should be able to learn what the potential return on their investment is by seeing what graduates from programs typically end up doing in their careers. Colleges can easily gather this information via alumni surveys. And fifth, since all students must pay something, applicants need to understand their best alternatives for aid. Schools waste a lot of money providing financial aid advice that students don't understand—as much as $400 per student in administrative costs, according to Noodle's analysis—while the students pay a steep price in time and frustration. "Let's take the whole financial aid process and make it user-serving," Katzman suggested. "I think it will put a lot of pressure on other schools to do the same thing."

Beyond the fees they pay Noodle, schools will have to invest a lot of high-level time and mindshare in these efforts. According to Katzman, "We would need the dean or the provost. We'd need the head of financial aid. And we'd need them for a while." But the return on that investment would be substantial. By bringing in the right experts, and even more important, bringing the schools in their network together to problem-solve together, they can distribute the costs as well as the benefits more widely.

Without a nudge from a partner like Noodle, this kind of collaboration is almost unheard of. "Schools were all built in silos," Katzman declared, "and they all think of themselves in that way."

But while some schools with similar programs may compete for the same students, the fact is, most only directly compete within a very small geographic range—a result of the reality that 75 percent of students attend schools that are within fifty miles of their homes. This means, in Katzman's words, that "everyone else is a potential ally." But how to get to that alliance? Or as Katzman put it, "How can we think of this as a network? How can our universities help one another?"

Noodle's website is one answer. It attracts about a half-million students per month who are looking for a college or graduate school.[4] If schools see themselves as partners in a network that supports those students rather than competitors, then students and schools alike will benefit.

Katzman offered a simple example of how a collaboration could work: "You have your own courses, but consider a little thing like a case study you develop, or an animation, a simulation, something that's really thoughtful and great. If you get four other schools out of four thousand other schools to use it, you just cut your instructional design costs by 80 percent. That's where this network can be really powerful."

Expanding Student Access and Support

Collaborations are key to Noodle's approach to the $20 billion market for employer-subsidized continuing education. A key example of this is the role it played in the September 2020 launch of WorkforceEdge, a "complete employee education management platform" developed by Strategic Education, Inc. (SEI).[5] In addition to the programs offered by SEI's two for-profit institutions, Strayer University and Capella University, WorkforceEdge also connects "select employers and their employees with degree programs from a network of higher education institutions" via Noodle Partners, according to *Inside Higher Ed*.[6] Tuition assistance typically comes in two forms—reimbursements to employees, or repayment of student loans. It is tax deductible for employers up to $5,250 per employee. But the processes involved in securing those benefits are so Byzantine in most companies that many eligible employees don't take advantage of them. WorkforceEdge streamlines the process by connecting potential students to a network of preapproved education providers, much as many health plans do with doctors, who are paid directly by the employers. SEI hopes that eventually all of its several hundred employer partners will use the platform, and Noodle Partners hopes to bring all of its university partners on board.[7] The WorkforceEdge endeavor is just one of a range of Noodle's innovative partnerships that widen the pipeline of students accessing higher education. While increased enrollment adds substantive value to those schools in the present, it also pays dividends in the future, as many of those students will continue to seek the benefits of higher education throughout their careers and lives.

Solutions Pursued

Help Universities Become Better Marketers

First, colleges must address their marketing problems. In a changing skills economy in which adaptability and critical thinking are seen as essential to success in the workforce, Katzman noted, "the best education we have is something like a liberal arts education that makes you agile and able to navigate disruption in whatever career you've chosen. But colleges don't tell that story." Noodle is trying to help colleges think more deeply about what "Liberal Arts 2.0 (or Liberal Arts 7.0 . . . after all, the liberal arts have been amended many times since the trivium)" could look like—and how it could be marketed more effectively.

Create Innovative Degree Offerings

As relevant as the liberal arts may still be in the workplace, college programs will also have to offer specific workplace credentials. In our interview, Katzman described a potential new type of degree—"effectively, the associate of a masters. It might be a twelve-credit specialist degree that is stackable towards a masters. It would be Title IV–eligible and could be offered by institutions of higher ed, but also by alternative providers." So long as all the schools that offer it agree about the competencies it provides, they could teach them in their own ways. But there would be reciprocity—"it will be stackable towards my masters, but it'll also be stackable towards ours." The idea of stackable credentials and credit transferability are not new; the American Council on Education (ACE) has been working on the latter issue since the 1970s.[8] But what Noodle is proposing would not just be recognized by higher ed institutions but co-created by them. And most important, "It'll be meaningful to an employer."

Help Universities Be Responsive and Aligned with Labor Market Needs

Specialist degrees and controlling costs are important, but in terms of the bigger picture, higher ed needs to be more responsive to the changing needs in the marketplace. Up until now, Katzman noted, higher ed was "not built to be responsive—rather, it's built to be consistent." The services Noodle Partners provides suggest one path to a different future. "I'm hoping Noodle will be the way that traditional universities are able to compete effectively against some of those new providers," he said. "You know, it's a big space, and it's not a death match. But those providers are tapped into a need, and higher ed wants to be tapped into it as well."

Full Focus: Alternative Model

- ENTER: Noodle provides its partners with lower-cost, clarified processes, and a broader pipeline of applicants.

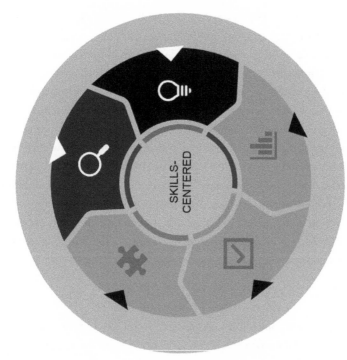

DISCOVER

Learners explore career pathways and competency mapping tools to understand where they are and where they need to be.

LEARN

Learners leverage a variety of educational resources to upskill and meet the needs of the current and future workforce.

ASSESS

Learners' abilities are assessed on the basis of demonstrated ability.

ENTER

Learners enter at various phases throughout their lifetimes.

CONNECT

Learners find or are recruited for jobs on the basis of validated skill data, ensuring that learners will be able to do what they are hired to do.

CREDENTIAL

Learners' abilities are recognized, validating skills in a transparent, contextualized, and standardized way.

Figure 4.1. Noodle and Alternative Model: (Enter + Discover + Learn).

- DISCOVER: Among Noodle's features are free twenty-minute admissions and financial aid counseling, and a streamlined approach to tuition reimbursement programs (in partnership with SEI) that will allow employees to take greater advantage of them.

- LEARN: By moving universities into the digital age, Noodle helps them leverage tools that allow them to provide better services at better costs. But they don't fundamentally change the learning design.

Limited Focus: Alternative Model

- ASSESS: All assessment still happens at the instructor level.

- CREDENTIAL: Same traditional degrees are offered, though there may be opportunities for universities to collaborate on new types of degree programs.

- CONNECT: While they partner with employers to provide traditional degree programs, Noodle doesn't facilitate the learning-to-employment transition.

Key Takeaways

- Students will continue to pursue traditional higher education, but high tuitions and complex and exclusionary admission processes pose steep barriers to entry.

- Collaboration is one way to attack the problem. Colleges and universities see all of their peers as competitors, but in fact they only directly compete with schools that offer similar programs within a close geographic range; everyone else is a potential ally. By sharing expenses and pooling resources, they can lower costs throughout the entire system.

- Cost and access, however, are just two of the challenges facing higher education. If the learning happening in the traditional model doesn't lead to success in the workplace, the value of degrees will continue to diminish. Students will benefit from innovations in learning designs that make them more relevant to employers.

Let's look now at a case in which innovation in learning design is taking place within traditional higher education.

Case Study 2: Practera

◎ Practera

Learner's Experience

I'm a part-time student at a community college. When I told my professor that I wanted to learn to code Java, he told me that as a way of providing students with real-world learning experiences, the department had recently partnered with Practera. I got an invitation to join the Practera platform and created an account. I saw that I'd already been added to the Java class, for which a project outline was posted. I was assigned to Student Team 4. I watched the project introduction video and learned that we were being tasked to come up with a new version of a user dashboard for a SaaS platform—that is, a software as a service platform on which a third-party provider hosts apps for distribution to customers over the Internet.

The next day in class, the professor introduced our "industry mentor," whom I recognized from the video. She works at a local tech company and seemed excited to work with us; she said the project submissions would really help her company, which has been rethinking its user experience. She presented a statement of purpose for the next few weeks, during which my team would design and code a new dashboard, while checking in periodically with the professor on technical issues and the mentor on project expectation issues. At the end, we would present our product to the mentor. Our collaboration would be via the Practera platform, which would capture data about how well we're working together and how far along we've come and make it available to our professor.

Over the next few weeks, my team met regularly via a video conferencing tool and the team chat function in Practera, following the project outline to stay on track. Every once in a while, we'd get pulse checks from our professor if it looked like we'd hit a roadblock, and feedback from the mentor on our progress reports. Sometimes we could tell she was really busy, but other times she was totally thorough.

On the day of the presentation, my team was really nervous. We were proud of our work, but what if the drop-down menu we'd created wasn't what she wanted? When she called us into the room, I grabbed our slides and took a deep breath.

About Practera

"There are points in people's lives where they suddenly realize, oh, wow, I need to get healthy. I need to progress. In the mental space, it's the recognition that I don't actually have the skills I need. . . . [Practera helps] universities build experiential learning into their degree value proposition . . . [to] offer mentoring and work experience programs that make their students more employable."

—Wes Sonnenreich, co-founder/co-CEO

Practera is an Australian education technology company that was founded in 2010 by its co-CEOs Beau Leese and Wes Sonnenreich. The two met while employed at Deloitte, where they had been tasked with starting an innovation program that would help Deloitte recruit new hires that were better prepared for the rigors of consulting. Deloitte had an internal two-year training program, but they wanted to offload some of that work on the universities that its new employees were graduating from. The program Leese and Sonnenreich designed partnered with universities to run case-study competitions and internships, among other things, and filled the need as intended.[9]

But managing those programs was extremely time-intensive. As Sonnenreich put it to me in our interview, they needed to "streamline and systematize the way in which we were running [it] . . . could we take the best parts of it and create a model that was scalable?" When Sonnenreich and Leese left Deloitte, it was with Deloitte's encouragement to do just that; in fact, Deloitte was the first corporate sponsor of what eventually became Practera. Fast forward to the present and Practera is partnering with dozens of universities and companies to run experiential learning programs. Powered by Practera's mobile-first platform, their instructional design methodology is deeply informed by learning science, feedback, reflection tools, and sophisticated analytics.

Though it was conceived from the employer's perspective, today Practera's customer is the educator. "We work with the educators because we believe that the ultimate accountability for the learning and experience rests with them," in Sonnenreich's words. Practera evolved to be "a learning platform first," purchased—on a per-student basis—by educators who "actually care about optimizing the learning outcomes of the students. We're selling to educators who actually want to make sure the students are developing skills and learning. They need to be able to audit what's going on, and they need to be able to control it and shape it."

Students benefit from Practera's project-based approach because they are solving real-world problems and exercising the professional skills they'll need in the workplace. Educators benefit from the student and team engagement data, which helps them better support student learning and cultivate work readiness. And employers benefit from the talent pipeline and the mentorship opportunities Practera provides for current or future managers.

Problems Addressed

ENABLE SCALABLE, HIGH-QUALITY EXPERIENTIAL LEARNING

To better explain this, let's rewind a bit to Practera's beginnings. At Deloitte and immediately after, Sonnenreich and Leese were thinking more about the corporation's needs than the students'. "We didn't understand the pedagogy," Sonnenreich admits. "But as we started to expand and to work with more university faculty and educators, we started to understand that what was missing from what we were doing was the learning side." They brought experts in education on board and began researching how they could do better. At the time, there was a growing movement in Australia toward work-integrated or experiential learning, which has since become a centerpiece of planning in most Australian universities. Colleges understood that they were not delivering outcomes that enabled students to succeed after graduation—the "skill gap" we sketched out in Chapter 2. "Work-integrated learning is about skill development and contextualization," Sonnenreich explains. Since then, "the trend toward work-integrated learning has been accelerating, first in Australia and now globally."

Because Practera emerged early in the game, an infrastructure to support scalable experiential learning did not exist. Sonnenreich and Leese began by offering services to support industry and educator collaboration, a la Deloitte's innovation program. "Over the course of several years," Sonnenreich explains, "we started to build our own tech to take away pain points that we felt internally." While the initial goal was to enable Practera to deliver services more effectively, the team realized that the software itself could be served directly to customers. "We started thinking," Sonnenreich reflects, whether what they had built "could be a software solution for our university customers to use, since they also have teams doing the same thing"—that is, "trying to run work-integrated learning, trying to scale up the programs."

That was the beginning of a journey to build out a SaaS platform that would reduce the complexity and cost of delivering high-quality experiential learning, while improving student outcomes by ensuring timely support, reflective practice, and regular feedback.

What does that look like?

For the student, it looks like being guided through a real-world project, sourced by an industry partner, via an education technology platform with learning content, communication tools, and prompts for feedback and reflection. The learning content is created by the educators, sometimes with the help of Practera's instructional design services, and takes three forms:

1. Formal learning content, delivered via the platform as text or video;

2. Workshop or meeting content, delivered in-person or, increasingly, via video conference sessions organized through the platform;

3. Feedback from learners, team members, peers, educators, and external coaches, mentors, and experts.

Feedback constitutes the most important element of learning content. Sonnenreich defines it as the "main delivery channel for learning because it contextualizes the theory to the practice through a tangible activity or work product." The student creates a deliverable using some guidance but, importantly, receives feedback throughout and after the process.

This experience is informed by the discipline known as learning science—and specifically by the underlying theory of experiential learning theory, as articulated by David A. Kolb in his landmark book, *Experiential Learning: Experience as the Source of Learning and Development*. In Kolb's words, "learning is the process whereby knowledge is created through the transformation of experience."[10] According to Kolb, learning is a cycle: sustain an experience, reflect on it, learn from it, try out what you've learned. "The emphasis on the *process* of learning"—my emphasis—"as opposed to the behavioral outcomes distinguishes experiential learning from the idealist approaches of traditional education and from the behavioral theories of learning created by Watson, Hull, Skinner, and others. Modern versions of these latter approaches are based on the empiricist philosophies of Locke and others. . . . Experiential learning theory, however, proceeds from a different set of assumptions. Ideas are not fixed and immutable elements of thought but are formed and re-formed through experience."[11]

Secondarily, Practera encourages constructive alignment in instructional design. In other words, start with what you want the student to know or be able to do, then devise teaching and learning activities that directly address those intended outcomes. The constructivist approach assumes that students make meaning from what they do in order to learn; real skill-building happens in that *process*. As Kolb suggests, this is in contrast to historical practice in the traditional college or university classroom, where the expert professor imparts knowledge that students passively absorb.[12]

Experiential learning, by definition and as supported by Practera, means that the student ends up with concrete evidence of his or her learning: a deliverable at the conclusion of a real-world project. Student competency is measured through expert evaluation of that evidence, typically by the educator. These expert evaluations are feedback against a rubric, which is often set up to measure competency against skills or achievement of learning objectives. The student also submits a self-assessment because reflection—especially self-reflection—is also an essential part of the model. "We realized self-assessment was really important, because we were taking the tools we used [for assessment] at Deloitte, which was for a performance review," Sonnenreich explains. "You would come into your performance review with a self-assessment based on the same rubric that you were being evaluated [against] by the reviewer, who was the professional. The self-assessment then contrasted with the reviewer assessment." So the assessment is not just based on a deliverable of a real work product; equally significantly, the student undergoes an assessment *process* that is similar to what he or she will experience in the workplace.

That said, the real value of experiential learning—that is, the human or employability skills it creates—is harder to measure. In a paper posted on the Practera website, Leese and Practera's VP of Learning & Experience Nikki James notes that "employability skills and work readiness extend beyond the development of foundational disciplinary knowledge to competencies and character qualities including collaboration, creativity, leadership and adaptability. Recently, transdisciplinary skills models have evolved and developed significant currency—for example the World Economic Forum's '21st century skills.' These competencies are best acquired experientially and are best demonstrated through the application of knowledge, skills, and responsibilities to new settings and complex problems."[13]

Leese and James emphasize that "to maintain distinctiveness and serve students, employers, and communities, Universities need to systematically encourage, challenge, and support students to apply, synthesize, and reflect on their use of knowledge in real-world situations."[14] The quality of those experiences really matters. So does the quality of authenticity. If students do not confront a situation that mirrors what they will face in the workplace, their skills will not transfer.

Delivering or participating in high-quality experiential learning is not easy, which is why shortcuts are usually taken. "I think the challenge for us—a frustration, but also an opportunity—is that it is human nature to trend toward mental diabetes, sugary snacks of learning where you feel like you're learning but aren't actually learning," Sonnenreich reflects. "The challenge is getting people to pay for quality." Taking shortcuts hurts students, but it also affects employers. Hiring someone without strong skills means the employer must either retrain or replace them—both expensive options. "I think the question is, do education institutions see it as their responsibility to offer a compelling solution to that problem?" Sonnenreich asks.

Ultimately, says Sonnenreich, "I don't know if we'll be a billion-dollar company off the back of trying to solve the quality problem, because the market doesn't seem to reward that as much as it rewards sugary snack manufacturers. We set out to actually try to move the needle on quality. Our challenge is to figure out how we're going to become big enough that we can have global impact in a world which is looking for silver-bullet solutions. The solution requires work; the educator has to think differently and be willing to commit to what is a complicated journey."

An essential part of that work is supporting educators as they absorb these changes in pedagogical theory and practice.

Support the Changing Role of Educators

"Any educator at any level—K–12, vocational, higher ed, or corporate learning—who is looking to add structure and quality assurance to a 'learning-by-doing' experience can benefit from our platform and services," Sonnenreich declares. But first, they have to know how to use it. Practera captures a wealth of data to inform educators' decisions on how and when to provide support and uses automated "nudges" to help them act as coaches to their students. The Team 360 component of Practera, for example, is a tool that many businesses use. Educators can use it, Sonnenreich says, to capture data at multiple points in time during a project and then lead discussions about how students' "self-perceptions and their teams' perceptions have changed over the course of a project. That's a very powerful idea, and it completely changes the role of the teacher, because now you're shepherding your students on a journey of self-discovery as they learn about themselves, how they work in teams, how others perceive them. It just opens up all these new dimensions. But if you don't know you can click on a button and get that functionality into your course with very minimal effort, you would never even think about designing your course around it."

Close the Skill Gap by Engaging Industry

The aim is to give students access to real-world learning experiences, including real-world feedback. The employers that supply it benefit in four ways.

First, brand positioning. Employers are keen to ensure that they can reach the students they are going to want to recruit formally later on. One way to do that is through the kind of outreach that work-based learning entails.

Second, recruitment. Engagement in work-based learning is a premier opportunity for measuring the capabilities of potential recruits and assessing their cultural fit with the organization.

Third, idea exploration. Student teams can be an excellent source of new ideas. When a company is pondering the business case for an initiative, engaging with motivated students in a real-world situation can potentially move the needle one way or the other.

Fourth, professional development. Engagement with students is a two-way street. Mentors and project leaders learn such valuable skills as how to give constructive feedback, articulate expectations and set scope, and motivate a team.

More broadly, when employers work with Practera, they help close the skill gaps in their own workforces. "It's not enough to know how to work in a team," Sonnenreich says. You need to know how to work in a team in the sector that you're in, how to apply the hard skills with the soft skills to solve problems in a particular area." The only way to do that, in his view, is "through experiential learning and evidence-based assessment," and for that, "you're going to need tools, but you also need incentive structures where it is in companies' and educators' interest to focus on high-quality evidence-based experiential learning and assessment."

Solutions Pursued

Integrate with the Tools Teams Use

Integration into the ever-expanding universe of work systems—Slack, Microsoft Teams, Salesforce.com, Google Workplace, Zoom, and more—is a primary focus for Practera, as it makes it easier for employers to engage students on projects while also improving their own skills. "Generally," says Sonnenreich, "the learning is around types of projects and collaborations where most of the work is not happening on the platform." Extracting information from all those different platforms is an essential Practera goal, but so is the need to ensure that those systems are "really very low friction."

Support More Automated Interventions

The aim is to achieve better outcomes, and to do so, Practera aspires to connect specific types of interventions with specific outcomes. Says Sonnenreich, "We've been letting the educators decide what interventions to do, but we've been collecting data on that so that we can start to analyze that and figure out what we should be doing or recommending. There are a few minor things we will automate, like overdue notices and things like that, but mostly we want [to] empower the educator to make better decisions or more timely decisions based on what's happening in the cohort."

Promote the Importance of High-Quality, Contextualized Experiential Education

Quality and scale outcomes are not typical standards for measuring educators, but Practera wants to change that. The company believes that quality at scale is both possible and affordable. Standing in the way is the status quo—the manual processes and mashup tools that educators typically use to run experiential learning projects. Practera is partnering with Academic Programs International to deliver experiential learning transnationally when students can't travel overseas, and with Northeastern University to develop a new, wholly experiential approach to corporate training.

Practera's goal is to be the world's leading platform for experiential learning at every level and in every context, from elementary school to corporate training, but it recognizes that the vast majority of community colleges and small to mid-sized companies cannot afford it. Sonnenreich believes, however, that "exemplars are going to step forward and show everybody that there's a commercially successful model." To support that, he says, it's important to "bring employers, learning and development teams, policymakers, education institutions, and executive leadership together to actually talk about how that's going to work."

Full Focus: Alternative Model

- LEARN: Power-scalable, high-quality experiential learning, supported by industry and faculty mentorship, and data analytics enhance the learning *process* through a deep focus on learning science and constructivist instructional design practices.

- ASSESS: Evidence-based assessment means students are judged on the basis of the value they deliver to a real industry partner.

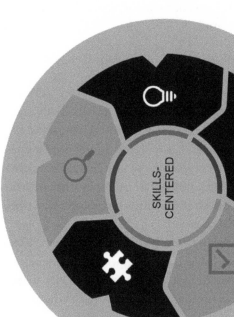

DISCOVER

Learners explore career pathways and competency mapping tools to understand where they are and where they need to be.

LEARN

Learners leverage a variety of educational resources to upskill and meet the needs of the current and future workforce.

ASSESS

Learners' abilities are assessed on the basis of demonstrated ability.

ENTER

Learners enter at various phases throughout their lifetimes.

CONNECT

Learners find or are recruited for jobs on the basis of validated skill data, ensuring that learners will be able to do what they are hired to do.

CREDENTIAL

Learners' abilities are recognized, validating skills in a transparent, contextualized, and standardized way.

Figure 4.2. Practera and Alternative Model: (Learn + Assess + Connect).

- CONNECT: Real-world projects give students a chance to navigate real employer demands and expectations, and a taste of how they would apply their skills in the workplace.

Limited Focus: Alternative Model

- ENTER: Since students access Practera via either an employer or an educator, they must already have an entry point into the system.

- DISCOVER: Practera is meant to support learning within a very specific context. While students develop transferable skills and are exposed to potential pathways to employment through industry mentorship, that is not its primary focus.

- CREDENTIAL: While it would be possible for microcredentials to be incorporated, Practera does not currently offer additional recognition of achievement for course or project completion.

Key Takeaways

- Students, especially adult learners, need opportunities to apply what they've learned in a real-world context. Practera makes experiential learning more scalable, adding value for students in traditional higher education who typically cannot access such learning through classes without an explicit practicum component or without dedicated time to a (usually unpaid) internship.

- Focusing on the quality of the learning process is absolutely key. This starts with educators, whose roles are shifting from that of the expert in the front of the room to that of a coach. This also has implications for instructional design. We can't rely on the knowledge-based learning theories that underpin most of traditional higher education; we need to use experience-based learning theory that allows students to develop the human skills they'll need to navigate real challenges in the workplace. It also requires a shift in assessment, from knowledge tests to allowing students to produce contextualized evidence of what they can do.

- Authentic experiential learning requires close partnerships between educators and industry. It is not as hard to get industry buy-in as is often thought, as there is a lot of value in it for the industry partner, too.

Where Practera sees experiential learning as the key to building work-ready competence, what does it look like when an entire university system is aimed at that goal? We'll explore such a model next.

Case Study 3: Western Governors University

Learner's Experience

I sign out of Slack and close down my laptop. My eyes need a rest. After a nine-hour day responding to my SaaS company's user tickets, I'm really feeling the itch to take the next step up in my career. That's why I enrolled in this online program: to get my bachelor's in business administration so I can apply for the project manager role that will open up soon on my team. I think I will really be able to put my strengths to use there.

When I was doing research on degree programs, I saw that most required a full four years, even though I'd earned some credits at the state college before I hit some personal challenges and had to go to work full time to help support my family. Now with a little one on the way, I can't afford to stop working and go back to school full time. But then I saw that I could finish in less than two years at WGU, even while working. Plus, the price was right. It was an easy decision, and I could get started right away.

Thanks to my years in tech support, some "Intro to Business" classes I took during my first foray into college, and nearly a decade of managing my family's finances I breezed through a lot of the courses. I'm a really quick learner and am used to juggling lots of responsibilities, so while it has definitely been rigorous, I'm enjoying the challenge of building new skills.

After a quick dinner, I open my laptop again and toggle over to my calendar. I have a call tomorrow night with my "program mentor." These calls are a huge part of what keeps me going. I had scheduled it to make sure I'm still on track to graduate in a couple of months, when that role finally opens up. I've been through this conversation a couple of times already, but it never hurts to quadruple-check.

About Western Governors University

"Higher ed institutions better get on this bus, because the demands of employers are changing. The demands of their students are changing, the profile of their students is changing, and the institutions that win are the institutions that are going to be able to clearly articulate the value of their programs and their associated services and align that value with what they're charging. That's the future."

—Marni Baker Stein, provost and chief academic officer, Western Governors University

"Traditional higher ed wasn't built for the realities facing many of today's students," Marni Baker Stein, the provost and chief academic officer of Western Governors University (WGU) bluntly declares.[15] Created by a group of western U.S. state governors in 1997, WGU "exists to provide equitable access to high-quality, affordable, and work-relevant higher education for all—bridging the gap between talent and pathways to opportunity." Its purpose is to provide work-relevant higher education to a growing demographic that is poorly served by campus-based models. More than 70 percent of WGU's enrollment is classified as underserved in one or more of four categories: ethnic minority, low-income, rural resident, or first-generation college student. Most are working full time. And most had completed some college previously.

That's why WGU starts new students at the beginning of each month, and allows them to complete their degrees at their own pace. It is why its straightforward admissions criteria take prior college and work experience into account (98 percent of the 46,718 students who matriculated at WGU between July 1, 2019, and June 30, 2020, transferred some existing credits into their degree programs).[16] And that is why its tuition is as low as it is, about $6,500 per year for most programs. It is charged at a flat rate, which means that students can complete as many courses as they are able to within each of its six-month terms at no additional cost (plus, students are eligible for Title IV federal financial aid). And all of WGU's degree programs are fully online and make full use of technology to support and facilitate learning.

WGU clearly fills a much-needed niche for students: Pre-COVID, its enrollments grew at a rate of 15 to 20 percent each year, and from March 1 to October 1, 2020—the core of the pandemic—WGU awarded nearly 30 percent more degrees than it did during the same months in 2019.[17] How well does it work for its graduates? In 2014, WGU partnered with Gallup to capture information about its alumni's longer-term outcomes beyond job placements and salaries. One key finding was the strong support alumni expressed for WGU's faculty model, particularly its program mentors, who begin meeting with students as soon as they matriculate. Sixty-six percent of WGU alumni strongly asserted the importance of having a mentor who encouraged them to pursue their goals and dreams, compared to just 34 percent of college graduates nationally.[18] Seventy-seven percent of WGU alumni compared to just 38 percent of college graduates strongly agreed that their education was worth the cost (a bachelor's degree at WGU typically costs $16,675). Within just four years of graduation, WGU alumni reported a $20,300 average increase in annual salary—an impressive return on investment compared to the national average of $8,200.[19]

Problems Addressed

REINVENT THE LEARNING THEORY TO MEET STUDENTS—AND EMPLOYERS—WHERE THEY ACTUALLY ARE

WGU pioneered what it calls "competency-based education"; it is still the only institution that offers competency-based degrees at scale.

What is competency-based education? WGU defines a competency as a set of skills that has value in either an academic or a professional setting.[20] Students advance as they demonstrate mastery, which they do by receiving a B or better on objective tests, papers, projects, or presentations. The competency-based standard means that they must master all of the subject matter in their degree fields before they can graduate.

WGU's sole purpose is to connect its graduates with opportunities in the workforce. By providing students with the skills they need to succeed, it addresses employer needs at scale, as a 2019 Harris Poll that surveyed three hundred employers of WGU graduates clearly showed:

- 96 percent said they would hire another WGU graduate.

- 97 percent said WGU graduates were prepared for their jobs.

- 95 percent rated the job performance of WGU graduates as excellent or very good.

- 98 percent said WGU graduates meet or exceed expectations.

- 95 percent rated the "soft skills" of WGU graduates as equal to or better than those of graduates from other institutions.[21]

Rethink the Traditional College
and University Structure

To understand how this "rethink" happened, we need to flash back to a hotel conference room in Park City, Utah in June 1995, where eleven governors of western states had gathered to address the "mounting problems of their states' universities."[22] Simply put, while enrollments kept rising, resources and infrastructure were not keeping up. If the states were going to maintain, much less improve, their university systems, where would the needed money come from?

As politicians too rarely do, they boldly embraced a lot of new thinking—such as capitalizing on technology to disseminate learning, valuing affordability, and bridging the widening gap between graduate knowledge and workforce needs—to "reinvent" the university as they knew it. They envisaged a new structure for faculty, with learning-process experts involved in curriculum development, subject matter experts providing content expertise, and program mentors coaching students one-on-one via telephone at least every other week. They imagined a new master curriculum, focused on what Stein described in our interview as "a set of programs and products and experiences" based on our "understanding [of] what employers need now and into the future." That includes enduring skill sets like "communication and critical thinking and sense-making," she explained, "but also technical skill sets. Based on that analysis, we create a set of competencies . . . which we tag and map dynamically to those skills. And we can actually give that degree or that stack of competencies a marketability score that's dynamic over time." To ensure that its programs meet the education needs of the economy at every level, WGU develops "transformative partnerships with corporate partners, community colleges, membership-based associations, and alliances to expand access to higher education for their employees while also supporting the partner's education and human resource business objectives." Another big part of WGU's rethinking was to become intensely data-driven. Key performance indicators focus on student experience and student success, are tracked on schedule, and are part of the WGU annual report—including twice-yearly student satisfaction reports.

Revolutionize the Credential to Give Students Insight
into the Value of Their Competencies

Working with the labor analytics firm Emsi, the university developed what it calls the Rich Skills Descriptor (RSD), "a contextualized syntax for writing skills," says Stein. A skills architecture team then went through "every single competency we have and tagged that competency description to marketable skills. This not only powers the marketability score of a particular competency, it also enables WGU to see whether the playlist of competencies that we've put together is complete." As of this writing, WGU is working with the Open Skills Network, a coalition of more than 150 employers and educational institutions it assembled, to develop technology to automate the process. Ultimately, WGU hopes to develop RSDs in collaboration with key employers so that WGU competencies are in employer systems, and employers' needs become the basis for WGU academic credits. Says Stein, "We're looking for a Rosetta Stone in this RSD approach."

All of this allows students to become savvier consumers of education. "They can start purchasing education from the start, and across their lifetime," says Stein, "based on what they need and who they want to become. And with the knowledge of the skills that are in demand, and the kinds of jobs that are out there, making that decision isn't a shot in the dark."

Solutions Pursued

Launch the Learning and Employment Record

WGU's Learning and Employment Record project (LER) will create a record of achievement for every WGU student that goes beyond the traditional academic transcript to include certifications, work accomplishments, and a description of accumulated skills, clearly documenting what students can do for employers, and not just the courses they've completed.

Closely connected is the ability to look at employer demand across zip codes nationwide to understand, for example, why a program that may lead to a job in one locale does not work in another, potentially extremely useful information for students.

Develop the WGU Achievement Wallet

Provost Stein explains the Achievement Wallet: "When students are assessed for a particular competency tied to particular skills, that competency is then wrapped in the Open Badge Standard 2.0. When they achieve that, they get not only an academic transcript but also a competency-based, life-skills-based achievement record that carries that intelligence with it. Because it carries that geolocated, dynamic intelligence with it, the wallet allows us to build in experiences that are value-adds for students: windows into their employability in the zip code where they live, windows into their employability plus gaps that they need to fill. So while it provides great intelligence for us about how to serve the students as well as regional workforces, it is a powerful tool for the students."

The Achievement Wallet also has profound implications for the lifelong learning journey, which can take a winding path through various employers and education providers. Says Stein, "If you're working at IBM or Walmart or another company that uses Workday and other HR systems, the portability of these achievements is important. Self-sovereignty is important. We've been able to test that out with prototypes of the Learning and Employment Record, and it works. It's super-exciting. We have established the plumbing to be able to do this. And I think that's great, not only for WGU but for the whole higher ed ecosystem."

The big problem with traditional higher education, Stein says, and the big problem that WGU is working to overcome, is the disconnect between academic achievements and skills. Employers haven't been doing skills-based hiring either. The system worked well enough when a college degree signaled that a graduate was ready for a job. But as the future of work changes, "this Duplo block, the degree, that has been the historical signal of readiness, just won't do anymore. I think everybody is waking up to that. But . . . there's a lot of work to be done to get from A to B."

Continue Engaging and Growing the Open Skills Network

Creating the Open Skills Network was transformative in its own right, as higher education has historically been so siloed. "It is separate institutions working for their own longevity and sustainability growth," says Stein, while what is needed now—and what the Open Skills Network can advance—is "a lifelong higher-education system with supporting infrastructure and services that is really aimed at the student."

Full Focus: Alternative Model

- ENTER: WGU's flexible start dates, digital delivery modality, and low price point make its programs much more accessible to working students, who make up a large population of learners.

- LEARN: By reorienting the university structure around the student—through specialized faculty and mentorship roles, a curriculum driven by skill demand, and competency-based learning—the student can leverage existing skills to move more quickly through the program and come out with marketable competencies.

- ASSESS: Since assessment is tied directly to competency and demonstration of skill, students are being measured against the same standards of readiness that apply in the workforce.

- CREDENTIAL: The Learning and Employment Record completely revolutionizes what students can present to show their learning. Powered by Rich Skills De-

DISCOVER

Learners explore career pathways and competency mapping tools to understand where they are and where they need to be.

LEARN

Learners leverage a variety of educational resources to upskill and meet the needs of the current and future workforce.

ASSESS

Learners' abilities are assessed on the basis of demonstrated ability.

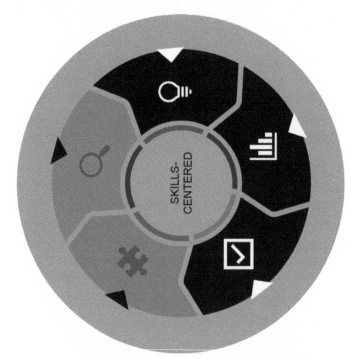

SKILLS-CENTERED

ENTER

Learners enter at various phases throughout their lifetimes.

CONNECT

Learners find or are recruited for jobs on the basis of validated skill data, ensuring that learners will be able to do what they are hired to do.

CREDENTIAL

Learners' abilities are recognized, validating skills in a transparent, contextualized, and standardized way.

Figure 4.3. WGU and Alternative Model: (Enter + Learn + Asess + Credential).

scriptors—standardized skills data that are contextualized through geotags and expressed in a syntax that has been pressure-tested to be viable across any labor market context—the LER gives students direct insight into the competencies and skills they have, the skills that are in demand, and the jobs that require them.

Limited Focus: Alternative Model

- CONNECT: Although the LER and the WGU Achievement Wallet will help students match their skills to opportunities, students are not applying for jobs or being recruited for them via WGU's platforms or tools.

- DISCOVER: Again, while the tools in development may ultimately make it easier for students to assess and fill gaps in their skill sets and decide on career paths, that is not a current function of their programming.

Key Takeaways

- "Scrapping" the status quo is a good place to start. It allows organizations to completely reimagine what it means to support lifelong learners, and it alleviates the friction that comes from changing existing processes and infrastructures.

- Smart partnerships are essential. Specifically, educational institutions should find employers who are willing to bet on big ideas and put them into practice; they should also look for funders who can back their collaborations. But partnership doesn't stop there. Partnering with *many* employers as well as with other educational institutions, using different tools and frameworks, ensures that whatever solution you come up with will not only be useful to you, but will support the entire learning-employment ecosystem.

- We need tools that allow us to respond in real time to both the broad needs of the labor market and the needs of specific students. If you want to be agile, forget static-text PDFs and slow-moving councils. Rely instead on machine-readable (and thus more easily updated and searchable) records and working groups that can implement, iterate, and collaborate to support the progress of all participants. Only when you are actually building something will you start to see what is missing . . . or what the real promise could be.

WGU represents a completely new approach to delivering a student-centered university experience. While it enables the "plumbing" that can connect skills and competencies built in the (virtual) classroom to employers, it hasn't yet laid the pipes. Handshake, however, is a company that is positioned to do precisely that.

Case Study 4: Handshake

ii Handshake

Learner's Experience

I had not expected my final fall semester of college to be all-virtual, but the pandemic is a fact of life. My career center is doing its best to provide us with virtual career fairs, remote resumé reviews, and application advising, but I'm having a hard time navigating my first full-time job search, especially now that I'm also competing with newly unemployed professionals with years of experience. When the career center sent out a message about Handshake, I figured it was worth trying—anything that might give me an edge.

I created a profile including my major (English Lit), my grades (pretty good), and my extracurriculars—an internship at an independent publishing house, writing for the school newspaper, and editing our school's feminist 'zine. I'm still not exactly sure what I want to do. I probably should have figured it out by now, but times are changing fast, and there aren't a lot of the publishing jobs I thought I might find. I'm really trying to avoid being a stereotype—you know, the unemployable English major.

Logging into Handshake for the first time after completing my profile, I was surprised to find a long list of jobs recommended for me. Some were from big names I recognized—The New York Times, Target, Amazon—but there were some unfamiliar companies posting job titles I'd never considered, like roles in HR, sales, and content strategy. The content strategy ones looked to be right up my alley. I saved a dozen of them to look into further and followed the companies that had posted the openings.

When I got a notification about a virtual career fair that one of those companies would be attending, I wasn't sure what to expect. I read about a dozen articles from Handshake and my career center about how to prepare and scheduled a one-on-one through Handshake with the HubSpot representative. I taped up a "help sheet" on the wall above my laptop screen: a list of well-researched questions, a reminder to maintain eye contact even if it feels weird, and a picture of Michelle Obama to make me feel more poised and confident.

The one-on-one went well and was less awkward than I had feared. I was surprised that they weren't looking for prior experience; they were looking for someone who could write and who had good intuitions about the kinds of information people would need. My Lit major was a sign that I could do the former, and my stint in campus journalism—plus, the rep said, my great questions—was a sign that I had the latter. And HubSpot, a small marketing firm, seemed like a really cool place to work; the rep spoke highly of its inclusive culture, and I could work remotely if I wanted.

Still, having heard all the horror stories about the job market and seeing some daunting requirements in similar job postings on LinkedIn, I was shocked when I was offered a formal interview. I definitely wouldn't even have thought to apply if Handshake hadn't suggested it, and my small school certainly wouldn't have been on their recruiting trail in "normal" times. It had seemed like such a long shot, but here I am. My interview is in two minutes. I give a nod to my Michelle Obama picture for good luck and click into the virtual interview invitation.

About Handshake

"My co-founders and I started Handshake to ensure that all students are able to find meaningful work, regardless of where they're from or where they go to school."
—Garrett Lord, co-CEO/co-founder

A startup that raised $74 million from such investors as the Chan Zuckerberg Initiative, Spark Capital, and Kleiner Perkins, Handshake aims to connect more than four hundred thousand employers with university students looking for internships, part-time gigs, or full-time work. Born out of the frustration of student job seekers who have yet to form their own professional networks, the company sees itself as an automated, third-party version of the college career center, but offering a breadth and depth of opportunities that few schools can match.

Its founders Garrett Lord, Ben Christensen, and Scott Ringwelski were fellow students at Michigan Tech University who were struck by the glaring inequalities in career opportunities for students across the country and the potential of software to bridge the gap. A cross-country road trip to look deeper into the challenges students face when applying for jobs affirmed their intent, and the three turned the trip into a voyage of persuasion, getting as many college career centers as they could to partner with them.

Since its formal launch in 2013, Handshake's network of university and employer partners—and its impact for students—"has grown exponentially," in its founders' words. "Within a few years, Handshake has become the leading early career community in the U.S."[23]

Evidence of its effectiveness came during a rebrand effort, when Handshake interviewed more than 100 stakeholders, including employees, students, employers and career center leaders. The survey affirmed that Handshake has been a gamechanger, enlarging the scope of possibility for both student job seekers and employers.[24] One unique feature of its program is it allows students to immediately identify and reach out to people who'd previously achieved internships a student is interested in. By the same token, hundreds of thousands of employers across every industry actively message students via Handshake, engaging them in ways they never could before. The data Handshake collects provides universities with unique insights into their graduates.

And Handshake is free to students; its revenue comes from the universities that partner with it. Companies can use Handshake for free or pay for a premium version.

Problems Addressed

LEVEL THE JOB MARKET PLAYING FIELD FOR COLLEGE GRADUATES
How do you get a first job without any experience? Or if you didn't attend an elite school? Handshake CEO and co-founder Garrett Lord experienced both frustrations first hand. As graduates of Michigan Tech—a school that Google and Apple and SpaceX recruiters tend to get to only after they've exhausted Harvard, Yale, and Princeton—he and his co-founders were determined to "democratize" the recruiting process. "LinkedIn is more of a mid-career tool, when you already have work experience and your professional network is established," Lord told one interviewer.[25] Even in a hot economy, it's hard for young adults to get on that first rung of the corporate ladder. A statistic from a Federal Reserve Bank of New York study bears this out: 41.4 percent of recent graduates are considered "underemployed" or are working in lower-level "gigs" that do not require degrees.[26] Handshake is made for students at smaller or less "prestigious" colleges that may not be on recruiters' radar screens. Its numbers are impressive: with over seven hundred colleges in its network, fourteen million students and recent graduates use it, as do nine hundred thousand recruiters, including, notably, all of the Fortune 500.[27] While Handshake's partnerships allow schools to better support their own students, any student with a valid .edu email address can sign up at joinhandshake.com to discover jobs and connect with employers, whether their school is a partner institution or not.[28] Democratization indeed.

Handshake proved especially helpful during the pandemic, when so much of recruiting and hiring went digital. Handshake allowed students to browse employers and schedule interviews ahead of virtual events, and get on employers' candidate lists for internships and jobs.[29] For students who need more experience with self-presentation, it allows them to schedule more informal sessions with employers, such as virtual office tours or coffee chats. As Lord puts it, "Talent is evenly distributed, [but] opportunity isn't. We want to help connect and bring more efficiency and equality to this process, regardless of who you know, regardless of what your parents do, regardless of what school you go to."

MAKE RECRUITING MORE EFFICIENT AND EFFECTIVE FOR EMPLOYERS

Employers invest heavily in campus recruitment strategies, yet they leave a lot of talent undiscovered. Handshake helps them fill the gap. One example of this, featured in a post by Lord on the Handshake website, is about Box, which began "creating more inclusive college recruiting practices. Since partnering with us, they've expanded their recruiting strategy from a core list of six colleges to more than 200 campuses across the country, are proactively engaging tens of thousands of students on Handshake, and are attracting a more inclusive, qualified, and engaged talent pipeline. Box has also seen their employer brand awareness among students spike by 70 percent thanks to their enhanced employer profile on Handshake."[30]

Achievement is also measured by advances in equality and fairness, and as Garrett Lord told an interviewer from Yahoo Finance, the change to virtual creates a lot more of both. The reason is simple: "Companies can reach out to far more women, far more Black students, far more Latinx students, conduct kind of a wider geographic net to find the right ideal candidate, as opposed to just their 10 or 15 core schools that they used to recruit at."[31] Virtual recruiting is not just more fair, it is more efficient—both in terms of better matchmaking and in terms of cost; it is simply cheaper to recruit virtually than in person.

Cheaper and better. The database keeps building up as network activity increases. Skills, prior experience, extracurricular projects and activities—all are fed into the platform. The platform makes it possible for companies to brand themselves as well—for example, by enabling employees to dialogue online with students from their alma maters. That can be a particular plus for smaller companies that don't have the bucks or the bandwidth to field teams of recruiters.

SUPPORT COLLEGE CAREER CENTERS

Support for college career centers is a top priority for Handshake. The aim is to provide them with a seamless process to connect potential employers to students. Its robust toolkit for doing so includes, among other things,

1. Ready-to-use presentations, videos, printouts, and promotional materials;

2. Blog posts about Handshake;

3. Resources to help students create an impactful Handshake profile and get career tips from students and recruiters;

4. Marketing tips for career centers to increase student engagement;

5. A virtual career fair launch kit;

6. Webinars.

Solutions Pursued

REMAIN VALUES-ORIENTED WHILE ENHANCING THE PLATFORM

Handshake adapts quickly, releasing enhancements every two weeks that support its six big-picture objectives:

- Put students first, democratizing access to opportunity.

- Focus on impact.

- Move quickly, but don't rush—in other words, stay aligned.

- Learn. Grow. Repeat.

- Act with empathy.

- Empower by diversity.

EXPAND STUDENT REACH TO HELP EMPLOYERS BUILD A MORE DIVERSE WORKFORCE

Handshake still has room to grow. An excellent first step is its plan to expand its reach to serve the more than six million students enrolled in community colleges and bootcamps, which are democratizing access to educational opportunities in their own right (more on that in Chapter 6).

GO GLOBAL

Twenty thousand students activated Handshake accounts during the platform's recent launch in the United Kingdom, where the company has partnered with eight higher education institutions (including the University of Cambridge, University of York, and University of Liverpool).

Full Focus: Alternative Model

- DISCOVER: As a tool that suggests jobs specifically for those without much prior experience, Handshake can lower barriers to entry for recent graduates and expose new career pathways that learners might not have previously considered.

- CONNECT: Handshake makes direct contact between (more) students and (more) employers possible, creating an accessible entry point to the workforce.

Limited Focus: Alternative Model

- ENTER: Learners must have a valid .edu address to join the platform, meaning they must already be enrolled at an educational institution.

- LEARN: While career advice resources are accessible via Handshake, they do not touch the students' learning experience at their institution.

- ASSESS: Assessment is at the educational institution level; Handshake asks students to self-report their qualifications.

- CREDENTIAL: Handshake does not issue credentials. Student affiliation with a credential-issuing institution is validated with an .edu email address.

Key Takeaways

- College graduates need better guidance to make the transition into full-time work. This may become even more the case as degree requirements fade, since traditional college graduates will have less prior work experience to lend weight to their applications. Giving students a means of direct access to employers who might not otherwise recruit from their campuses can introduce them to best-fit options that don't depend on existing networks or work experience.

- The hiring process is becoming more virtual, as is the workplace. This is an opportunity to democratize access, as it encourages employers to focus on candidates and what they can bring to the table, rather than on their school. This still requires alignment, however, between the skills the student is developing and the skills the employer needs. Leveraging data about successful hiring can help inform better matchmaking.

- Career centers are also adapting to today's hiring practices, giving students better tools to find viable pathways to employers. Coaching students on how they can best represent themselves virtually is essential.

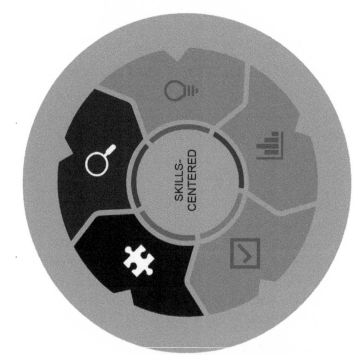

DISCOVER

Learners explore career pathways and competency mapping tools to understand where they are and where they need to be.

LEARN

Learners leverage a variety of educational resources to upskill and meet the needs of the current and future workforce.

ASSESS

Learners' abilities are assessed on the basis of demonstrated ability.

ENTER

Learners enter at various phases throughout their lifetimes.

CONNECT

Learners find or are recruited for jobs on the basis of validated skill data, ensuring that learners will be able to do what they are hired to do.

CREDENTIAL

Learners' abilities are recognized, validating skills in a transparent, contextualized, and standardized way.

Figure 4.4. Handshake and Alternative Model: (Discover+ Connect).

Concluding Thoughts

This chapter looked at four different organizations that aim to preserve the traditional college degree by increasing its relevance and value as a gateway to a career. Noodle seeks to expand access to the college or university pathway; Practera is helping to transform the classroom experience so that it better imparts skills that are transferable to the workplace; Western Governors University reimagines the college or university structure altogether; and Handshake is a platform to connect college or university students to their first jobs. The case studies raise a number of core points.

First, partnerships among educational institutions and between educators and employers are essential. "Breaking down silos" is becoming a cliché, but it is the only way to ensure a smooth transition from learning to working and back again, through what promises to be a lifelong cycle.

Second, the quality of the learning process matters. Students need contextualized, real-world learning experiences in which they can directly apply the skills and competencies their education develops. This requires innovations in learning theory—specifically, in the form of experiential learning and competency-based models.

Third, educators' roles are also changing. Educators must be tuned in to the labor market as, increasingly, they assume the task of coaching students through the reflective process of applying what they are learning to their future careers. Incentive structures must shift accordingly.

Finally, higher education needs to be more agile. Curriculum design must be more responsive to labor market demands, and educators and administrators need to seek out and use dynamic data to inform program development and student support.

The case studies reveal a wide range of tools and strategies that stakeholders within institutions of higher education can use to address each of these needs. In the next chapter, we will explore the tools and strategies employers can use to support employees in what will, of necessity, become a process of lifelong learning.

⑤

EMPLOYER PARTNERSHIPS

While the changing world of work has inspired a number of startups to enter classrooms in bids to influence the roles of educators, the organizations examined in this chapter are explicitly moving education into the workplace. The reason is both simple and urgent: 40 percent of employers complain that their employees cannot do what they need them to do. To address this mismatch, they can either hire more appropriately skilled candidates or upskill their existing talent, which is both cheaper and a safer bet. Employers are also under increased pressure to hire and support more diverse candidates. To do so, they need to open up nontraditional recruitment channels and support the growth and progression of the people they bring in. As a result of these pressures, companies are investing more in learning and development, which is seen as directly affecting their bottom lines.

This chapter explores the tools and strategies employers are using to find the right candidates, to gain better insights into their workforce's skills, and to provide additional learning opportunities to their employees. As in Chapter 4, we tell the story through four case studies.

Case Study 1: ZipRecruiter

ZipRecruiter

Learner's Experience

Thanks to COVID, I was laid off from my "Customer Success" job yesterday. I need to get a new job—and fast! Rent in Boston is too expensive to go even a week without a paycheck. My job search starts today.

I update my LinkedIn profile—"Open to opportunities to help customers succeed"—and run a Google search for "job sites." I click on the first result: "ZipRecruiter: Job Search—Millions of Jobs Hiring Near You." I type in my name and email address to get started and enter "customer success" as a keyword. First up: a "Client Success Manager" role in Boston.

I loved my last job, and I was good at it. I loved helping clients make the most of our company's SaaS platform, coaching them as they learned to use the tools that could give them the answers they needed, helping them navigate change management, and showing them the value our platform provided. I really felt like a partner to them and not just a vendor. Based on the job requirements I saw in this "Client Success Manager" posting—business acumen, excellent client-facing skills, problem-solving abilities, and strong work ethic—I think I'd be a good fit. I click an "Am I Qualified?" button to see what ZipRecruiter thinks.

I'm presented with a list of skills the employer has listed as important for the job and am instructed to include them, if relevant, in my resumé. I scroll through my resumé—already open on the other half of my screen—to make sure they're all there. I add a few missing keywords that fit with my abilities, save the file, and upload it to "Apply" as prompted. My profile is autopopulated with all of my experience, and I notice it has pulled out keywords to populate a "Skills" section, too. One more click to confirm the information, and my application is submitted. One down.

Luckily for me, ZipRecruiter is showing me a long list of other jobs I might consider. Before I do that, I click into my "Profile" section and scroll through it. The "Skills" section, again, catches my attention. I'm prompted to "Verify" my skills, meaning I can ask a friend or colleague to vouch for me. I send a request to my former boss; she was bummed that the team was downsized and offered to help.

I notice I can also click into e-learning content to build new skills. Might as well take advantage of the opportunity to beef up my repertoire, now that I have some time on my hands, even if only—I hope!—for a few days. I know how important it is to be able to work with the product team to solve clients' problems, so I filter for product management courses and enroll in an option from edX. As enthusiastic as I usually am to learn something new, I'd really hate to become a full-time student again.

It looks like that might not happen. There's a message waiting for me already.

About ZipRecruiter

"You see repeated statements by employers that they're having real trouble hiring and finding the people with the right skills for their jobs. At the same time, especially during recessions, you see millions of people saying they're struggling to find work. It's clear the two sides of the market don't always meet each other very well. And that's because the jobs that are looking for people are often looking for different things than the people who are looking for jobs."
—Julia Pollak, chief economist, ZipRecruiter

ZipRecruiter is a two-sided marketplace that matches the right employers to the right job seekers. Its value proposition is that it reduces the "friction" of a search by enhancing both sides of the equation, supplying employers with full skills profiles while offering job seekers both appropriate jobs to apply for and a wide range of value-adding information about companies, occupations, and salaries. Importantly, it is easy to use and always up to date. It is also free for job seekers; businesses pay to post jobs.

All of which may explain why ZipRecruiter, which has positioned itself as "the smartest way to hire and look for a job," is as of this writing the fastest-growing online employment marketplace and the number-one-rated job search website and mobile application, outstripping its rivals LinkedIn, Indeed, and Glassdoor, which offer different features and pricing structures.

Problems Addressed

MAKE IT EASIER FOR EMPLOYERS
TO HIRE THE RIGHT CANDIDATE

Much has been said and written, in this book and elsewhere, about the skills gap in today's marketplace and about what that portends. ZipRecruiter's Julia Pollak told me that the term "skills gap" is "very, very controversial among labor economists," and that the ZipRecruiter approach to the issue rests on a very specific meaning. Pollak, who is herself a labor economist, points out that when employers have a need for a particular skill or set of skills that their existing employees do not have, there are other people elsewhere who do have those skills or who are capable of mastering them. That isn't a gap; it is a mismatch.[1]

It's a lot like the dating market, she continued. "You can have the same number of single men as single women, to use a very heteronormative example, and still have lots of people who can't find their soulmate. And that's because you can't just match numbers. When we speak to employers, and if you look at all of the surveys and the Federal Reserve Board's Beige Book, even in a recession you see repeated statements by employers that they're having real trouble finding and hiring the people with the right skills for their jobs. At the same time, especially during recessions, you see millions of people saying they're struggling to find work. It's clear the two sides of the market don't always meet each other very well. And that's because the jobs that are looking for people are often looking for different things than the people who are looking for jobs. And so there isn't a perfect match. There are often geographic mismatches or skills mismatches. There are also, of course, differences on pricing; job seekers are typically looking for a higher wage and more generous benefits than employers are prepared to provide. And so you often have unemployment and vacancies, and they don't meet each other that swiftly and smoothly."

Enter ZipRecruiter, the matchmaker. Using artificial intelligence-driven algorithms to determine whether candidates are good matches for jobs on the basis of their skills and experience, ZipRecruiter's Search Engine Optimization team creates company pages, job pages, and salary pages that provide information about employers, occupations, and earnings—all aimed at giving candidates a clear idea of what they are in for—an essential first step if employers are to attract the right candidates.

Make It Easier for Job Seekers to Get the Right Job Offer

Anyone who has been through the job search process—probably most readers—knows that it takes time to find, evaluate, and apply for jobs. Information about both employers and jobs tends to be imperfect and asymmetric. Learning precisely which skills each job requires, and assessing which match job seekers' skills and experience, makes job searches faster, safer, and more likely to succeed, especially for those who don't have the benefit of an existing network they can tap for contacts and introductions

Make It Easier for Job Seekers to Upskill in the Right Direction

Online job search tools like ZipRecruiter also help students make better-informed decisions about their education, claims Pollak. "You can now browse all the job openings in the United States and find out quite easily who's hiring in your city or what skills they need. You can figure out quite easily what is required to become a cybersecurity expert, for example. Job postings will typically list a whole bunch of certifications, and if that's the kind of job you want, you have to find a way to get those certifications."

ZipRecruiter has also developed partnerships that ease job seekers' access to appropriate educational resources. A job seeker creating or updating his or her ZipRecruiter job files will be invited to browse a curated menu of courses that could conceivably improve their eligibility for the job in question, or for jobs at a higher level of skill or requiring a different skill. Partners in this effort include edX, Coursera, Skillshare, SkillSuccess, Udacity, and GoSkills. In addition, the ziprecruiter.com blog contains hundreds of articles with advice and guidance on how job seekers can create the best possible profiles.

Solutions Pursued

Strengthen Feedback Loops Between Job Seekers and Employers

Over time, the intelligent algorithms will become smarter about letting candidates discern the strength of their candidacy for a job—and, if needed, how to build up and buttress their application.

"Right now," Pollak said, "it's a two-sided marketplace with employers on one side and job seekers on the other. . . . In the future it could grow to be a three-sided marketplace, where there are even stronger feedback loops between job seekers and employers." ZipRecruiter's current algorithms and tools are just the beginning. "I imagine that all of those features will become a lot smarter over time," Pollak said. "The more interactions you get, the more the platform learns, and the smarter and more tailored those recommendations can become."

Educate Employers About How to Help ZipRecruiter Facilitate Better Matches

While ZipRecruiter can ease a lot of the friction in the hiring market, employers cannot be passive participants. Pollak describes two key steps employers can take to ensure their workforces have the necessary skills.

The first is to "clearly articulate the skills that you need on your job postings" so that candidates can self-select appropriately and, if needed, upskill to become more attractive prospects. "I think the first and most important thing for employers is to figure out which skills they actually value and need among their own workers and then communicate those very, very clearly in job postings. This means not just saying 'We need Excel skills,' for example, but clearly saying which Excel skills, like pivot tables, or which specific licenses and certifications."

This level of specificity—made possible by the expanding landscape of credentials for precise skill sets—can help employers stop using imperfect proxies. For example, Pollak asks, "Is five years of past experience really important? Or is someone with one year of experience who has figured out how to ace the key skills the most valuable kind of employee you get? I would encourage employers to move away from silly measures like years of experience, which don't necessarily translate into skills and competence."

A second step is to provide training in-house. "If employers are determined to meet their skill needs," Pollak suggests, "they need to be willing to invest in their talent to help those who are in the door develop the right set of skills." Partnering with course providers can be one approach; Pollak points to the RAND Corporation for an example of one extremely successful partnership, but whatever the source of the educational content, investing in training can have huge benefits.

Some examples from recent history illustrate the efficacy of this approach. The first is the labor market shifts that took place during the Great Recession. According to Pollak, "many employers said that there was a skills gap and that was the reason they weren't hiring people. But what we saw over the course of the ten-year expansion was that as the labor market got tighter and tighter, employers did continue to add jobs and they often did that by investing in training and raising wages, which drew more and more workers off the sidelines and into work. So, many people will say, you know, there is no skills gap. Employers can fill vacancies if they're prepared to invest in creating those skills."

Another example is Facebook, which started life as a desktop application. When Mark Zuckerberg decided its future would be mobile, the first applications it developed "were really bad," according to Pollak, until he "realized that in order to develop the right kind of apps, he would need everyone to learn how to code for iOS. They didn't have the skills in-house. They also didn't really know how to hire contractors with the skills. And so they basically put everything in the company on hold and brought in lots and lots of trainers. They had everyone go through a rigorous training, a coding bootcamp. It was a huge cost, a huge investment. And you know what? That's why everyone is on their phone today looking at Facebook."

Finally, Pollak points to the manufacturing industry. "We have lots of examples where regulations have forced manufacturing companies to adopt new standards. They've had to train workers to implement those standards—sometimes overnight. And it's happened successfully. So we know it can be done."

Yet many employers, Pollak adds, hesitate to invest in employee skill development. Some worry "that those employees will then be more employable elsewhere" and will leave for a bigger paycheck, taking those expensive skills with them. While there are ways to lock employees into the relationship—for example, with contracts that specify that they must remain with the company for a certain period of time or pay back the training costs—research suggests that investing in employees actually increases employee retention and enhances performance.[2]

Pollak acknowledges the difficulties and expense. "Expecting employers to be saviors of the education system is probably too ambitious," she admits. But they must decide what their candidate should be able to do on day one and what they are willing and able to invest in developing their skills. To the extent that they clarify their list of requirements, the matching facilitated by ZipRecruiter will be that much more effective.

A Utopian Vision: Power a Perfect Skill Market

In Pollak's vision of ZipRecruiter's future, a job seeker logs on and is presented not only with a list of available jobs, but—based on the job seeker's skills—a choice of salaries. "You can have the job at a lower wage, given that you don't yet have the key credential needed, or you could earn that credential and have the job at a higher wage." The platform would provide a list of courses and costs along with reputation ratings, via student and employer reviews. After making the cost-versus-payoff calculation, the applicant would decide whether to invest in their own education or apply at the lower level and trust the employer to provide the training. "I think overall economic well-being would improve greatly if there were more transparency and more information-sharing," Pollak says. "And the best way to share information when things are so complex and everyone has different incentives is through a market mechanism and through a price structure. If there was some way to put a price on these things, that would make a huge difference."

Pollak admits that "it's going to be a while before we get there." In the meantime, she urges applicants to not let the perfect be the enemy of the good. "You can already learn a pretty great deal about which skills have the greatest bang for the buck." Take earning a drone license. Google the typical time it takes to pass the drone operator test—say, fifteen hours—and the approximate cost—about $150. Then search for drone operator jobs on ZipRecruiter and see if there are any near you, what they entail, how much fun they look like they'd be, what they typically pay. That's one option; now play with it: "It would take me fifteen hours and $150, and I'd be able to take photographs of farms and construction sites and homes for retail websites and a pretty cool range of interesting things." Compare that with another option—say, a nursing license. How many years does that take? What's the cost? Which path looks more appealing, all things considered? How recession-proof is it? There's so much information available, she says, that, if trained to think about their choices in the right way, an individual can really come up with a decision that is just right for their life and career.

That is why it is important that people be coached to think about the job search process in this way. Teachers are one potential source of this coaching, as Pollak notes: "I think every lecturer and teacher should encourage people to think about the future and not just to think about the assignment that's due on Monday that will be thrown straight into the trash." She offers some hopeful advice as well: "I wish that professors would be more entrepreneurial about encouraging their students to do work today that actually matters. To build planes that could actually fly. Not to just write some essay, but to write it as a blog post that they actually publish to build a portfolio of work so that they start to think of themselves as adults in the world of work, where work has value and is not just checking a box and going from one stage to the next."

It is a view of education that asks teachers to assume responsibility for something that has not been considered a part of their jobs before. Teachers, says Pollak, must help students understand "that education is partly a stepping-stone to get somewhere." They can advance that understanding by showing students how "what they're doing now connects to what they'll be doing in the future." The same kind of coaching should be available in the workplace. It can come from managers, from People Ops teams, from peers within teams—just so long as the conversation is informed by the right data.

Full Focus: Alternative Model

- ENTER: Anyone can create a ZipRecruiter profile—for free—and use the information to inform their next steps.

- DISCOVER: Individuals can match their skills with employer needs, determine skills they need to develop, and find resources for learning the needed skills. These tools will improve over time.

- CONNECT: ZipRecruiter's primary purpose is to connect job candidates with employers; it is where the organization and its platform shine.

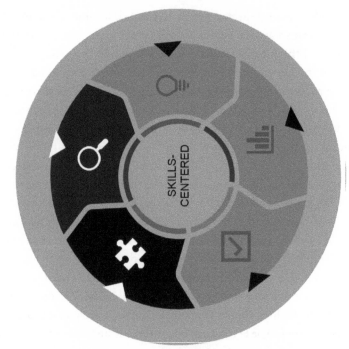

DISCOVER

Learners explore career pathways and competency mapping tools to understand where they are and where they need to be.

LEARN

Learners leverage a variety of educational resources to upskill and meet the needs of the current and future workforce.

ASSESS

Learners' abilities are assessed on the basis of demonstrated ability.

ENTER

Learners enter at various phases throughout their lifetimes.

CONNECT

Learners find or are recruited for jobs on the basis of validated skill data, ensuring that learners will be able to do what they are hired to do.

CREDENTIAL

Learners' abilities are recognized, validating skills in a transparent, contextualized, and standardized way.

Figure 5.1. ZipRecruiter and Alternative Model: (Enter + Discover + Connect).

Limited Focus: Alternative Model

- LEARN: While it partners with course providers, ZipRecruiter is not primarily an education provider.

- ASSESS: Although individuals can get their skills verified through the platform, they must demonstrate their abilities outside of it.

- CREDENTIAL: Validated achievements can be promoted at ZipRecruiter, but it does not issue credentials.

Key Takeaways
• The skills "gap" is actually a skills "mismatch." Employers can right-skill their workforces by creating job postings that specify skill requirements precisely—as opposed to such proxies as degrees or years of experience. Employers can also invest in training their workforce, which, if done right, can lead to higher performance and retention. • Decision making about career next steps benefits from transparent data about skill or credential requirements, education provider costs and reputations, and labor market trends. • Precise and transparent data needs to be coupled with coaching on how to make sense of it. While educators should play a role in this coaching, so should employers, especially regarding opportunities to progress within the company.

Case Study 2: Degreed

ᚖ degreed

Learner's Experience

Since starting to work remotely, I've developed some new routines. Instead of listening to a podcast on the train in the morning, I take a walk and listen to a TED talk or a video. Sometimes it's directly related to my job—I'm a robotics engineer—so there is always room to learn about the latest technologies, and sometimes the relationship isn't quite as clear (I have listened to more Brené Brown talks than I can count). But I always find that it is related to my work somehow.

After I laced up my shoes this morning I logged onto Degreed to find today's video. I chose one on time management that seems, well, timely. My calendar is packed, and I've been having a hard time juggling all my different projects. My walk takes me past my favorite coffee shop, where I pick up my usual order, and through the park down the street, where I see a few neighbors sitting on some appropriately distanced benches. Even though I'm an engineer—the stereotype would suggest I might not have the best people skills—I miss our casual chats; now, I wave from afar.

I make my way back home and read the suggested article. I learn about some good tricks; I jot down some notes and action items that I'll try out today. I mark the resource as read, and give myself a Level 1 mastery rating, my lowest option. I definitely still have room to improve.

As I get started on my daily tasks, I can see that some of those tricks really are helpful. I can already breathe a bit easier knowing that my to-do list is prioritized and that I have a plan for when I'm going to cross each item off the list. This is something I might be good at if I practice it a little bit more, especially with the rest of my team.

I click into the time management skill to see what related opportunities I might have to put this stuff into practice. There are a couple of cool stretch projects I might be able to take on if I really master this time management thing.

Tomorrow morning's walk-and-learn agenda: RACI charts—Responsible, Accountable, Consulted, Informed.

About Degreed

"Managers need to have a different mindset around who employees are. They're individuals, not your people on your team that you own. . . . They are people you are borrowing for a period of time. And part of your job should be to help them grow and develop."
—Chris McCarthy, CEO, Degreed

In the introduction to their 2018 book *The Expertise Economy: How the Smartest Companies Use Learning to Engage, Compete, and Succeed*, Degreed's chief learning officer Kelly Palmer and co-founder David Blake write that "the world of work is going through a large-scale transition—much like the transition we went through from the agricultural economy to the Industrial Revolution. We are now in the age of digitization, automation, and acceleration—an age where critical skills and expertise will be an imperative for us to succeed."[3] They cite a 2018 McKinsey Global Institute report asserting that "the task confronting every economy, particularly advanced economies, will likely be to retrain and redeploy tens of millions of midcareer, middle-age workers."[4]

The ZipRecruiter case study made the point that employers can and should take a more active role in right-skilling their workforces, and that managers are uniquely positioned to act as coaches through employees' lifelong learning journeys. Degreed is a tool that can help managers gain the insights they need to be more effective coaches, while helping them achieve their own learning and career goals.

Degreed is an education technology company that, in the words of its website (degreed.com), "connects learning and career growth to business opportunities through one single, fluid skill-development experience, so your organization and your people are always ready to clear the next big obstacle." It does this by aggregating learning content, data, projects, and job listings in one easy-to-access place. Curated plans and pathways enable users to access resources related to potential career steps as well as personalized development opportunities. These resources are gathered from a wide variety of sources, depending on the user's interests, role, and skills.

On the employer side, Degreed's powerful analytics give companies a full view into all the learning and development their employees are pursuing so they can better gauge the supply and demand of skills within their workforce—and how to bridge the gap between the two. By assessing capabilities with Degreed's suite of skill measurement tools and strategically aligning them to the business, employers can connect people and their skills to in-demand projects and opportunities.

In our interview, CLO Palmer told me that Degreed was originally built as a consumer product for individuals. This changed at the suggestion of the company's first corporate client, Bank of America, but Degreed continues to serve individuals. "This is a really important distinction," Palmer said, "because a lot of education technology that's out there is not for the individuals. It's for the HR organization or for the company to track compliance training and things like that . . . the vision first was all around learning."[5]

The individual learner's journey through Degreed has three phases. The first, says Palmer, is about helping people understand how much there is to learn, and that they can learn from a variety of sources. Phase 2 is about "identifying what skills people have and what skills people need"—in other words, skills assessment. And phase 3 is about creating an internal skills-based career marketplace to recommend stretch assignments, projects, and jobs to the individual employee. "It's learning skills and connecting them to opportunities," she summarizes.

Problems Addressed

PROVIDE ASSESSMENT TOOLS AND LEARNING OPPORTUNITIES FOR INDIVIDUALS

Before developing new skills, it's important that individuals take stock of the skills they already have. For a quick snapshot, employees can self-assess using an array of tools that Degreed provides, including the Lumina Foundation's Connecting Credentials framework.[6] To go deeper, employees can use Degreed's Skill Review product. "That's very performance-based," Palmer says. It's useful "if you want a more rigorous way to evaluate whether or not people have skills based on what they've actually done."

Degreed also incorporates other indicators and credentials into the mix that Palmer calls "signals." "For example," she explains, "Pluralsight does a lot of content for technical people, and they have a product called Skills IQ. EdX has nano degrees and micro degrees. A lot of people are using badges. What we do is we bring in all the signals and help people see where you are, personally, on your skills."

Once their baseline skill set is established, users can follow pathways toward career opportunities—teams, roles, projects—that interest them and determine the specific skills they would need to be qualified to pursue them. Then, Degreed's algorithms surface specific resources that can help make up the variance. Degreed does not create its own educational content; it curates the best options from a wide array of resources spanning different platforms and providers (some of whom we will explore in Chapter 6).

As Palmer and Blake write in *The Expertise Economy*, "[I]f you expect people to learn, then you need to know what makes them tick from both a cognitive and motivational perspective. . . . You have to solve for context, personalization, and motivation for successful learning."[7] Enabling the individual to drive his or her own learning and understand the "why" behind the learning experiences is essential for keeping that individual motivated. As long as learners meet the intended outcome of skills development, when they learn or what resources they use is less important than demonstrating they can use those skills in practice and in context with their team.

Such an approach adds a key layer to the overall body of learning theories already touched on in this book. Specifically, the idea that learning may proceed across peer networks and leverage a wide array of resources is central to *connectivism*. Theorized precisely as a framework for the digital age, the principles of connectivism George Siemens outlined in his 2005 book *Connectivism: Learning as Network Creation*—finding patterns in chaos, leveraging networks and connections to create new innovations, and self-organizing and adapting as new information is discovered—apply with singular relevance to a platform that facilitates self-exploration, peer-to-peer learning, and the pursuit of learning that is meaningful in context.

As Siemens wrote, "The starting point of connectivism is the individual.

Personal knowledge is comprised of a network, which feeds into organizations and institutions, which in turn feed back into the network, and then continue to provide learning to the individual. This cycle of knowledge development (personal to network to organization) allows learners to remain current in their field through the connections they have formed."[8] Connectivism suggests the need for new tools that can help individuals sift through limitless resources, share their knowledge with their peers, clarify where they have room to develop, and otherwise "flourish in a digital era,"[9] precisely the role that Degreed aims to fill.

Grant the Employer Insight into the Workforce's Skills

Degreed's powerful analytics give employers a full view into the learning and development happening within their company. With organizational skills heatmaps across fifteen hundred skills, employers are equipped for highly strategic workforce planning. Most important of all, however, is the value that the company culture sets on lifelong learning. There is never a shortage of tasks to do in the moment. If learning is not central to the mission, then that will be people's sole focus. But if opportunities to expand and explore skill sets are front and center of every project, it is almost impossible to avoid learning something new. What Degreed provides is a record of exactly what is being learned. With such a wealth of data, it is easy to set benchmarks for team skills and growth and make better investments in people, and it is easy for a manager to be the coach his or her team needs.

Connect Individuals to Opportunities on the Basis of Their Skills

Degreed acts as a career marketplace with skills as the currency. From the individual's perspective, it provides clarity as to the skills that are needed for each opportunity. "With Degreed," explains Palmer, "people start thinking about themselves in terms of skills. My employability is based on the skills that I have and what I know; that translates to projects, roles, and opportunities."

From the employer's perspective, Degreed's granular data edges out the proxies and biases that all too often insinuate themselves into human capital decisions. Instead, you can now see who has the necessary skills and who can be better supported in the right direction. "I talk about old work models versus new work models," says Palmer. "In the former, managers are used to command and control and telling their employees what to do, when to do it, and how to do it." With the skills-based model, "managers are the linchpin to really making this successful."

Solutions Pursued

Enhance Transferability

Employees change jobs, companies, and even careers faster now than ever. They should be able to carry their skill information with them. Platforms like Degreed help make that possible.

Bring Clarity to "Human Skill" Assessment

"If you think about how work is changing," says Palmer, "the half-life of technical skills is really around two years, if not less. I argue that because machines are going to take over a lot of the automated tasks . . . human skills are going to be much more important. And they're the transferable skills. I call them power skills."

We have yet to learn how to measure those "qualitative" skills objectively, but we are making progress. Says Palmer, "There's still a lot of work to be done, but I feel like it's where we should be focusing."

Continue to Advocate for Changing People Management Practices

The traditional manager's role needs to be disrupted. "Today," says Palmer, "we reward managers for what they get done and what deliverables they offer, not how they're developing their people."

Hiring practices might also benefit from some disruption—by eliminating unnecessary degree requirements and basing hiring decisions on what people can do, not where they learned how to do it.

As the algorithms powering Degreed's and other systems' analytics get smarter, more and more traditional manager roles will be automated. But at the end of the day, human managers must decide who to recruit for a project or who gets the promotion. To make the most equitable and effective decisions, they need to be educated on how to leverage the data, and incentivized to use it wisely.

Full Focus: Alternative Model

- DISCOVER: On the basis of their skills, individuals can explore opportunities available to them and find out where they need to bridge gaps. Employers can do the same at an organizational level.

DISCOVER

Learners explore career pathways and competency mapping tools to understand where they are and where they need to be.

LEARN

Learners leverage a variety of educational resources to upskill and meet the needs of the current and future workforce.

ASSESS

Learners' abilities are assessed on the basis of demonstrated ability.

ENTER

Learners enter at various phases throughout their lifetimes.

CONNECT

Learners find or are recruited for jobs on the basis of validated skill data, ensuring that learners will be able to do what they are hired to do.

CREDENTIAL

Learners' abilities are recognized, validating skills in a transparent, contextualized, and standardized way.

Figure 5.2. Degreed and Alternative Model: (Discover + Learn + Assess + Credential + Connect).

- LEARN: Degreed curates learning content that is relevant to the individual at a certain place and for a certain purpose.

- ASSESS: Degreed allows individuals to self-assess and powers peer and manager assessments. It also offers highly robust performance-based assessments.

- CREDENTIAL: Degreed powers skill certification and also brings in other validated "signals" of achievement—nano degrees, digital badges, and Skills IQs.

- CONNECT: Employers make human capital decisions based on skills data, minimizing bias and ensuring that learners get the opportunities they need and deserve.

Limited Focus: Alternative Model

- ENTER: While Degreed also has a direct-to-the-consumer product, it is most effective when used in the context of an employer, where the peer and organizational connections can be made.

Key Takeaways
• Given the diminishing half-life of skills, individuals will miss out on opportunities if they stop learning. They need tools that surface the right learning resources at the right time.
• Adult learners, especially, need to be motivated. They need to know *why* they are learning something and have opportunities to put it into practice. Adult learners are also navigating chaotic, networked, and connected learning landscapes; rooting learning in connectivist learning theory acknowledges this reality and empowers learners to make their own meaning, using their peers and a wide variety of resources.
• The changing landscape of learning also changes the role of the manager or employer. If employers don't get involved in coaching their employees—leveraging skills data to make human capital decisions—and in incentivizing *people* growth alongside *profit* growth, they will not reap their workforce's full potential.

In the next case study, we'll look to a different model, one that connects learners with educational resources.

Case Study 3: Guild Education

GUILD

Learner's Experience

I got a job as a Chipotle crew member during my junior year of high school. Like most high school students, I wanted a little extra cash because I was saving up for a car. I definitely didn't expect to be here four years later. But I've earned more than money— I'm almost half of the way through college, and Chipotle is paying for all of it.

This is a really big deal for me and for my family, as I will be the first to gradu-ate college. I wasn't sure this would be an option for me, as I couldn't imagine a world where I could stop earning an income to pursue an education. It's only possible because I can do both.

I'll have been at Chipotle for seven years by the time I earn my diploma. My manager just used the same benefits to earn her second degree in business, and she's on her way to managing a multimillion-dollar business unit for the com-pany. I can definitely see a career path for myself here; they've invested in me, and if I can keep moving up the ladder, I can earn enough to someday support a family. I'm not sure another company would do what Chipotle has done to help me further my career.

About Guild Education

"We found a win-win, where we can help companies align their objectives with helping their employees achieve their goals."
—Rachel Carlson, co-founder and CEO of Guild Education[10]

Where Degreed brings in a wide variety of skill-specific learning resources, Guild Education addresses a pain point felt by working students striving to earn a different kind of credential: a GED or college degree. According to Guild's website, there are more than thirty million working adults without high school diplomas in the United States; 70 percent of Americans do not have col-lege degrees. Rachel Carlson and Brittany Stich founded Guild Education to help that population further their educations through their employers' tuition benefits.[11]

We got a peek into this marketplace in the Noodle case study in Chapter 4. Guild works with three key stakeholders: employers, the students or would-be students who work for them, and the academic institutions that partner with Guild to serve those students. The overall aim is to provide high-quality, low-cost educations with a minimum of friction. Guild also provides best-in-class academic coaching, ensuring that students have support throughout their educational journey.

"There's a whole generation of Americans who have lacked access to quality education," says C. J. Jackson, Guild's communications director, "and the routes that they take to—for lack of a better phrase—'self-medicate' for that can be destructive or not constructive at a minimum. One of the things that Guild does is give people who face different economic imperatives or have different opportunities a chance to maintain their priorities and balance them with their own desire for social and economic mobility."[12]

Problems Addressed
MAKE IT EASIER FOR EMPLOYEES TO MAKE THE MOST OF TUITION BENEFITS

In addition to offering administrative support for students who are using tuition benefits to earn a degree, Guild works to ensure that the programs are high quality, and that the students can realistically complete them.

Which schools make the cut? "There's not one litmus test for institutions we partner with," says Jackson, "but these are attributes that we look for: Do they offer programs that our employers want? Are they offered in a manner that makes it easy for a working adult to do it? Do they help meaningfully to expand the range of options that we can offer? Do they provide an affordable product?"

The aim is to support educational programs that provide a potentially transformative experience for employees. Jackson relates, "We recently announced a partnership with Paul Quinn College, which is our first historically Black college and university. Paul Quinn is led by a president who really thinks three dimensionally and expansively and innovates, and our employer partners really wanted to be able to offer that experience to our potential students."

Another concern is quality. "Quality is based on outcomes," as Jackson puts it. "It's based on extensive research about which institutions provide students with the best and most meaningful way to get the credentials they need to advance their careers and economic opportunities."

Add it up: accessibility in terms of cost, delivery, and content, plus a promise of quality and successful outcomes. By curating educational options that fit that bill, and by streamlining the administrative processes, Guild makes it easier for employees to transform their lives.

Meet Working Students Where They Are and Guide Them Through Each Next Step

Meeting working students where they really are means, first and foremost, helping them find programs that are made to serve them instead of putting them in charge of the filtering process.

Guild's partner employers and educational institutions have opened the door to further education, but the employee must be the one to walk through it. If there is no clear direct career benefit to an employee for completing an education program, then even with tuition assistance the offer is often not particularly attractive, according to Anthony P. Carnevale, director of the Georgetown University Center on Education and the Workforce, as quoted in the *Inside Higher Ed* study.[13]

Via its robust coaching team, Guild ensures that students' educational choices are aligned to their goals. This is especially important for students who are pursuing their first weighty credential. In some cases, employees are pointed to additional education to meet specific employer skill needs. "In those cases," Jackson says, "it's less about what the major is or what the skills are than it is about the career benefits that come with having a particular credential."

"There's a huge opportunity and return on investment in education in general that is underrealized for tens of millions of Americans," says Jackson. "It doesn't need to be as hard for them as it is. You shouldn't have to claw and fight to get a degree if you feel like a degree is going to help you."

Drive Benefits for Employers

"The largest employers in the United States all, generally speaking, have some form of an education benefit," Jackson asserts, "but they haven't really thought about it in terms of a tool for recruitment or retainment and ways to achieve their corporate strategy." That's an oversight that Guild aims to correct. "A small investment in learning and development or education benefits has a disproportionate impact on other aspects of your bottom line, which is something that we've seen borne out time and again with the companies we work with. We work primarily with HR and people executives, but candidly, I think their CFO should pay more attention because if you make an investment here, it ends up bringing down a whole bunch of zeros elsewhere in the equation. I think when people realize what having a robust education strategy can do, if they optimize it the right way, it really changes the way they think about their benefits programs. It goes from being sort of like a cost anchor to a potential cost cutter or cost center."

Guild dramatically proved that point when it released a case study of one of its employer partners, Chipotle. Chipotle turned to Guild because, like many in the restaurant industry, they were paying a high cost for their employees' high turnover rate. Specifically, they had an annual turnover rate of 145 percent for hourly workers within six months on the job, and it was having a big impact on customer service and efficiency.[14]

Chipotle saw partnering with Guild as an opportunity to design a benefit that aligned with their purpose to "Cultivate a Better World." After launching their "Cultivate Education" program in 2016, which provided hourly employees with up to $5,250 in tuition reimbursements per year, "Chipotle found that those who took advantage of their education benefit retained at 90 percent"—a rate 3.5 times higher than peers who did not engage with the program."[15] This meant improved restaurant stability, as many employees who received their education stayed at Chipotle longer and were promoted to management position.

Chipotle was so impressed by the results that, in 2019, it took major steps to deepen its commitment. The benefits program was expanded to cover 100 percent of tuition costs up front for seventy-five different degrees in business technology, degrees that "align with Chipotle's priorities and give employees the chance to gain the skills and knowledge necessary to succeed in an evolving job market," as the case study put it.[16]

The results were powerful. "Not only were more crew members able to access education, but Chipotle found that employees who participated in the program were 7.5 times more likely to move into management positions than non-participants."[17]

Chipotle's success was made possible in part by the close partnership of Guild's employer solutions team, which digs into trends in learning and development and works with companies on "what their problems are and best practices to solve them through education," says Jackson. "We work really closely with the companies that we partner with to figure out what skills they need and then add programs accordingly. For example, Walmart wanted more health and wellness degrees, and we've added different language programs. We're constantly adapting to what companies and employees need."

Guild publishes its own research, white papers, and trend line reports. According to Jackson, some of that research is "oriented around getting employers to understand that they don't need to hire people with BAs. They can kick along their educational journey by hiring them without a degree and supporting their entrance into a college completion program. Employees of organizations that support them in that way are more loyal to their employer, but they're also attaining skills and academic advancement through the program."

For employers, Jackson speculates, education and learning are strengths you want your employees to have across their entire lifecycle with you. Investing in learning pays dividends both "for you and for the individual that you employ and care about and who is a part of your corporate family."

Solutions Pursued

ADD EMPLOYER PARTNERS TO SERVE AS MANY STUDENTS AS POSSIBLE

Guild's list of employer partners is constantly growing. According to Jackson, "There are eighty-eight million workers in the United States who need more training and advanced learning to keep up. And we're not there yet. But that's the goal."

ADD EDUCATIONAL PARTNERS TO SUPPORT THOSE STUDENTS IN AS MANY WAYS AS POSSIBLE

Guild's partner institutions run the gamut from traditional universities to providers of certificate and shorter-form programs and even boot camps. Movement in that direction is purposeful; Guild aspires to connect students to the educational opportunities that fit their unique needs, and not all students need a bachelor's degree. "The biggest issue is ensuring quality and proving that it will materially increase students' ability to be employed or make more money," says Jackson. (Chapter 6 looks at some high-quality alternative education pathways and providers that may provide such value.)

LEAN INTO THE MISSION AS THE LEARNING AND EMPLOYMENT LANDSCAPE CONTINUES TO CHANGE

Guild's student enrollment increased 25 percent between March and the fall of 2020—the height of the COVID pandemic. Guild has also worked closely with students who were close to completing their degrees but were laid off by the employers covering their tuition payments; the Guild intervention helps connect these students with another employer within the Guild network who could pick up where the previous one left off.

Guild is truly mission-driven, and its recent certification as a B Corporation speaks volumes about just how central that mission is to how it operates.

Full Focus: Alternative Model

- ENTER: Guild helps employees and employers get the most out of tuition reimbursement benefits, while ensuring that students enter, or reenter, their educational journeys in the right place and at the right time.

- DISCOVER: By partnering with employers to achieve their goals, guiding students through direct coaching, and publishing thought leadership studies on broader trends in learning and hiring, Guild helps students assess their present situations and consider where they want to go.

- CONNECT: Working students juggle education and part- or full-time work. Taking full advantage of tuition reimbursement keeps employees on the job and improves their chances of being promoted as they apply what they've learned.

Limited Focus: Alternative Model

- LEARN: Learning is provided through Guild's educational institution partners.

- ASSESS: Assessment is done at the point of learning.

- CREDENTIAL: Credentials are issued by the educational institution partners.

Key Takeaways

- Too often, tuition benefits go unclaimed because the process is difficult to navigate, the right programs are hard to find, and employees see no clear or direct line between education and progress in their careers.

- Streamlining the process and ensuring that both employers and employees understand the benefits can lead to higher employee participation, which in turn means higher employee retention and lower recruitment costs for the company. It also helps students gain skills that are important to the company and aligned with its broader mission.

- Connecting students to good-quality education requires deep partnerships between employers and educational institutions. Working students are looking for low-cost, accessible, flexible programs that are built to support their needs. Increasingly, the most viable options for meeting these goals are found in traditional degree-granting institutions.

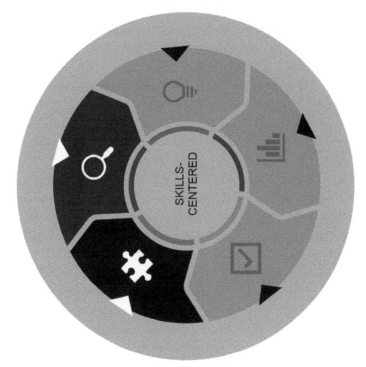

DISCOVER

Learners explore career pathways and competency mapping tools to understand where they are and where they need to be.

LEARN

Learners leverage a variety of educational resources to upskill and meet the needs of the current and future workforce.

ASSESS

Learners' abilities are assessed on the basis of demonstrated ability.

ENTER

Learners enter at various phases throughout their lifetimes.

CONNECT

Learners find or are recruited for jobs on the basis of validated skill data, ensuring that learners will be able to do what they are hired to do.

CREDENTIAL

Learners' abilities are recognized, validating skills in a transparent, contextualized, and standardized way.

SKILLS-CENTERED

Figure 5.3. Guild Education and Alternative Model: (Enter + Discover + Connect).

In the final case study of the chapter, we will look at a different kind of approach to connecting students with learning pathways, one integrated in the workplace and offered in collaboration with a single educational provider partner.

Case Study 4: Ernst & Young

Learner's Experience

It's my second year as an EY consultant. I felt out of my element when I started; I was thrown into situations I was completely unequipped to confront, and I needed to learn—a lot, and fast.

At this point, I have not only participated in but led conversations about artificial intelligence, data analysis, and block chain technology—with just one exception (blockchain) things I didn't have a clue about before I joined EY. And not just theoretical conversations—our clients are actually looking for advice on how to leverage these tools to enhance their businesses.

Luckily, I have had constant access to the learning content I needed to prepare for those kinds of projects. And I haven't had to pay a cent—or to worry about whether I was getting the latest information my clients would expect me to have mastered.

Before starting at EY, I had been curious about blockchain technology. My biggest frustration, though, was the lack of resources to learn about it. I had to be scrappy, attending meetups and learning the lingo of the developers in that space. It seemed like they were the only ones who actually knew what it was or could do. I ran into countless numbers of people in that space who thought they had a great idea about how blockchain technology could save the world, but no one was actually building anything, least of all well-developed educational resources so the world could actually understand what it was in for. At some point, I hit my threshold; without actually learning how to code, there wasn't any further I could go.

So, when I started at EY and saw all the learning resources that were available, including about blockchain, that was where I started. But I didn't stop there. I've earned thirty-five micro credentials at this point through the EY Badges program, and I am well on my way to a full MBA. Good thing I didn't start with business school right out of undergrad: I'd probably be a hundred thousand dollars in debt, and I'd still have had to learn all of this when I got here.

I expect to earn my full MBA by the end of the year. While the idea of add-ing to my resumé a degree from Hult International Business School is exciting,

I know it's just the beginning. I have a full toolkit to keep growing at EY. Who knows where my learning will take me?

About EY (Tech MBA)

"I'm committed to preparing our people for the future of work so they can lead our teams and clients through disruption and grow their careers. As a champion of our D&I efforts, I believe we must seek out people with diverse backgrounds and unique experiences who can contribute to our highest-performing teams and provide exceptional results for our clients every day."
—Trent Henry, Global Vice Chair of Talent, Ernst & Young

The venerable firm Ernst & Young is a multinational professional services network and one of the Big 4 consulting firms, along with Deloitte, PwC, and KPMG. Not only among the Big 4 but actually among *all* organizations, it is unique in that it offers a fully accredited, free MBA for all of its people, regardless of their location, rank, or prior educational backgrounds: the EY Tech MBA, from Hult International Business School. Says Trent Henry, EY's "Global Vice Chair of Talent," "this is the very first program of its kind, and it truly sets us apart from our peers, not just among the Big 4 but in the entire business world."[18]

The EY Tech MBA by Hult combines academic learning with real-life experiences. All of the learning also meets EY's wider digital accessibility policies, thereby providing access to people with a diverse range of vision and hearing abilities. Its curriculum is built around the future-focused skills most in demand by EY's clients to enable their technology needs. The mastery of these skills is combined with a core leadership methodology and the required business skills of any MBA. It is all delivered through the EY Badges program, in which EY develops and curates learning content from the best industry learning providers.

EY Badges deliver digital credentials via Credly's Acclaim platform. Students choose which badges they would like to study, then achieve credentials by completing the required learning and, most important, applying that learning in practice. The learning is delivered virtually via an EY Badges platform integrated with the organization's learning management system—SAP Success Factors and Jam.

Badges are reviewed every quarter, so that the curriculum is as relevant and future-focused as possible, while the fact that it is self-directed means that EY people can build and regularly update their skills in a way that suits them. In addition to completing the EY Badges program, students must write a number of papers and complete a final "Capstone Project." Hult International Business School provides a quality and assessment methodology; all items of learning are approved by them. Hult also directly manages the final Capstone Project stage of the program.

As Trent Henry sees it, the degree benefits both EY's people and EY itself. Employees master the skills that help them better serve clients while gaining a fully accredited qualification from one of the world's top business schools. The talent marketplace recognizes that EY is fully invested in the development of its people. And clients recognize that EY's people at every level are as knowledgable and well-prepared to serve as it is possible to be.

Problems Addressed

KEEP WORKFORCE SKILLS UP TO DATE SO EMPLOYEES CAN SERVE CLIENTS MORE EFFECTIVELY

The goal is to keep EY people up to date on the future-facing skills that are most in demand from clients, as assessed by EY's business leaders. The learning is delivered when it's needed, in a context in which it can be immediately applied. The learning for each area of EY Badges is curated by "Domain Owners," subject matter experts who review the available learning, develop the curriculum, and update the curriculum every four months.

Equally significant, the learning model is appropriate for adult learners. "In terms of the curriculum, it is very practical and focused on 'learning by doing.' EY people in the process of completing the MBA need to demonstrate practical examples of how they have utilized their learning in real-life business situations," says Henry.

And the learning doesn't stop with graduation, as it might in a traditional educational environment. Rather, those who have achieved the degree continue to have access to the Badges learning platform, so they can continually plug into updated learning content. They are also considered alumni of Hult and therefore "have access to the same opportunities as other Hult alumni," Henry says. Moreover, EY people who have successfully completed the MBA can serve as sponsors and mentors for their colleagues within the EY Tech MBA community, providing support to current employee-students and gaining mentorship experience that is important to building their management skills.

Assess and Contextualize Learning Through Applied Demonstration of Skill

Candidates must demonstrate practical application of their learning, which means they are tested in real-life, on-the-job experiences. A Hult-approved assessment matrix enables senior staff to evaluate how well students have embedded their learning, both with clients and via internal projects. In addition to codeveloping the assessment matrix, Hult International Business School is thoroughly involved with the design of the program. Hult contributes content from its own syllabus and is responsible for assessing and grading candidates.

The objective of the Capstone Project is to demonstrate the integration of concepts learned throughout the program in one of two ways:

1. A strategic opportunity for EY: candidates choosing this option will need to identify a new strategic opportunity for EY globally, or in their region, using the knowledge and skills they gained in their pursuit of the EY Tech MBA.

2. A new social impact enterprise to address a societal challenge: candidates who choose this option will be required to develop a business plan for a social impact enterprise that addresses the current year's challenge for the Hult Prize, as detailed at www.hultprize.org.

Aligning assessment with metrics that matter to the company means that EY immediately reaps the rewards of having a better-prepared workforce; the assignments submitted by program participants deliver value on the job.

Grant Portable, Meaningful Credentials

EY believes the MBA is, and will continue to be, a highly regarded qualification that can give people an excellent grounding in business skills. But while the MBA is the final credential, learners earn badges throughout the study process that speak to what they know and hence what they can do. Over the course of completing the MBA, they will build a portfolio of various levels of achievements in various content areas. They can focus on their personal preference areas, but they must also attain the required breadth across three pillars: technology, leadership, and business. Allowing students choice in their areas of study is important because it drives engagement and allows them to develop their own self-selected pathways through the content. In addition, it means that they can use those credentials to tell their professional story.

Companies spend an estimated $20 billion each year on tuition benefits for their employees.[19] But as noted earlier, without direct career benefits, employees may not take full advantage.[20] EY's approach—partnering with an accredited institution to provide learning that is practiced and assessed directly in the workplace—provides employees with the motivation that is needed, while completely eliminating the friction of typical tuition reimbursement channels.

Solutions Pursued

EXPAND TO REACH MORE EY PEOPLE

EY will continue to grow its education programs. "During the COVID-19 pandemic," says Henry, "we saw a 40-percent-plus uplift globally in the use of our online learning resources. The virtual and flexible nature of the EY Tech MBA by Hult means people can study wherever and whenever they want, at their own speed." Looking forward, a key success metric will be the number of people completing the MBA. "By the end of 2021, we expect to have awarded over a hundred MBAs, and we expect this to grow to around a thousand by 2023," Henry says.

CONTINUE TO HOME IN ON FUTURE-FOCUSED SKILLS

The premise of the program is to stay current; this requires an ongoing process of feedback, iteration, and further development. Though technology is important, its scope is much wider. In the future, Henry says, "we think there will be an increased focus on . . . broader purpose-based skills—for example, diversity and inclusion, and sustainable business practices."

DEVELOP A CULTURE OF LEARNING

As we saw in the previous case study, it's not enough for companies to simply make educational resources available to employees; employee development must be a cornerstone of their business objectives, and incentives must be aligned to encourage employees to participate. As Henry puts it, EY's MBA "is part of our wider strategy to enable our people to build the careers they want, in a way that suits them—which we call 'It's yours to build.' We want to encourage and enable our people to have a growth mindset, where ongoing learning is part of the foundation of the career experience. Further, we believe that curiosity is a key attribute for everyone to keep up with the uncertainty and disruption in the world today. Asking better questions is key."

Full Focus: Alternative Model

- ENTER: While learners must be employees at EY to participate, once they're

DISCOVER

Learners explore career pathways and competency mapping tools to understand where they are and where they need to be.

LEARN

Learners leverage a variety of educational resources to upskill and meet the needs of the current and future workforce.

ASSESS

Learners' abilities are assessed on the basis of demonstrated ability.

ENTER

Learners enter at various phases throughout their lifetimes.

CONNECT

Learners find or are recruited for jobs on the basis of validated skill data, ensuring that learners will be able to do what they are hired to do.

CREDENTIAL

Learners' abilities are recognized, validating skills in a transparent, contextualized, and standardized way.

Figure 5.4. EY and Alternative Model: (Enter + Learn + Assess + Credential + Connect).

in the door, all barriers to accessing additional learning are removed.

- LEARN: Learners can leverage high-quality, future-oriented learning content curated by EY in collaboration with Hult.

- ASSESS: Learning is measured by an assessment matrix that is based on real-world, contextualized criteria that are meaningful to EY. Learners develop a portfolio of evidence of what they are capable of.

- CREDENTIAL: Learners earn skill-specific micro credentials and potentially a full MBA, both from trusted brand names.

- CONNECT: The learning is applied immediately and directly to the learner's work, delivering value to the company and its clients.

Limited Focus: Alternative Model

- DISCOVER: While learners can create their own pathway through the program, the skills they build are directly aligned with their clients' and employer's needs. Exploring career pathways is less important than enhancing performance within their current roles.

Key Takeaways
• Partnering with a trusted educational provider—in this case, Hult International Business School—can alleviate the burden of creating and assessing learning content while ensuring that outcomes are directly in line with business objectives.
• Lowering barriers to entry is an essential first step but it is not the only one: creating a culture of learning and growth is key to engaging the entire workforce.
• Applied assessments create opportunities for learners to put their skills into practice in real time, leading to more accurate measures of what the learner can do and more immediate benefits to the company.

Concluding Thoughts

Traditional four-year colleges are failing to meet two critical goals—providing reliable pathways to employment for as many qualified students as possible, and ensuring that the skills they graduate with are relevant and transferable—and more important still, that potential employers recognize them as such. The four case studies in this chapter profile organizations that address these issues from the employers' side of the equation. ZipRecruiter uses algorithms to develop more precise matches between the skills that an employer needs and those that candidates have, simplifying job searches, helping candidates source programs that can close their gaps, and spurring colleges to align their course offerings with relevant skills. Degreed connects employees to courses and programs that allow them to continuously develop on the job, while Guild Education partners with employers and educators to provide workers with frictionless opportunities to earn degrees and certifications that are paid for through their employee benefits. Finally, Ernst & Young provides all of its employees with the opportunity to earn the EY Tech MBA. All four reflect the understanding that companies must not only strive to hire the right candidates, but support their continuing growth and progress.

In the next chapter, we will look at programs that are geared to individuals who neither need nor want college degrees, but who wish to acquire the skills that will qualify them for the high-skill, high-pay jobs that are the high-tech equivalents of the building and construction trades.

6

SOLO DISRUPTORS

So far, we have explored innovations within higher education and companies that are designed to break down barriers to entry and enable learners to develop in-demand skills that can strengthen and advance their careers. These are valuable initiatives, yet they do not entirely meet the needs of a market moving at great speed. Nor do they respond to the needs of individuals who neither want nor need a college degree, yet lack the qualifications they need to apply for the jobs they see as most desirable. The alternative educational pathways we explore in this chapter provide learners with skills and knowledge that translate into immediate employment.

The need for such pathways is conspicuous. "Demand for digital talent outpaces the supply," says Kathy Mannes. Mannes, vice president at the education and workforce development nonprofit Jobs For the Future, notes that there are "hundreds of thousands" of digitally intensive jobs that remain unfilled because of a lack of skills—jobs that call for more education than a high school diploma but don't require a four-year college degree. "In the field of IT support alone," Mannes said in 2019, "there are 215,000 open roles in the United States."[1]

As for who or what is responsible for that, Mannes lays the blame squarely at the feet of the country's education system, which has not moved fast enough to adapt to the needs of a rapidly changing economy. "Generally, we have pretty structured, traditional ways of entering jobs," Mannes says. "Employers need to onboard people more quickly with the skills that they need right away."[2]

The marketplace has responded with a number of promising initiatives.

Sean Gallagher, the founder and executive director of Northeastern University's Center for the Future of Higher Education and Talent Strategy, notes that the decade 2010 to 2020 saw significant experimentation in postsecondary education, with both colleges and noninstitutional educational providers developing micro credentials, digital badges, and certificate programs for skills training, "shorter, more modular, more job-market-aligned credentials that are more affordable."[3]The companies profiled in this chapter are developing four different pathways to those credentials: industry certifications, apprenticeships, bootcamps, and self-guided courses. None of them requires an existing degree or current employment, and all lead to better employment options. Together, they offer a checklist of best practices that can help consumers and employers alike as they learn to navigate this new territory.

Case Study 1: Google

Google

Learner's Experience

I'm Rey Justo. Before the COVID-19 pandemic, I had one of the highest-paying jobs I've ever had as the Lead Installer for a fireplace installation company. But once the pandemic hit the US, I became unemployed for the first time in my life and lost my home. The only jobs I was able to find were jobs that couldn't pay the bills. And finding similar work to my previous job was extraordinarily difficult as my entire industry was impacted by the pandemic. As a consequence, I had to move in with my grandparents where my wife, our four children, and I shared one room.

I always had a passion for tech but fitting in college courses to pursue it wouldn't work with my family life and full-time job. I enrolled in the Google IT Career Certificate with a nonprofit called Merit America and they helped me earn my certificate at my own pace in less than six months and connected me with a coach, a group of peers, and employers. It was so flexible it allowed me to navigate my very busy life and still have plenty of time for my family. The program taught me how to build on skills I already had. And because the course was created and taught by current Google employees, I knew everything I was learning was relevant to the industry.

Enrolling in the Google IT Career Certificate gave me the confidence boost I needed. I received interview requests for jobs in IT starting the very next day after completing the certificate. I got a dream job as a developer-in-training at Zennify—a cloud technology consulting firm—and was able to purchase my first home. As an apprentice at Zennify, I am making more money than I was as a lead at my previous job. It's an incredibly rewarding feeling and my family is very proud of me.

About Google (Grow with Google)

"We are proud that our certificate programs are a driving force in the alternative education and skilling space and in creating equal economic opportunities for nontraditional learners. We are both humbled and excited to be part of the changing landscape that is focused on diversity, equity, and inclusion as we think about the future of education and the future of work."
—Lisa Gevelber, chief marketing officer, Americas Region, Google, and vice president of Grow with Google

Grow with Google takes individuals with no related work experience to entry-level job readiness in less than six months. Courses are offered online on the Coursera learning platform; the Google Career Certificates they award provide on-ramps into high-growth, high-paying jobs that don't require college degrees. Google debuted its first Career Certificate, in IT support, in 2018 to help create upward economic mobility for historically underserved groups. Eighty percent of the program participants in the United States reported a positive career impact within six months.[4] In keeping with its goal to be accessible to all, Google worked hard to lower barriers to entry. Would-be learners log into grow.google.com to find available courses and pay $39 per month to cover Coursera's platform fee. Google earns no revenue from the program and funds a hundred thousand need-based scholarships; Coursera also supplies financial assistance and waives the fee for students registered at schools and universities, since they can access the program via Coursera for Campus. Ungraded content (videos, readings, practice quizzes) is available for free via audit mode on Coursera, and video content can be found on You Tube's Google Career Certificates channel. Learners must score 80 percent or higher on all graded assessments in order to be awarded the end-of-program credential.

Among a fairly wide range of industry certifications—including from such widely recognized technology companies as Cisco and Microsoft—Google Career Certificates claim to be unique in numerous respects. First is their accessibility. While an individual can pursue a certificate completely online on a part-time basis, there is also the option to enroll in cohort-based learning available through nonprofit partners, community colleges, and career and technical high schools. Second, they "build for the job." The company applies task and skills analysis to discern the precise needs for each entry-level role, then vets it with subject matter experts at top employers. Third, the courses are created and taught by Google experts. The company takes justifiable pride in the rigor and depth of its curriculum and on what it calls the "product agnosticism" of its programs. Mastery is evaluated through hands-on exercises, capstone projects, and extensive assessments—150 for the IT Support Professional Certificate. And finally, a hiring consortium of more than 130 national employers, including Walmart, Best Buy, Bank of America, PNC Bank, the Cleveland Clinic, Sprint, Hulu, Intel, and Google itself, taps directly into the program for entry level job candidates.[5] As noted above, 80 percent of certificate holders report such positive outcomes as a new job, a raise, or a promotion.[6]

Natalie Van Kleef Conley, the product lead for Google's IT Support Professional Certificate, notes that the program provides "a strong entry point for nontraditional talent into tech."[7] This is particularly the case when courses are offered at community colleges that enroll significant numbers of low-income students and young people of color.[8]

Google is aware of other best-in-class online learning offerings, and in some cases it collaborates with them. For example, CompTIA, a nonprofit trade association for help-desk technicians and tech support specialists, offers a highly regarded CompTIA A+ certification. Learners who complete the Google IT Support Professional Certificate and pass the CompTIA A+ certification exams receive a dual credential from CompTIA and Google—a double-whammy badge that can be posted on LinkedIn to catch the attention of potential employers.

For the two-thirds of Americans who do not have a four-year college degree, a Google Career Certificate is a pathway to fast-growing, well-paying jobs.[9] But it may also jump-start the pursuit of a degree. The Google IT Support Professional Certificate has secured a credit recommendation from the American Council on Education's (ACE) CREDIT program, the industry standard for translating workplace learning to college credit. Learners can earn a recommendation of twelve college credits for completing the program, the equivalent of four college courses at the associate degree level.[10]

Problems Addressed

Open Doors to High-Growth, In-Demand Jobs for Underrepresented Populations

Google places great emphasis on its inclusive curriculum. Its learning design incorporates nontechnical videos showcasing the personal stories of Google employees from diverse backgrounds and underserved groups—an IT special-ist turned security engineer from the deaf community; several female execu-tives; and a veteran of the U.S. Navy. Holders of Google's first Career Certificate, the IT Support Professional Certificate, are similarly diverse. Fifty-eight per-cent are Black, Latino, female, or veterans. Forty-five percent are in the lowest income tercile (reporting an annual income of $30,000 or less), and 61 percent do not hold college degrees.[11] Google also works with partners who provide cohort-based learning environments. Among these are nonprofits, community colleges, and career and technical employment high schools that distribute Google certificate programs in their classrooms as part of an effort to provide their students hands-on, applied skills toward future careers. Google has also partnered with such nonprofit organizations as PerScholas, Year Up, Goodwill, Merit America, USO, and Student Veterans Association among others. Funded by grants from Google.org, these organizations offer Google Career Certificates and wraparound services to support learners.

Throughout the program, Google learners have access to

- A suite of Google-created resumé and interview prep videos;

- Downloadable resumé templates appropriate for each career field;

- Forums to connect with other learners.

Upon completion, they have access to

- Free, virtual interview practice;

- A job board that features local, regional, and national open roles in related fields.

Develop a Workforce with In-Demand Skills

Google takes pains to ensure that its programs reflect current industry stan-dards and needs. As earlier noted, the learning content for each Career Certifi-cate is developed by Google employees who are experts in these career fields, and vetted with top employers to ensure that graduates will be job ready. The goal is to define the skills and knowledge required for a particular job. Training programs are practice-based, enabling learners to engage in a dynamic mix of hands-on and interactive assessments.

Support a Transition to More Equitable Hiring Practices

Programs that focus on job training, skills matching, and employer connection not only position learners for specific fields but prepare them for the shift to skills-based hiring rooted in competency-based assessments. Google is working toward more equitable hiring practices by applying the same or greater weight to Career Certificates for some entry-level roles as it does to four-year degrees. The company also hosts a number of apprenticeship programs that give participants the opportunity to "earn as they learn."[12]

More broadly, Google works with national and local workforce organizations like the National Association of Workforce Boards and the Society for Human Resource Management to connect with talent acquisition decision makers nationwide. Through these partnerships, Google aims to create greater awareness of its certificate programs while promoting a more equitable model for hiring managers across the United States.

Solutions Pursued

Expand Career Certificate Offerings

The IT Support Professional Certificate's success paved the way for an expanded suite of certificate offerings, which can be found on Google's website (https://grow.google/certificates/). Recent new entries at the time of this writing include

- Data Analyst: a position with an average entry-level salary of $67,900;

- Project Manager: with a median annual wage of $59,000;

- UX Designer: with a median annual wage of $58,600.

Strengthen Relationships with Even More Delivery Partners

Because community colleges have unparalleled reach in their communities and play a critical role in workforce development, Google—in partnership with JFF, which we will learn more about in Chapter 7—has scaled its Career Certificate programs to more than a hundred community colleges.[13]

Expand the Hiring Consortium Network

Since buy-in from employers is key to Grow with Google's success, it aims to add to its hiring consortium. There are no restrictions regarding company size or annual hiring minimums, and companies can count on substantial benefits (see https://grow.google/employers/), including

- A robust candidate pool of highly qualified talent, many from nontraditional backgrounds;

- Exclusive access to the job board for Google Career Certificate holders, both to post open entry-level roles and to review learner profiles;

- Invitations to participate in interview days and email campaigns about open roles;

- A "Google participating employer" digital badge post on the company website.

Full Focus: Alternative Model

- ENTER: There are no prerequisites to entering the learning process here. There are no requirements for a degree, previous knowledge, or prior work experience, and the nominal monthly fee can be covered by scholarships.

- LEARN: Learning content is created by subject-matter experts and validated by top employers to ensure that it is aligned with current needs.

- ASSESS: Assessments are interactive and hands-on, and participants must receive a grade of at least 80 percent to pass.

- CREDENTIAL: The credential earned carries the weight of the Google name, which is trusted globally. In concrete support of its value, Google equates it to a college bachelor's degree in its hiring practices.

- CONNECT: A huge emphasis of Google's Career Certificates is connecting learners to employment opportunities via career support resources and the buy-in of the Grow with Google Hiring Consortium.

Limited Focus: Alternative Model

- DISCOVER: Google Career Certificate students explore their career options before they enroll. They have made up their minds about what pathway they are pursuing, and see the certificate as the most efficient and effective way to get there.

DISCOVER

Learners explore career pathways and competency mapping tools to understand where they are and where they need to be.

LEARN

Learners leverage a variety of educational resources to upskill and meet the needs of the current and future workforce.

ASSESS

Learners' abilities are assessed on the basis of demonstrated ability.

ENTER

Learners enter at various phases throughout their lifetimes.

CONNECT

Learners find or are recruited for jobs on the basis of validated skill data, ensuring that learners will be able to do what they are hired to do.

CREDENTIAL

Learners' abilities are recognized, validating skills in a transparent, contextualized, and standardized way.

Figure 6.1. Google and Alternative Model: (Enter + Learn + Assess + Credential + Connect).

Key Takeaways

- Industry certificates offer up-to-date training for in-demand roles. Since they carry the weight of the certifying brand, the trust in the brand translates to trust in the learners' abilities, which are proven through demonstration of the skills they will need to put into practice in their jobs.

- While other nondegree credentials can validate abilities, industry certifications are backed up by employers who commit to hire certified individuals. This makes industry certifications a reliable investment for learners—especially if they are embarking on a new career path.

- Other partnerships are essential to the support of nontraditional students. Delivery partners at such local educational nexuses as community colleges and trade schools, for example, can support cohorts of students, while nonprofit partners can provide wraparound services to ensure that students have the resources and support they need to complete the program. The importance of supporting students holistically cannot be overstated; it is key to creating a more diverse and equitable workforce.

In the next case study, we'll see how industry certifications can be leveraged to connect learners with specific career opportunities via apprenticeships.

Case Study 2: Apprenti

APPRENTi

Learner's Experience

I've had a tough time settling back into civilian life. As a veteran, I have faced and overcome challenges that many couldn't dream of, yet those experiences don't often translate well on a resumé. I've been an Uber driver for the past year, but that's not how I want to spend the rest of my career.

When I learned about Apprenti through my Veterans Administration center, it seemed like a great way to get my foot in the door of a career that I could get excited about. I passed the competency assessment with flying colors—I was always good at math—and I've honed my problem-solving and emotional intelligence skills through my service. I had a successful interview with Apprenti's staff, and my research into the Apprenti network of "hiring partners" paid off too. At least it seems that way, since I was selected after my first interview for an apprenticeship as a data center technician at Amazon. I couldn't believe it. Just months ago, I never would have imagined this could be possible.

I'm going through an intensive online program of technical training first, then I dive into a year of paid on-the-job training. Since I'm not getting paid yet, I'm still bootstrapping, but luckily I qualify for Basic Allowance for Housing through the VA, and as long as I cook the meals, my sister is paying for groceries.

I'm a hard worker, a fast learner, and a team player. The technical training has been challenging, but I know it will be worth it once I get in the door at Amazon and can prove myself as an employee. I can't wait for another opportunity to contribute to something bigger than myself.

About Apprenti

"It's no wonder we complain we don't have enough qualified talent. It's because we're not willing to make it. I spent about a year understanding the ubiquitousness of two things: one, not enough tech talent anywhere, and two, lack of diversity at all ranks. . . . There's just no investment level that the country could make to scale the number of people we need to produce domestically. And so we were going to have to stand up a secondary system."
—Jennifer Carlson, co-founder and executive director, Apprenti

National understanding and awareness of apprenticeships have increased since President Barack Obama's 2014 call to action during his State of the Union address. ApprenticeshipUSA provided funds for states to "develop strategic plans and build partnerships for apprenticeship expansion and diversification."[14] Apprenticeship.gov defines apprenticeship as "an industry-driven, high-quality career pathway where employers can develop and prepare their future workforce, and individuals can obtain paid work experience, classroom instruction, and a portable, nationally-recognized credential."[15] Though most Americans think of the skilled trades or Europe when they think of the word, its definition does not specify any particular industries or contexts. Apprenti is a 501(c)(3) not-for-profit company that has taken it upon itself to create an apprenticeship model within the technology sector—a "secondary system" that is parallel to and not competitive with colleges. It acts as a middleman between potential trainees and companies by assessing applicants, matching them with available positions at their hiring partners, and undertaking the training they need before they can start.

There will always be a place for an expansive university education, Apprenti co-founder and executive director Jennifer Carlson says, but as the cost of a bachelor's degree continues to rise, more Americans are opting out, unwilling to take on the debt needed to complete something that has no guaranteed employment outcome. And while no one contests the *intrinsic* value of a well-rounded education, more has remained the same in higher education than has changed, widening even further the divide between graduates' skillsets and the work needs of employers.

In Europe, roughly 40 percent of the population completes university.[16] In the case of Germany, more than 50 percent of those who don't start apprenticeships.[17] Apprenticeship works. In the building and construction trades, for example, "by the time you move on to what they call a journeyman, the person with those years of experience [has the] equivalent of a college degree, and can very quickly be making high five figures to start, completely equitable with the tech sector and just a simple choice of preference. Why look at that as any better, worse, or different than what we do?" asks Carlson. "There's dignity in that."[18]

The fact is, technology companies need skills. Necessity breeds invention, so employers and third parties are creating code academies and bootcamps to provide them. While Carlson concedes that not all of them are good options, she believes that as in any free market, "the good will rise to the top in time, the bad will die or be acquired and fade away." The more industry sees these alternative on-ramps as viable (and that is increasingly the view), the more consumers will choose them over more costly options.

The apprenticeships that Apprenti enables are hybrid classroom and hands-on training systems that allow their participants to quickly learn the technical skills that are needed to begin a career in technology. Employers gain a diverse, prescreened pool of highly competent individuals who will spend at least a year learning their systems. Apprentices gain a pathway into a long-term high-wage career at low to no cost.

Carlson explains that "there isn't a model out there for us to follow in a nontraditional sector that's done it before. . . . The hospitality sector is doing this, but their job types are so different from ours, and their consumption of entry-level talent, which is sadly largely minimum wage, is very different. We can't use them as a benchmark. This means everything we do is feel your way through it, try it, see if it works." Essentially, we "look at (a) what is the gap we need to fill, and (b) who are the likely partners who can fill it? Is this something we want to internalize or externalize? We're not going to be another social service organization; I don't want to replicate work that's already being done by workforce boards and other nonprofits. . . . I'm happy to pilot and beta something, but I'm not willing to do it if we can't scale it operationally in every market."

Close partnerships with employers are key. "Our role," Carlson explains, "evolved to being the intermediary. Companies, for the most part, are not ready to reshape their current in-house HR and recruitment systems to accommodate apprenticeship." So while the employer specifies the requirements, Apprenti pulls together the resources to find, train, and—ideally—fund the apprentice through that initial training. Building the entire model from scratch has its benefits. "We went through those first painful steps," Carlson recalls. "We presented employers with a blank piece of paper and said, 'Tell us what you want.' After getting back a whole host of things that couldn't be executed or looked just like today's world, we took key learnings, started filling in the paper, and gave them an opportunity to weigh in on changes. Suddenly, we got far more meaningful data: 'Tweak this, do this differently, that's not as relevant as you think it is, this is more what we want.' And that allowed us to now do what we do when it comes to the classroom training." It's a matter of iteration, Carlson concludes. For "every single cohort, we're able to iterate what we did last and what we need to do this time to continue for improvement."

This ability to evolve in real time on the basis of employers' changing needs is not typically found in universities. As Carlson dryly notes, "Higher education . . . is not synonymous with the word nimble." She feels no discomfort in calling higher education "a broken system. I'm not saying it can't heal, but part of the reason we don't use community colleges everywhere or the college system everywhere—and even where we do partner, it's on the nontraditional, noncredit-bearing side of the house—is the lack of flexibility for accreditation." As an industry-backed consumer, Apprenti has the ability to influence the education market. With the exception of industry-created credentials like Linux, CompTIA, AWS, or CISCO certifications, Apprenti rarely takes its curricula off the shelf. "We are a consumer on behalf of employers who have promised employment. Thus we have control to ensure that the employer or industry gets its needs met," Carlson says.

The Apprenti program model follows a constructivist-connectivist approach, meaning it is designed to teach students to look for patterns and identify sources of information that can solve the pertinent problems of the job. With a project-based learning environment and a relatively minimal number of traditional tests or quizzes, Apprenti models the work environment in the classroom. "This helps us observe interpersonal traits and knit the apprentices into a community that can rely on each other," Carlson maintains, "in much the same way the apprentice will need to be self-sufficient on the job even with the mentorship and supervision of more experienced staff." In the accelerated Apprenti environment, the objective is not to jam two to three years of course content into three to five months; rather, it is to instill good habits for critical thinking and problem solving. Most skill development will occur through hands-on experience on the job.

Core competencies are established on the basis of the primary job duties, allowing for variation across employers. Apprenti provides objective measures of performance that reflect attainment of the theoretical and practical skills needed to succeed in the workplace. Typically, there is an entry-level industry certification attached to that skill set, which validates Apprenti's instruction through an impartial third party. In other cases, the competency is based on performance metrics inherent in the role—for example, the number of support tickets resolved or closed, the number of successful contributions to a code repository. In other cases, it could be based on an evaluation of a benchmarked project simulation or a mock interview loop covering the technical skills needed for advancement. Training is delivered through a combination of community colleges—typically, on the continuing-education side of the colleges' operations—certified corporate trainers, and code academies willing to meet Apprenti's requirements and the employers' training needs.

In addition to creating training curricula, Apprenti helps employers address another key need: attracting diverse talent. "While our focus is working with employers to secure apprenticeable headcount," says Carlson, "our function is to deliver people of color, women, veterans, and persons with disabilities—all underrepresented groups." Apprenti conducts outreach in each market in a hands-on way, working with local community-based organizations, community colleges, and other nonprofits whose services focus on similar target groups. This has yielded an applicant pool with greater than 84 percent diversity.

From a disability standpoint, Apprenti worked with the Wheelhouse organization and the U.S. Department of Labor's Office of Disability Policy to audit its website's accessibility. "We've ensured that the program meets all criteria for public accessibility," Carlson says, "so it can be completed using school, library, and other institutions where computers are publicly accessible." She adds that the site has been set up "to scale to your device, so you can take the assessment via your telephone or a tablet, though it may take a little longer."

Importantly, the cost to participate as an apprentice is free as of this writing. Employers pay Apprenti a fee for sourcing diverse talent and for managing the training process. Most hiring employers pay half of the tuition costs for the classroom training needed to get an apprentice prepared, and the rest is subsidized by state and federal grants and through private philanthropy.

The model has proven successful by virtually every measure. Completion rates are 88 percent.[19] Job placement rates are at or above 50 percent. Retention rate with employers is 80 percent,[20] and 75 percent of employers return to Apprenti for candidates year after year, allowing for company changes, mergers and acquisitions, and the like. So, it is surprising that Apprenti has few peers. Some other organizations perform similar functions in other industries; FAME (www.fame-usa.com), for example, has established a similar record of success in the manufacturing industry. But overall, the market is thin.

Carlson does not expect it to stay that way. "As an intermediary, we do not really have many peers. I do expect that to change, and rising tides are needed to help all ships, so I respect the need for more of us. Employers want consistency in the delivery and application of any model they employ. Enterprise-level companies are already exploring how to scale nationally and operationalize globally. This model delivers an industry-certified credential, which no training provider outside of higher education can offer. Further, employers are fatigued at the number of solutions approaching them that are all one degree left or right of the last promising the same outcome. Our role is to consolidate all of that and make consumption easier for the employer, and if preferred, help them internalize the whole process."

One reason some may hesitate to enter the market is the scale at which an organization functioning in Apprenti's role must operate. The list of partnerships it wrangles is daunting. "We work with a little bit of everyone in partnership," Carlson says, "a range of training entities; public workforce organizations; government agencies at state and federal levels; community-based organizations, which work with a wide range of people we would like to place; and philanthropies—who help to underwrite some of the costs." What partnership needs, in her view, is "transparency, alignment to objectives, [and] clearly defined roles and responsibilities." And then, she says, "it's just *go*."

Problems Addressed

DESTIGMATIZE AND RECONTEXTUALIZE APPRENTICESHIPS

"I think there absolutely is a stigma that the industry to this moment is still struggling with," Carlson says. The term "apprenticeship" seems to make just about everybody think of the building and construction trades, so she tries to assure people that it is just like a "residency in medicine or clerking in law. . . . It's just . . . a combination of classroom and hands-on experience."

The other side of the conversation, however, is a little harder to confront. It is what Carlson calls "the prevailing idea in the U.S. that our higher education system is the ultimate outcome." Carlson's response is to show that the Apprenti model results in a raise of one and a half to twice as much of an individual's income within eighteen months. Why, she challenges doubters, "are you clinging to this old paradigm?"

For anyone needing a nudge to accept apprenticeship-style applied learning as an equally viable model to traditional higher education, Carlson offers a persuasive argument. "I will go so far as to call out that I think the trade school of the technology sector, the applied learning model, if you will, is MIT. It's Stanford. It's Carnegie Mellon. It's Georgia Tech. It's those ranked schools known for being the best. At the end of the day, those people are getting true hands-on skills, have built things, sold things, filed patents—you name it— before they've even graduated. That is trade school. That is the original trade school."

Make Tech Hiring More Equitable and Efficient

For applicants, it's all about access. Apprenticeship is a gateway to a high-wage career that does not require years of education and potentially hundreds of thousands of dollars for admission. Apprenti removes barriers for people with the aptitude to prove their worth, and at the same time, works with companies to shift from simply consuming talent to building it.

Apprenticeship can also help undermine the tech sector's hiring bias. In creating Apprenti, Carlson was forced to confront the sector's bias against non-college graduates, and more troublingly, certain cultures. To the extent that Apprenti delivers competence, that bias will fade.

Employers' hiring systems are built around company-to-company recruitment, higher education or college recruitment, and third-party systems that procure talent on the basis of stated need. The technology sector is not adept at screening prospective talent for skill sets and an ability to learn. Apprenti manages a highly diverse talent pipeline that is prescreened for aptitude and teachability. This bolsters employers' confidence in those candidates.

Apprenti does face some challenges. The greatest is companies' lack of transparency when it comes to tracking and quantifying their recruiting costs. Apprenti has begun a longitudinal study by requesting blind data on the costs of internal-versus-external recruiters, nonreported costs like stock and signing bonuses, benefits, relocation, and the like. As no two companies account for these costs in the same way, and there is no cost allocation for the time that mentors spend managing their apprentices, it is difficult to compare the value of apprenticeship as a talent development system against the standard college ranking system—or any other system. Carlson claims that "anecdotally," apprenticeship seems to provide employers with "a 23 percent to 27 percent savings over traditional hires," but she admits that the figure is highly conjectural. Hard data would help her make her case.

Scale is also a challenge. The tech industry, she concedes, has been slow to adopt apprenticeship. It is growing, but at a snail's pace—unusual, claims Carlson, "for a sector that generally moves at light speed on new options."

Convincing employers to make the shift often depends on internal champions. "More often than not," Carlson says, "we're starting with the CTO or the CIO. They own the budget headcount and the pain of the work not getting done. And frankly, they're more pragmatic about if the person can do the work." HR departments, the group typically overseeing credential requirements, are all about risk management, so it's hard for them to loosen their dependency on the four-year degree. But with the help of a high level executive sponsor, she says, "it becomes a mandate."

The lack of reliable data also stymies employers' ability to do "more predictable funding," says Carlson, another cloud over the advance of apprenticeship. Absent a full cost-benefit analysis, employers tend to revert to recruiting methods they can estimate more predictably. Which is why Carlson believes her biggest challenge of all is "a sustainable funding mechanism."

Tackle Policy Challenges

According to Carlson, "Apprenti fills in the gaps that companies don't want to deal with on the regulatory side." That can get very complicated.

The fastest way to grow apprenticeships, she says, would be to tie consumption of apprenticeships to the consumption of H-1B visas. "We have eighty-five thousand H-1B visas a year, and sixty thousand of those come to the tech sector," Carlson says. "If you just make it like-for-like, you don't have to get industry-centric. This means if we suddenly need more stevedore engineers next year and they start consuming more visas, then we can advocate for more apprenticeships in the shipping industry."

Employment regulations can be difficult for employers to navigate; for example, as a federally regulated and protected class, apprentices are not easy to fire. Add in the H-1B visa concern and the issue of pay bands, which don't allow companies to take advantage of the wage differential of an earn-and-learn model (until Apprenti helps them find a workaround), and you have what Carlson wryly calls "employment lawyer heartburn."

"The Department of Labor sometimes wonders why nontraditional sectors are having so much difficulty standing apprenticeships up and moving more quickly to get it going. . . . These legal and regulatory worries are part of a whole litany of things that, because the system wasn't built with apprenticeship in mind from the get-go, it's having to backtrack to figure out how to work around."

Apprenti is deeply involved in the policy conversation. Carlson applauds Congress for "trying to figure out the right methodology," and is eager to supply what information she can "on education, employment, anything they can get that can help them inform policy." Politics, as always, can be a sticking point. As Carlson notes, the H-1B topic is also partly an immigration issue, which, on its face, "has nothing to do with the Labor Department or with the health committees. So you're going to have to go pull in other departments like immigration and naturalization to figure out how to make that work in other parts of legislation that have nothing to do with labor law."

Another substantial hurdle companies face is background check clearance. "Big companies," says Carlson, "are always looking for people who already have a background check clearance. So many tech jobs require it. For example, if you are working in high-security data centers, they can't put you to work until you have your background clearance. Right now, they can sponsor you to get that, but it costs tens of thousands of dollars for each background clearance, and . . . it's taking over a year to get a clearance. If they can't put you to work, you're just sitting on the bench for that time, [while collecting] a salary."

Solutions Pursued

NORMALIZE TECH SECTOR APPRENTICESHIPS AND EXPAND ACROSS OTHER SECTORS

Apprenti's five-year goal is to place five-thousand-plus apprentices annually, and to grow from there into other support business lines to ensure employers have the tools they need to successfully manage the system. A second goal is to look beyond tech to stand the system up across other sectors.

Move Toward a Secondary Education Model in Which Apprenticeships Are a More Viable Option

An expansion across sectors would require a reinvention of the secondary education model to create more vocational pathways. Carlson envisions a "very clear laddering system in your junior and senior year in high school, exposing kids to a thousand hours a year of job experience in a particular sector." She recommends presenting students with twelve "industry verticals—for example, health care, financial services, high tech, building and construction trades—and then having them pick four and spend a semester in each." Such exposure would allow students to "learn earlier what they like and what they don't like," thus informing "a better choice coming out of high school" between university or apprenticeship.

Carlson describes how this laddering system might work in the nursing field. "For some, the first outcome might be going straight to nursing. For others it might be home health care, but then home health can lead into a nurse's assistant, and a nurse's assistant to a phlebotomist, and a phlebotomist to an LPN, and then becoming an RN. They don't have to jump from the base to the top, they should be able to ladder their way through it."

Create Opportunities for Collaborative Problem Solving

Apprenti works hard to bring the right people to the table and act as their intermediary with employers. Its future will involve bringing those companies into direct contact with each other, so they can learn from one another and collaborate on solutions. It will also continue to work across the table with policymakers, specifically about a funding model that would allow apprenticeships to scale upward. She hopes for a solution in which the federal government, the apprentice's state, and the employer each pay a share of what it will take to keep an individual apprentice in the classroom. "That's the apprentice's skin in the game," she says. "They have to take care of themselves, and that's five months without a paycheck that they're going to have to figure out."

Full Focus: Alternative Model

- ENTER: Anyone who scores higher than 80–85 percent on the skills assessment, which is focused on math (algebra with some geometry), logic, critical thinking (are you a good problem solver?), and emotional intelligence is entered into the candidate pool. No degree is required, and anyone can access the option regardless of employment status.

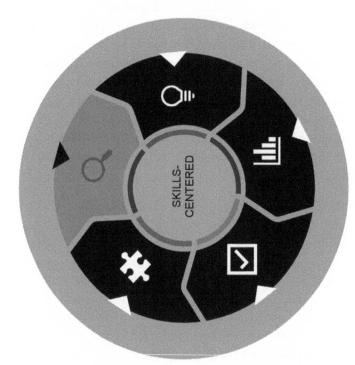

DISCOVER

Learners explore career pathways and competency mapping tools to understand where they are and where they need to be.

LEARN

Learners leverage a variety of educational resources to upskill and meet the needs of the current and future workforce.

ASSESS

Learners' abilities are assessed on the basis of demonstrated ability.

ENTER

Learners enter at various phases throughout their lifetimes.

CONNECT

Learners find or are recruited for jobs on the basis of validated skill data, ensuring that learners will be able to do what they are hired to do.

CREDENTIAL

Learners' abilities are recognized, validating skills in a transparent, contextualized, and standardized way.

Figure 6.2. Apprenti and Alternative Model: (Enter + Learn + Assess + Credential + Connect).

- LEARN: Learning happens in the classroom and on the job, using both a constructivist and connectivist approach.

- ASSESS: Assessments are psychometrically sound, industry-vetted, and verified to ensure they translate to real-world success.

- CREDENTIAL: The learner earns an industry certification.

- CONNECT: Learners are directly connected to an employer while learning, giving them a direct path to employment if they are successful.

Limited Focus: Alternative Model

- DISCOVER: Pathways are focused; career discovery happens before pursuit of the apprenticeship. A more aligned secondary education system would allow learners to explore their options and choose their path more wisely.

Key Takeaways
• The apprenticeship model is a proven success. Look at Europe, where almost 70 percent of people pursue a vocational track versus 30 percent who pursue a college degree, or to the building and construction trades, which already have nondegree pathways that lead to high-paying jobs.
• The U.S. educational and employment systems were not built with apprenticeship in mind, so there are structural obstacles to its widespread success. Among these obstacles are funding models for secondary education that are pointed toward the four-year college as the single viable option. Policy changes on that front will be essential.
• The word "apprenticeship" carries a stigma as a second-tier option to traditional college. The tech sector can lead the way away from this perception; many companies already see viable nondegree paths into technology as equally dignified as and, in many ways, preferable to the traditional college or university education.

Tech apprenticeships, we've seen, leverage bootcamps as educational providers. In the next case, we'll take an in-depth look at the model.

Case Study 3: General Assembly

Learner's Experience

I was devastated when the theater where I worked closed its doors. I've been working on Broadway for fifteen years; it was an abrupt end to a journey I had expected would last a lifetime. So it goes, these days; time to move forward.

A few years back, I had attended an amazing event at a General Assembly campus—a Black female founders forum—and I'd been getting emails ever since. One of the emails, promoting an event on programming for nonprogrammers, was at the top of my inbox the day the theater closed. If I can call myself anything these days, it's a nonprogrammer. So, I signed up.

When I went, I was surprised by how interesting the job opportunities looked, and I was wowed by the pay ranges—some into six figures, which is more than I would have made in two years in theater. I signed up for the immersive program on the spot.

I knew it would be a lot of work—the event had promised as much—and I would expect nothing less, considering I had exactly zero experience in coding. It was like drinking from a fire hose. I was overwhelmed, but I was also more energized than I'd been in years. I found myself feeling excited to jump into class each day, unsure what that day's challenge would be.

I'm halfway through the course now, and the tone has shifted. I still feel a little wobbly in terms of my actual coding skills, but it's starting to come together through the projects. It's the same kind of feeling I used to have when I was acting, once the costumes were ready and the set was designed and up. That's when things would start to feel real. I'm starting to pick up on nuances in the code and in the problem that I'm being asked to solve, and although I had started out without even knowing what a coding language was, now I'm starting to feel like I'm at least conversational—like I know how to ask the right questions.

As I look toward the month ahead, I'm reminded of that feeling I used to get just before opening night. After months of fumbling over lines and tripping over my feet, that feeling of confidence, the butterflies in my stomach that meant I was ready would always come. No matter how challenging my role was, I always knew that with enough practice and preparation, that feeling would arrive, and then nothing could shake me. No matter what happened under the lights, I knew we'd make magic happen.

I'm not there yet. But I know I'm getting there and I'm ready to shine.

About General Assembly

"We're not a one-size-fits-all solution, but I think we are part of a growing body of entities and providers that are helping to sort of move the conversation in a different direction."
—Jake Schwartz, co-founder and CEO, General Assembly

General Assembly (GA) is a global education company that supports both individuals looking to transform their careers by learning new skills and companies in need of high-quality talent in such areas as digital marketing, software engineering, and product management.

As student loan debt climbs, the value of a traditional college degree has been called into question. GA provides an alternative pathway to a lucrative career that can take as few as twelve weeks and costs significantly less than college.

In 2020, nearly half of college graduates were still looking for work, almost a year after graduating.[21] Some of that had to do with COVID, of course. But a 2019 Gallup survey of GA Immersive graduates paints a very different picture. One year after they finished, their average salary was $69,127. Five years post-graduation, GA Immersive graduates averaged $107,059 per year. In a report of its outcomes for the 2018–2019 year, a majority of Immersive graduates had more than doubled their incomes within five years after completing their studies.[22]

That said, the vast majority of students come to General Assembly with some college, and many have four-year degrees. All General Assembly students, with few exceptions, bring with them some professional experience, whether working at a big law firm, performing on Broadway, working at a nonprofit, or serving as a barista. GA works closely with students to package their past work experiences with their new skills to make a case for the unique value proposition they provide to employers.

The bottom line is that General Assembly can either replace or complement a traditional degree, depending on the individual's goals, by providing the technical training required to launch a career in technology, data, or design. To that end, GA has two businesses. One is a consumer business that provides education and training directly to individuals looking to explore a new professional path, build a new skill, or change careers altogether. This is delivered at GA's retail campuses globally, as well as through partner relationships in markets where the company has what it calls "a flexible presence"—for example, in a coworking space.

Second is the GA enterprise business that works within companies to assess, train, and deploy new or existing talent. Working with these hiring partner companies, thirty-five of which are in the Fortune 100, GA maps out ways to reskill existing teams and develop clear talent pipelines externally. These engagements can range from a few days of programming on digital mindset for executives to full upskilling and reskilling programs for employees. Think of this as an outsourced and extremely hands-on version of what Degreed outlined in Chapter 4, or what the training component of an Apprenti apprenticeship might include. "Rethinking the Build vs. Buy Approach to Talent," a report commissioned by GA and prepared by Josh Bersin, senior advisor of Whiteboard Advisors, articulates the value proposition to employers that invest in General Assembly's enterprise solutions.[23] This case study zeros in on General Assembly's consumer business, which has no previous employment requirement and is thus accessible to all. Consumers choose from an array of courses, ranging from free workshops and events to full-time, twelve- to fourteen-week Immersive programs aimed at placing students in new roles. The pricing varies. A two-hour workshop on "programming for non-programmers" may cost a few hundred dollars, while part-time upskilling programs (typically forty to sixty hours of live instruction) cost around $5,000. Immersive reskilling programs (typically four to five hundred hours of live instruction) can cost as much as $15,000.

While some individuals pay out of pocket, General Assembly has a number of financing options. Some students receive scholarships or loans via GA's Catalyst program, some have partial or full financial support from their employers, and others apply their military benefits through the G.I. Bill. The percentage of self-funding students is declining; as of this writing some 18 percent of students use scholarships and about 11 percent GA's Income Share Agreements, loans paid back out of students' future salaries.[24]

GA's instructors are practitioners in tech, business, data, and design. An instructor management team prepares them to deliver the content in the classroom; it also provides ongoing coaching and support—for example, by helping them develop performance improvement plans for struggling students.

Immersive students benefit from an outcomes program that provides support at every step of the job search process, from resumé-building to interview prep. Career coaches and partnership development experts provide personalized advice and strategies that help students develop skills in networking and branding. GA alumni have ongoing access to mentor support as well as networking events and job boards.

Says GA's Tom Ogletree, GA's VP of Social Impact and External Affairs, "I think more and more you'll see people looking for education that effectively prepares them for a sustainable career. As a result, there will be a greater emphasis on education that both results in tangible benefits for the individuals who go through the program as well as education that is doing all it can to be accessible and foster the spirit of diversity.[25]

"Our core mission," he affirms, "is to help people find meaningful work; we are successful to the degree that we are able to accomplish that." One component of GA's success is its scale. As disclosed in its outcomes report covering the period 2018–2019 (released in May, 2020), GA has 950 staff at 32 locations in seven countries, and more than 1,500 active instructors. During the period covered by the report, it trained nearly 10,000 individuals through part-time offerings, and hosted 338,000 learners at short-form workshops and events. Its alumni community includes "former Olympic athletes, musicians, lawyers, baristas, stay-at-home parents, teachers, refugees, journalists, accountants, and many, many more."[26] 91.4 percent of Immersive students participating in the career services program found a job in their field of study within 180 days of graduation, according to the report; 99.7 percent did so within twelve months. Five years after course completion, a majority of Immersive graduates had more than doubled their income, with an average increase of 106 percent.[27] "The fact that we have been able to scale so rapidly while upholding our outcomes rates," says Ogletree, "is a testament to the success of our model."

Problems Addressed

CREATE AN ACCESSIBLE WAY FOR LEARNERS TO DISCOVER A CAREER PATH

Tom Ogletree has a tale to tell.

"A lot of General Assembly's history," he begins, "comes out of the experience of our co-founder Jim Schwartz. He went to an elite college. He graduated with this fancy degree. He sort of thought his ticket was written. And then he landed in the world of work and realized he didn't know how to do anything. Feeling lost and lonely in the world of work, he got his MBA to actually become hirable. And I think his view was like, something is wrong with this picture where I have to go to graduate school to get actual skills. And oh, by the way, in my MBA program, I really only spent the first semester in deep learning. The rest of it was networking, experiential learning, et cetera.

"So in 2011 we were founded as we were sort of coming out of the last recession, where you had a lot of overeducated, unemployed folks trying to figure out how to make their careers make sense after feeling the setbacks of the recession. At the same time, there was this whole emerging community of entrepreneurs, technologists, and designers building businesses and launching new careers. So, the original idea was a coworking space to bring together early-stage startups. And part of it was to sort of replicate the experience of the university common room, the sense that by bringing people together and having people bump into each other and interact with one another, you could facilitate good ideas, connections, et cetera.

"I think one of the things seized on early on was this real hunger for people to just learn about what these new career opportunities were, what this looked like in the world. So, they started offering classes and workshops on how to break into a startup or how to start a career in tech. And they were selling out one after the other, after the other, after the other."

The next phase of General Assembly's journey grew out of the success of the exploratory courses, says Ogletree, as they began "to think about creating something like an accelerated 'post-baccalaureate' in coding so that somebody who wanted to break into tech, but didn't want to go back to school, could do so really quickly. Initially they worked with more traditional higher ed providers. But they found that students didn't respond to that; it was learning from practitioners that was really important, to contextualize learning in a way that's actually going to be applicable on the job." These opportunities are accessible, too, although there is a formal admissions process for twelve-week Immersive programs. It starts with an applicant filling out a form on the GA website that states what the applicant is interested in, his or her learning preferences, and experience to date. From there, applicants receive a course syllabus and get connected to an admissions counselor, who walks them through the program(s) offered, financing options, and next steps for enrolling.

The enrollment process typically consists of

1. A preliminary interview;
2. A student task that demonstrates aptitude and enthusiasm for the discipline;
3. An in-person interview to review the task;
4. Preliminary enrollment;
5. Precourse work (before class);
6. Formal enrollment.

In order to ensure that GA programs are accessible to people from all walks of life, GA has made it a priority to expand into smaller cities. In addition to launching pop-up campuses, GA has also been ramping up its remote offerings. These make it possible for students to engage fully online while participating in select community upskilling initiatives.

GA also prides itself on its wide range of financial support programs. Through its Catalyst program, the financial vehicle for GA's Income Share Agreements, students can take a career-changing Immersive course at no up-front cost, which they pay back once they land a full-time job with a salary of $40,000 or more. This tuition model is not unique—other bootcamp programs, such as Lambda School (www.lambdaschool.com) and Thinkful (www.thinkful.com), operate under a similar model. GA has also awarded more than $22 million to students in need as a way to help increase diversity in tech and beyond.

The majority of GA offerings are in-person and hybrid; the pandemic sent all programs online for the duration (online classes are designed to replicate the in-classroom experience and facilitate real-time feedback and discussion). GA also offers "On Demand Learning Paths," online classes that are self-paced for learners looking to gain a new skill or skill set at their own pace.

Create the Talent Needed in the Workforce

With experienced instructors active in their field, GA's curricula are constantly updated. A full-time team of product leaders and instructional designers conducts market research to identify demand and works with subject matter experts to build, test, and validate curricula, piloting, launching, and sunsetting programs as needed. Some courses are co-designed by industry partners, for example, a 2019 partnership with Microsoft to train fifteen thousand workers in artificial intelligence and machine learning skills, and to develop a career pathways framework for these disciplines.[28]

With the aim of readying individuals to apply new skills and technologies immediately in the world of work, students create portfolios of work product that can be used in the context of job interviews. Student assessments are designed in partnership with GA's Standards Boards, which are made up of practitioners. More than any particular skill or technology, GA aims to impart a learning and growth mindset to students—that is, an orientation toward problem-solving, a willingness to take on new or entirely unfamiliar challenges with confidence, a comfort in seeking out answers independently with the support of colleagues, and a tolerance for ambiguity and failure. To that end, GA instructors only act as traditional teachers for the first half of courses. After that, they become the boss. The work they assign is project-based and independent, and the requirements for resourcefulness and self-starting far more rigorous.

At the end of the day, General Assembly learners are not just building a set of skills, they're getting prepared for a role. Ogletree points to the history of two-tiered traditional higher education: learning to think at a liberal arts college, learning to do at a vocational school. General Assembly combines the best of both worlds: learners emerge with strong skill sets and an ability to deliver immediate value to employers, but they also have the vital critical thinking skills and resilience to be "consistently effective in a rapidly evolving job market where the shelf life of skills is shrinking. That adaptability is not always necessarily instilled in the context of higher ed."

Build Trust with Employers

GA is partnering with Fortune 500 companies to change the ways that industries approach skills-based hiring. Executives understand that the workforces' skillsets will need to be updated and refreshed continually. To meet this need, GA has streamlined the search process, one of the key pain points for companies in need of talent. GA's role-specific Standards Boards provide businesses with a framework they can use to determine what it takes to be a component software engineer, digital marketer, AI specialist, and so on.

GA faces significant competition; companies like Coursera, edX, Codecademy, and more offer online courses, coding bootcamps, MOOCs, and alternative training programs. Tom Ogletree contends that "what sets GA apart has been our proven track record when it comes to job placements and career services, as well as our vast global alumni and hiring network that supports our students well beyond graduation."

Solutions Pursued

Continue to Extend Reach

The aim is to equip global employers with the tools needed to reskill and up-skill their teams while supporting the growth of diverse talent pipelines. Tactically, that means expanding the pools of applicants to be trained, while growing the number of companies GA works with across industries. GA also seeks to deepen its collaborations with the public and private sectors to open more pathways to good careers in high-demand, fast-growing fields.

Increase and Enhance Resources for Students

This starts with making courses accessible remotely. That effort is well under way, with all GA career coaches trained in remote coaching and curriculum delivery. The job search game has changed with the transition to remote hiring, as well. GA helps its graduates identify how to shift job search processes, advising them to watch industry trends, grow their community networks, build their skills, and shift expectations around weekly job search success. The application process may be slower, says Ogletree, "but we encourage an increase in online networking and expanded industry learning."

And General Assembly continues to work toward finding and implementing sources of funding for students. As this book goes to press, GA is working with its loan partners to ease the financial burden of loan repayments. It is also adding new mental health resources for students and graduates through a partnership with Ginger.io.

Deepen Partnerships

Partnerships are of particular importance to GA, which delivers weekly insights and engagements to its teams, conducts regular outreach to growing industries, and routinely looks for new ways to support its hiring community.

Reskilling partnerships to train laid-off workers is just one example. In addition, GA is working to establish a framework for community reskilling initiatives that it intends to scale to cities around the United States and beyond. In Atlanta, for example, GA is partnering with Accelerate: Atlanta, Microsoft, Accenture, TechBridge, and such civic partners as the Office of the Mayor and the Metro Atlanta Chamber of Commerce to generate job and training opportunities for the communities most underserved and underrepresented in tech.

Full Focus: Alternative Model

- ENTER: Piggybacking off General Assembly's exploration resources, qualified candidates can enter the job market through the company's Immersive programs, which have a remarkably high job placement rate.

- DISCOVER: GA's free career exploration resources are an accessible starting point for discovering what options exist and how to enter high-growth markets.

- LEARN: The learning is hands-on, project-based, and industry-led. Learners develop not only technical skills but also the critical thinking, resilience, and adaptability that is so important in today's workforce.

DISCOVER
Learners explore career pathways and competency mapping tools to understand where they are and where they need to be.

LEARN
Learners leverage a variety of educational resources to upskill and meet the needs of the current and future workforce.

ASSESS
Learners' abilities are assessed on the basis of demonstrated ability.

ENTER
Learners enter at various phases throughout their lifetimes.

CONNECT
Learners find or are recruited for jobs on the basis of validated skill data, ensuring that learners will be able to do what they are hired to do.

CREDENTIAL
Learners' abilities are recognized, validating skills in a transparent, contextualized, and standardized way.

Figure 6.3. General Assembly and Alternative Model: (Enter + Discover + Learn + Assess).

- ASSESS: Learners produce work product portfolios that demonstrate their readiness for the job. The portfolios speak for themselves, but they are also judged within a framework that is aligned with—and validated by—employers.

Limited Focus: Alternative Model

- CREDENTIAL: General Assembly does not necessarily offer an industry-vetted credential, but it has built trust with employer partners such that its programs have high credibility.

- CONNECT: It is up to the candidate to do what is needed to do to be hired. Thanks to the training and support candidates receive from GA, their placement rate is close to 100 percent.

Key Takeaways
• Both technical and human skills are important in today's workforce, and both can arguably be taught through smart curriculum design that puts learners in a work-like environment where they are expected to be resourceful and adapt to unexpected changes.
• An obsessive focus on outcomes—outcomes that are audited by globally trusted partners—can establish trust in an educational space that is still coming into its own. This trust effectively guarantees a return on investment for learners and for the employers who hire them.
• "Collaboration," as Tom Ogletree has said, "is key to addressing the global skills gap. No single actor can successfully address the problems facing today's employers and workforce." GA's success opens a space for others to emulate its model across a range of sectors and contexts.

In the final case study of this chapter, we'll look to a type of education provider that has already been noted in a number of contexts: online course providers. These serve as upskilling resources for employers, as delivery mechanisms for industry certifications or bootcamps, or—and it is in this context that we will explore them—as self-guided learning options for individuals.

Case Study 4: Udemy

ʎʌ Udemy

Learner's Experience

Having just graduated from high school, I'm pretty tired of sitting in classrooms being taught about things I don't find relevant to anything other than a standardized test. My parents and guidance counselors weren't too happy with my decision to take a year off before deciding what my next step would be, but I just don't think I want to sign up for another four years of absorbing information and spitting out answers that I'm not sure I really care about.

As compensation for disappointing my parents, I promised them I would take some online classes to figure out what I wanted to learn more about. I browsed a bunch of options—Googling "online classes" is a pretty ridiculous approach, I know—and pretty much decided to just point and click. I landed on Udemy. There are over a hundred thousand courses listed there . . . surely I could find something interesting.

The first question I was asked on the platform was what I want to learn. I have no idea. I typed in "career exploration" and got back 2,883 hits—guess I'm not the only one in this boat. I filtered for free options and 227 came up. The one I clicked on was called "Career Navigator: A Manager's Guide to Career Development," created by Shelley Osborne.

The list of learning outcomes seemed to align pretty exactly with what I need right now. I could learn about introspection (which my therapist would love), goal-setting (which my parents would love), and mentorship (which my guidance counselor would love). The instructor said she used to work as a high school English teacher, so I figured she'd have at least some understanding of where I am coming from. The course had received a rating of 4.4 stars out of five, and the reviews were all along the lines of, "Love this course! Really great insight on what to think about when starting your career journey or feeling stuck!"

I enrolled. It's a good starting point, but I know eventually I'll need to pick a direction to actually start growing in. Maybe this will start me thinking in a more productive way. Or maybe I'll decide I want to be a career coach. Unlikely, given where I am right now, but who knows? Right now, all doors are open.

About Udemy

"I think it's really important to remember that the word for that high school or university graduation ceremony is 'commencement.' It's a beginning. And we kind of gloss over that. We don't do a lot of explaining to folks that learning is going to keep happening, needs to keep happening, in our jobs."
—Shelley Osborne, vice president of learning, Udemy

We've referred to online course providers throughout previous case studies. We touched on Coursera, for example, which delivers content in partnership with ZipRecruiter and Grow with Google. Degreed functions as an online content provider when it surfaces learning content to spur learners through pathways. We mentioned edX as another player in the upskilling space in the General Assembly case study. Now, we're going to take a deep-dive into one of the largest online learning marketplaces, Udemy.

Like many similar platforms, Udemy offers solutions targeted at a variety of audiences:

- Individual consumers, who choose from courses listed on Udemy.com

- Employers upskilling their workforces through Udemy for Business subscription solutions (among them Adidas, General Mills, Volkswagen, SurveyMonkey, and thousands more)

- Government employees and public servants learning through Udemy for Government (including the Civil Service College of Singapore, the County of Los Angeles, the Government of Jalisco, and more)

Expert practitioners of all kinds may also seek to apply their knowledge and teaching skills as Udemy and Udemy for Business instructors. The focus of this case study is Udemy's direct-to-consumer tools, specifically those designed to build employable skills. "We're proud that students all over the world rely on Udemy to learn new skills," says Shelley Osborne, Udemy's vice president of learning."[29]

Instructors set the prices for their courses, which range from $12.99 to $199.99 per course. "We have courses in more than sixty-five languages that can be viewed on the web, on a mobile device, Apple TV, and through Chromecast," Osborne continues. "In addition, our students are able to download and view our courses offline, as well as change the video quality for low-bandwidth environments. Our instructors can share their knowledge globally by uploading their own captions or by using machine-captioning. In addition, we offer a Q&A

feature where students can directly interact with the instructors, ask questions, and make sure they understand the topics they're learning."

All of the offerings are based in a learning design theory created by Udemy's team of instructional design and learning and teaching experts, and include such features as sending reminders to students to encourage them to make learning a habit, delivering course content in easily digestible, bite-sized videos, and encouraging instructors to participate in course Q&As. "We believe that self-driven learning creates unlimited opportunities," Osborne asserts, and that means "empowering learners to decide how they learn, and what course choices to make as they navigate their future." Machine learning and data science make it possible, says Osborne, "to deliver dynamic learning journeys that are not just relevant to current professional needs but [that] anticipate a user's potential needs in the future."

Udemy was built, says Osborne, "for how people want to learn wherever they are, in their own time frame." This is essential in a world in which, according to a Deloitte study, the half-life of skills has fallen to about five years.[30] That means that in a career lasting around fifty years, employees will need to reinvent themselves as much as ten times. Without trying to replace or replicate a traditional academic experience, Udemy helps people gain the skills and competencies that can keep their careers advancing—and do so in a way that is convenient, practical, affordable, and effective.

Problems Addressed
DEMOCRATIZE LEARNING AND TEACHING

Udemy is focused on democratizing access to expert knowledge. That is apparent, first, in the sheer scope of its offerings: some fifty-seven thousand expert instructors teaching more than 150,000 continuously updated online courses, with topics ranging from software and mobile development to data science, and from leadership to team-building.[31]

Significantly, Udemy's offerings are determined by what learners and instructors deem worth sharing. Anyone can teach on Udemy," says Shelley Osborne. "You just need to be an expert in what you know. And I think that really does help us attach to those learning goals because we're unlocking people all around the world."

EMPOWER LEARNERS TO BE THE CREATORS
OF THEIR OWN LEARNING JOURNEY

Shelley Osborne was a high school teacher for nearly a decade before obtaining a master's degree in education focused on adult learning and gamification. Her experiences in the classroom shaped the connectivist approach to learning and development that she espouses today. As she puts it, her teaching was a "continual attempt to define, refine, and control access to knowledge, access to content, and access to learning." But it never entirely worked: "Those kids always found a workaround. They always managed to find their way outside of this controlled environment we tried to make for them. And I walked away from that experience learning that it's like trying to control the tide. Really. You can't stop it. Things are always changing. . . . And I'm more interested in helping individual learners find that way for themselves."

Today, she says, it's important to "rethink . . . the competencies we're teaching versus the straight facts or the skills." Premier among these competencies is what Osborne calls "learning agility . . . a set of behaviors that we have to practice and master." These are the "human skills," and among them Osborne cites "how we respond to failure . . . how we ask for feedback . . . how much we're willing to practice. And I think it's possible for us to reframe it not as this soft sort of nuanced thing that's not achievable, but as a series of repeatable, consistent behaviors we can tackle in moments where we're learning. And that also comes down to not thinking about failures or mistakes as failures or mistakes, but as learning, and continuing to use those as sort of iterative processes. . . . The more we give ourselves awareness into what we're doing, how we're thinking and how we're approaching things, the better we are at becoming learners."

Learning agility means thinking about how you think, what you have learned, and what you need to learn next as a way to sharpen your own critical thinking ability—essential, Osborne implies, in a world of "more job mobility, a need for folks to change what specifically they're doing. So, in terms of how we think about providing education, I think we really have to make sure that education is far more dynamic, far more personalized."

For Udemy, that means "designing learning in such a way that it is relevant and useful to all learners. They're not going to watch an old video. Learners are expecting more from us. We have to create content that really does meet them where they are, that's engaging, that's personalized, that's contextualized."

Use Data to Inform Course Development

"Democratizing learning includes giving the power to the students to identify what quality learning is through a continuous feedback loop," says Osborne. She adds, "We really love to see their reviews and their feedback. We're hearing directly from those individuals taking those courses, how they're progressing through it, what the overall impact is. They're sharing those stories with us directly."

What is learned in those "reviews" becomes a mechanism for individual instructors and for overall quality assurance. "We have such an open marketplace," Osborne says. "It lets the learners decide and drive what high-quality content is, and it anchors it far more in impact and value for our learners than a perceived prestige that may or may not be there."

Solutions Pursued

Expand Reach and Continue to Enhance Tools

Udemy's numbers keep rising, demonstrating the expanding need for Udemy's kind of dynamic education.[32] While the COVID-19 pandemic accelerated the company's growth, Udemy believes the trend will be long-lasting. Continuous learning to upskill or reskill is fast becoming a requirement in the world of work. Udemy sees its content model as the right solution and aims to continue its leadership in providing breadth, quality, and freshness of content. The company is making significant efforts to expand its footprint in global markets.

Zero in on Learning Outcomes

"Ensuring that learning outcomes are at the forefront of our strategy and our roadmap" is Udemy's primary focus, says Osborne, and "open, democratized access." Osborne hopes her fellow educators will join her and Udemy in their quest to create lifelong learners. "Traditional education isn't . . . equipping everyone with everything that they need," she says. Educators need to "see ourselves as part of an ecosystem of lifelong learning."

Full Focus: Alternative Model

- ENTER: Democratizing access to learning—and, uniquely, teaching—is Udemy's core mission. This is a completely accessible entry point.

- DISCOVER: Learners can not only explore pathways but create their own. They have access to important data to inform their decision: the feedback of

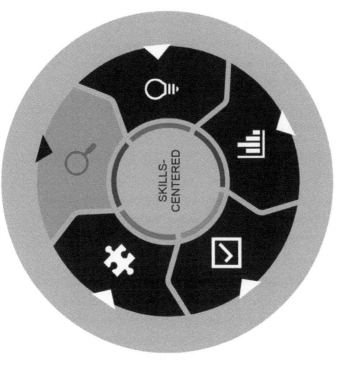

DISCOVER

Learners explore career pathways and competency mapping tools to understand where they are and where they need to be.

LEARN

Learners leverage a variety of educational resources to upskill and meet the needs of the current and future workforce.

ASSESS

Learners' abilities are assessed on the basis of demonstrated ability.

ENTER

Learners enter at various phases throughout their lifetimes.

CONNECT

Learners find or are recruited for jobs on the basis of validated skill data, ensuring that learners will be able to do what they are hired to do.

CREDENTIAL

Learners' abilities are recognized, validating skills in a transparent, contextualized, and standardized way.

Figure 6.4. Udemy and Alternative Model: (Enter + Discover + Learn + Assess).

other students and previews into course content. Being put in the driver's seat empowers students to develop their learning agility.

- LEARN: Learners choose the kind of learning content that matches their preferences and needs and have a chance to inform the development of that learning through their feedback.

- ASSESS: Learning is measured through in-course assessment tools.

Limited Focus: Alternative Model

- CONNECT: Though the Udemy for Business solution places the learner in the work context, the direct-to-consumer tool leaves it up to learners to position themselves in the workforce.

- CREDENTIAL: While credentials could be issued for course completion, they are not inherent to Udemy's experience.

Key Takeaways

- Creating firmly structured pathways for learning leads to mediocre outcomes for everyone instead of great outcomes for all. We need to meet students where they are and allow them to explore content that is meaningful to them.

- Again, we see connectivism shining as a learning theory that cultivates important human skills—what Osborne in this case has dubbed "learning agility." We need to put learners in the driver's seat so they can take ownership and reflect on what they already know, what they are currently learning, and what they need to know next. That is called lifelong learning, and it is a competency that can be practiced and repeatedly refined.

- We need to allow learners to create their own paths and to crowdsource curriculum development through their feedback. This is a drastic departure from traditional learning models that consider the teacher the owner of the curriculum; it means that teachers, too, need to recognize their changing role in the lifelong learning model.

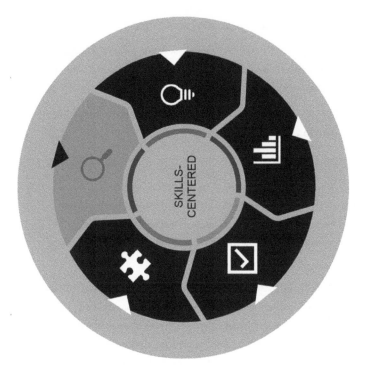

DISCOVER

Learners explore career pathways and competency mapping tools to understand where they are and where they need to be.

LEARN

Learners leverage a variety of educational resources to upskill and meet the needs of the current and future workforce.

ASSESS

Learners' abilities are assessed on the basis of demonstrated ability.

ENTER

Learners enter at various phases throughout their lifetimes.

CONNECT

Learners find or are recruited for jobs on the basis of validated skill data, ensuring that learners will be able to do what they are hired to do.

CREDENTIAL

Learners' abilities are recognized, validating skills in a transparent, contextualized, and standardized way.

Figure 6.4. Udemy and Alternative Model: (Enter + Discover + Learn + Assess).

other students and previews into course content. Being put in the driver's seat empowers students to develop their learning agility.

- LEARN: Learners choose the kind of learning content that matches their preferences and needs and have a chance to inform the development of that learning through their feedback.

- ASSESS: Learning is measured through in-course assessment tools.

Limited Focus: Alternative Model

- CONNECT: Though the Udemy for Business solution places the learner in the work context, the direct-to-consumer tool leaves it up to learners to position themselves in the workforce.

- CREDENTIAL: While credentials could be issued for course completion, they are not inherent to Udemy's experience.

Key Takeaways

- Creating firmly structured pathways for learning leads to mediocre outcomes for everyone instead of great outcomes for all. We need to meet students where they are and allow them to explore content that is meaningful to them.

- Again, we see connectivism shining as a learning theory that cultivates important human skills—what Osborne in this case has dubbed "learning agility." We need to put learners in the driver's seat so they can take ownership and reflect on what they already know, what they are currently learning, and what they need to know next. That is called lifelong learning, and it is a competency that can be practiced and repeatedly refined.

- We need to allow learners to create their own paths and to crowdsource curriculum development through their feedback. This is a drastic departure from traditional learning models that consider the teacher the owner of the curriculum; it means that teachers, too, need to recognize their changing role in the lifelong learning model.

Concluding Thoughts

This exploration of four paths to employment or job readiness that don't require a college degree sparks a number of observations. Role-based industry certifications, which carry the weight and trust of globally recognized brands, constitute an accessible entry point for learners.

Apprenticeships—a model that works in some sectors in the United States and more so globally—are expanding as another viable option. Although restricted by stigma and a lack of regulatory clarity, they are the most protected and supported of the four paths under existing policy. Bootcamps are an increasingly familiar, popular, and trusted entry point, but learners need to choose programs wisely, on the basis of an objective assessment of learner outcomes. Finally, self-guided learning gives lifelong learners a chance to develop their learning agility and to take ownership of their own pathways.

All four case studies showed the importance of learning theory. If we dipped a toe into constructivism and experiential learning theory with Practera in Chapter 4, and were exposed to connectivism with Degreed in Chapter 5, the cases of Chapter 6 dig deeper into what those theories look like in practice and the benefits they supply to learners in the form of both practical and human skills.

Finally, these four studies emphasize the importance of partnerships for learning approaches that are not rooted in traditional higher education or established by a company, since the provider needs to build credibility with employers if they are to connect their learners to opportunities. Subject matter experts, employers, educators, policymakers, and learners all deserve a seat at the table, and all must have access to available data if they are to make wise decisions about what educational resources to invest in.

In the final chapter of case studies, we'll focus a little more on the key players in the ecosystem-level conversation. We'll discuss the language and infrastructure underpinning a skills-based lifelong learning model, and we'll look at two different but successful models of partnership that are aiming to break down silos and streamline the lifelong learning experience the new world of work requires.

7

BRIDGE-BUILDERS

Alternative models of learning embrace a variety of players, all of them working to expand access to education, enhance learning within traditional higher education and on the job, and create fresh, imaginative pathways to high-quality employment and the reskilling and upskilling it demands.

One element that's loomed large in every case study presented so far is the importance of partnerships—of the connections alternative learner providers forge with employers, learning material creators, industry experts, junior colleges, and more. While no one-size-fits-all model has emerged, they all support the need to break down the silos that isolate players from one another.

This chapter studies four players who are creating an infrastructure that helps partners in doing just that—connecting, communicating, and working together to their mutual benefit. Whether they are translators, creators of interoperable technologies, or the working groups and connectors that support the ecosystem of alternative education, I call them bridge-builders. Each case study considers how well the organization in question adds capacity to, builds leverage, and complements the other players in the system. As previously noted in Figure 3.16 in Chapter 3, the Career Pathway Model shows how bridge-builders facilitate the entire alternative learning process.

Case Study 1: Emsi

.ıl· Emsi

Learner's Experience

I've been a call center professional for the past fifteen years, but I'm about to be replaced by an AI bot, and I need to make a change. Luckily, I've had some fore-warning; my company's HR department understands that this transition is re-ally going to hurt, so the more heads-up the better. But HR is also strapped for resources and can't help everyone on my team find new jobs. Instead, they pointed us to an Emsi SkillsMatch tool so we could figure out what to do next.

In the tool, I'm asked to select a goal. My options are "Explore New Career Paths," "Level Up in my Career," "Find a Job," or "Learn and Explore." I definitely don't want to level up, so that one's out. I'm not sure I'm feeling up to learning and exploring, either, and finding a job immediately seems like a stretch. Exploring new career paths seems like my best bet—for starters anyway. I'm prompted to add my education: associate degree in business administration, in progress (those plans fell through the cracks last year).

Next: skills. I paste in my resumé so the tool can extract skills for me. It finds customer relationship management, problem solving, and business administra-tion, among others. Some I select as a skill I have, some I select as a skill I want, and some I don't touch. Some I don't actually recognize; I click more info and up comes a definition of that skill. Helpful. Before I move on, I get a pop-up asking me if I have any related skills; I select a few more that apply and click exit.

The next screen is a surprise: I have a ton of matching career areas. IT Support (match score: three out of five stars), Education Administration (two stars), Office and Administration Services (three stars). I click into "Education Administration"; even though I haven't spent a ton of time in school and the match has a lower rating, I like the idea of being in a learning environment.

The next page is even cooler—I'm actually starting to feel impressed. It lists the top in-demand skills in Education Administration, highlighting those I have, those I want, and those I don't have. It's a pretty even balance. I see educational opportunities on Coursera and edX that I could pursue if I wanted to build those missing skills. I also see job postings, and one of them matches a ton of my skills: "Customer Experience Manager" at the University of Washington, which is just a few miles from where I live. I click and am taken straight to the job application page.

Maybe this transition is a blessing in disguise. I never would have imagined this option as a next step. I'm not sure I'll get the job, but now I'm motivated to try. That's a new feeling for me. Guess it's time to step outside my comfort zone.

About Emsi

"We believe that people who are doing things they enjoy, that people will pay them to do, and that they have the right education to do, will have fulfilling careers. And with big data, we can identify that sweet spot for as many people as possible, because it's different for everyone out there. That's what we're all about at Emsi."
—Andrew Crapuchettes, CEO of Emsi[1]

Emsi's role in the alternative education model can be summed up as "translator." An affiliate of Strada Education Network, Emsi aims to ensure that higher education providers, public sector workforce or economic developers, and enterprise staffing and talent acquisition companies—and all the people those organizations serve—are speaking the same language when they communicate with one another. Specifically, that is the language of skills—the heart of our model and the underpinning of everything this book seeks to convey.

Emsi's website (https://skills.emsidata.com/about) puts it simply: "Emsi's mission is to use data to drive economic prosperity. To do this, we inform and connect three critical audiences: people (who are looking for good work), employers (who are looking for good people), and educators (who are looking to build good programs and engage students)." The objective is "a deeper connection" among people, employers, and educators.

Emsi Skills is the language of that deeper connection, and it focuses on two big problems:

1. A rapidly changing labor market that existing data and taxonomies struggle to keep up with

2. An on-going communication failure in which people, education, and work often find themselves misaligned and struggling to understand each other

In the first instance, that of the rapidly changing labor market, the issue is that jobs have long been defined by the U.S. Department of Labor's Standard Occupational Classification (SOC) codes or by O*NET, the department's online system, a function of the Employment and Training Administration. Although both work well, the data quickly go out of date and therefore do not provide much insight into emerging jobs or register the quick changes occurring inside the classifications themselves. In addition, SOC codes often lack the detail or nuance needed by employers and colleges that are looking to create up-to-date curricula.

The second problem, the communication failure at the core of the skills gap, underlines the need for a common language among the people who need to acquire skills, the educators and other learning providers who want to train them, and the businesses that want to employ those skills.

Take the example of a college that is equipped with a great business program but that fails to identify to either businesses or students the most important, in-demand skills that it provides. Across town, there is a company seeking to hire a client relations manager. Management isn't sure the job advertisement has captured all the skills needed, but they give it their best shot and just list whatever they can think of. At the same time, an alumnus of the college's business program, currently employed as a retail floor manager, submits an application for the client relations manager position without actually understanding which of his skills pertain and therefore which to include on his resumé. The chain of miscommunications results in massive labor market inefficiencies.

Emsi's solution is simple: a common skills language. "You're a client relations manager? Wonderful! And what do you actually *do*?" The answer is best expressed in terms of skills: leadership, problem solving, project management, and more.[2] Emsi Skills equips the ecosystem not just with the raw data needed to "skillify" communication, but the data literacy that is needed to write a job description, a syllabus, or a resumé that are not only precisely and accurately worded, but that can be understood by the people that they are intended for.

Problems Addressed

Gather Skills Data

A rapidly changing labor market makes it difficult to keep up with the changing skills landscape. To respond, Emsi has developed an open skills library that captures the evolving lexicon of skill terms (along with the associated certifications, hard skills, and soft skills) used by today's employers in job postings, and by working professionals on their resumés and online profiles.

In developing this library, Emsi prioritized several key characteristics:

- Machine-readable data: Interoperability is key. Once Emsi Skills can be incorporated into a variety of other platforms and tools, institutions can embed their credentials into the common language, thereby equipping learners with a transparent, shareable record of the skills associated with their learning achievements.

- Real-world foundation, expert curation: As of this writing, Emsi has gathered more than thirty thousand skills from hundreds of millions of online job postings, professional profiles, and resumés. It meticulously cleans and fact-checks each skill and updates every two weeks.

- Connection to the labor market: Each skill is connected to relevant labor market insight, including the top job titles and companies posting for that skill, the job postings trend line over the last twelve months, and even specific, live job postings requesting that skill. The aim is to help learners and educators see and share each skill's market relevance.

All skills in Emsi's Open Skills Library reflect current common usage. Rather than impose a taxonomy on them, Emsi lets its classifications arise organically from the skills and the relationships between them. The reason? The rapidly changing nature of the labor market means that any preexisting categories will quickly go out of date.

DEVELOP A SHARED SKILLS LANGUAGE BASED ON THE GATHERED DATA TO HELP EVERYONE UNDERSTAND EACH OTHER

"We have three separate planets that are trying to align," says Rob Sentz, Emsi's chief innovation officer. "We have a home ecosystem; every person has their own culture and way of interacting. We have a work ecosystem, which has a completely separate cultural way of interacting. And then we have an education ecosystem, which has yet another separate way of interacting. These three planets . . . are radically dissimilar in how they relate and speak to each other. . . . resumés, learning content, and job postings struggle to speak to each other or to find value in one another. . . . A skill is the descriptor of work that can be put into each one of those documents."

A partner to many of the organizations we've featured already, Emsi is a major supporter and data provider backing the development of Learning and Employment Records used across organizations, as, for example, discussed in the WGU case study in Chapter 4. "As a company," says Sentz, "our mission has always been connecting people, education, and work—and LERs are an important, tangible way to make that vision a reality. If adopted widely and implemented effectively, LERs have transformative potential for learners, employers, and educators."

The benefits of a common language seem self-evident:

- Learners can document and share the skills and competencies they learn, whatever the learning model, even prior to degree attainment. This translates to greater flexibility in making the transition into and out of education and work over a lifetime, and to greater clarity on how to upskill or reskill to advance.

• Employers gain more precise insight into the relevant skills and abilities of job applicants and current employees. That means more efficient and effective matching of applicants with job openings and of current employees with appropriate training opportunities.

• Educators can better serve their learners and employer partners by providing more transparent learning records that surface the work-relevant skills learned in each course or program, while institutions can better recognize and award credit for skill-based learning completed at other institutions, even nontraditional or work-based training programs. As learners come to experience and expect the benefits of LERs, it will become increasingly important for institutions to offer them.

How to do this: gather the skills data. Make sure people are using the same language in their living documents. Finally, create the infrastructure that pulls all of those documents together and gets them to speak to one another. That infrastructure—and the key to interoperability—is the LER.

Numerous players agree. For example, the T3 Innovation Network, an offshoot of the U.S. Chamber of Commerce Foundation, piloted an LER program aimed at empowering individuals "with a validated record of their skills and competencies in a way that all employers can understand." And the Labor Department's American Workforce Policy Advisory Board declared in a September, 2020 white paper that "skills have emerged as a common vocabulary and an important currency that add value to learning achievements, work experience, and other credentials issued to an LER."[3] When the Chamber of Commerce and the U.S. Labor Department are on the same page about something, it's fair to say that the "something" is pretty impressive.

For colleges and universities, articulating course content and learning outcomes in terms of work-relevant skills—"skillifying" appears to be the agreed-upon term—is a huge enabler of interoperability, because it helps academic programs align more closely with both the labor market's supply side—earners looking for work—and demand side—employers looking for people.

To this end, Emsi has created the Open Skills Application Programming Interface—API—a software intermediary that allows two applications to talk to each other so that organizations might "extract skills from raw text within job postings, resumés, professional profiles, and course descriptions," in the words of the Emsi Skills website. "Once we extract those skills, you'll be able to read them . . . in the language they're written in: the language of the real world. Now that we're speaking the same language, we can take your data and compare it with our massive database of postings, resumés, and profiles. We'll be able to tell you whether your students are actually learning the skills they need, which companies are looking for people with these skills, and more. Colleges can align curriculum to the ever-changing job market. Schools and organizations can help students and job seekers craft more powerful resumés that showcase skills that are in demand. And businesses can create better job postings that target the best candidates."[4]

EDUCATE EVERYONE ON HOW TO UNDERSTAND SKILLS DATA AND USE SKILLS LANGUAGE

It is impossible to overstate how important it is to address this issue: data are useless if we cannot interpret and act on them. So "we train and educate all the people we work with to illuminate data and show how to use it," says Rob Sentz. Actually, that starts at home. "Our own employees need to figure out how to communicate it, and the market needs to understand it," Sentz concedes. Although his title is "Chief Innovation Officer," a lot of his work focuses on addressing this communication gap. "I'm spending a lot of time on the distribution, communication, and education side of the data," he says.

It is time well spent, for once it "clicks," skillification creates huge benefits for the entire ecosystem. Simply put, says Sentz, "You can optimize the documents on all sides."

At the individual level, Emsi typically works through organizations or schools that are already teaching or reaching out to learners. Emsi's Resumé Optimizer tool enables users to optimize their qualifications to better fit the labor market, while the SkillsMatch tool, highlighted in the "Learner's Experience" section at the head of this chapter, helps learners understand the connection between what they are studying, the skills they're developing, and where those skills are in demand, so they can better determine the learning content they need to invest in to further their careers.

The flexibility of the SkillsMatch tool, which can curate skills out of past job experience, translate them into future job opportunities, and note immediate opportunities both for jobs and reskilling, hearkens back to Chapter 5 and the ideal futuristic perspective envisaged by labor economist Julia Pollak of ZipRecruiter. Rob Sentz puts it this way: "Because we have so much data—about a hundred-million-plus job postings and zero-million-plus résumés and profiles—if somebody says 'I'm a technical writer,' for example, we immediately surface all the skills related to that title based on the skills that people who have that job say *they* have. Then, for all the skills surfaced related to that job, it's just a matter of the person selecting which skills they do or don't have, and suddenly we have a very clear profile of that person. It starts with what experiences you have had and helps you go do that next thing. And people don't realize that the thing that they've done has value to the next thing they might need to do. But education-to-work is very nonlinear."

At an educator level, Emsi also helps schools "skillify" their curricula so they can close the gaps between what they teach and what the market needs. Emsi also helps them evaluate the demand for their existing programs or the need to develop new programs. "The trick," says Sentz, is that "we have to convert the learning content into a skills language, which is not something that a lot of people have ever done. What we're doing is reading learning content with faculty and helping them convert it to skills. . . . Faculty . . . care dearly about their curriculum. They understand it deeply. That's where they live. They're not really living in the labor market, but they do live in what they're teaching. We're trying to bring all the stuff we have on skills to their curriculum and go back and forth with them to sort of flesh out, like, when you say this, this is actually this kind of skill. Or if you add this skill to your program, it would really check these boxes."

Those familiar with higher education governance can imagine that this work could be challenging. But Sentz emphasizes that the schools deciding to partner with Emsi are already on board. "I think the schools that have invested in it are definitely working to change those programs. No postsecondary school works with us if they're not already invested in program development or program changing. It could be that they've got an existing set of courses that they're just trying to update. Or it could be that they're trying to evaluate courses to add something new. But they're all trying to invest in skills-based learning."

Liberal arts schools, in particular, have a huge opportunity to benefit from "skillifying" their curricula. According to Sentz, "100 percent of job postings mention human skills, and they're dominated by communication management, leadership, critical thinking, and problem solving." That is the sweet spot of the liberal arts. "Their strength is how much they *do* develop human skills." This book's very first case study, of Noodle Partners, gave voice to the assessment that colleges—and particularly liberal arts colleges—are notoriously bad marketers in terms of communicating the return on investment they provide. Tapping into Emsi's data can help them uncover the connection between the human skills they teach so well and the labor market value of those skills. That might also help liberal arts schools better identify opportunities for program enhancement into the more technical skills, which are also important, so that learners can add value on day one on the job. "We've seen things come together where the trades need as much of the humanities as possible and the humanities need their people to learn the trades as much as possible," says Sentz. "The phrase I would use is the 'foxy hedgehog.' The fox is the generalist, and the hedgehog is specialist. Our economy needs people who thrive as generalists but who have a few areas of specialization."

Breaking down education into skills offers yet a further benefit—it uncovers broader themes and a greater range of potential pathways. Instead of thinking about what you majored in or a job title as a path to employment, thinking instead about skills puts the focus on what problem or problems an individual is equipped to solve. Sentz gives an example: "Two of our best data scientists are actually music majors, and we would have never said, 'We're going to select you to do this job because of the degree you have.' What we did is ask, 'Is this person good at solving this problem, and do they have skills that really fit the needs of the job?' Thinking in terms of the problems you're uniquely suited to solve for other people is a really good way to think about it that I think helps the human skills side of the house."

Finally, what about the employer? An employer working with Emsi can optimize job postings to focus on the skills that are most important to it. That is quite different from what we see today, which is often a "Frankensteined" list of requirements based on the skills and experiences of many ideal employees, resulting in fairly unrealistic and very expensive qualifications. "A lot of our work," says Sentz, "starts with the actual practitioners, administrators, or people in HR or the public sector. The first step is giving them data that allows them to understand, for instance, the skills that are needed in their area or the major gaps that are occurring there." That shapes their policies or investments as they realize where they may need to develop a program or seek a partnership to fill those gaps. "A lot of our work can be characterized as a gap analysis. After that, it turns into working more directly with the people that those organizations need to help."

Solutions Pursued

Help Companies Better Understand and Make Use of Their HR Departments

HR departments get a lot of heat for current hiring practices, yet according to Rob Sentz, it's not their fault. Companies aren't built around HR; HR is secondary to the company's actual function. HR teams are typically small and given few resources. Consider their responsibilities—everything from recruiting and hiring, learning and development, diversity and inclusion, and payroll and benefits administration to buying a new appliance for the break room. "It's just a super hard job," says Sentz. "Most HR people have like ten jobs. HR isn't really well supported or well structured."

Emsi has for some time been collaborating with HR guru Josh Bersin—met earlier in our General Assembly case study in Chapter 5—to "try to highlight the ten key characteristics of HR so that they can better understand the key things they're trying to accomplish," and to determine which skills they need to do those things. Sentz puts it in the form of a strategic question: "The big picture here is that if talent is the most valuable asset of a company, how does the company not have a five-year talent plan where it has a five-year financial plan?"

What would a better talent plan look like? "Employers are having a really hard time finding people," Sentz says. One effective approach, advises Sentz, is "backing off on the requirements and getting to the core human skills that are so important. . . . That helps you expand your perspective and expand the number of candidates." Second, he says, "focus a little bit more on building from within. It's actually cheaper." And third, audit job titles. "There are companies that only employ a thousand people and have five hundred different job titles. Their whole HR system is a mess." If HR roles are better defined, and HR teams are better equipped, they can start to clean it up.

Clarify and Analyze Labor Market Trends

Emsi routinely performs, analyzes, and publishes research on trends in the labor market. For example, a collaboration with Strada Education Network's Institute for the Future of Work resulted in a December, 2019 paper titled "The New Geography of Skills." Emsi also updates its open skills library every two weeks, ensuring that the common language everyone is using stays grounded in reality. This updating work is incredibly important; as our Chapter 4 case study on WGU made clear, one problem with shared frameworks is that they are usually locked into static documents that are neither machine-readable nor updatable.

EXPAND NETWORK AND COLLABORATIVE EFFORTS

Emsi is involved with just about every working group in the ecosystem of thinkers about the future of work and education. (We'll explore one such group—the Open Skills Network—later in this chapter.) Emsi's vast datasets are huge assets in these global efforts to align the "planets" of employers, educators, and workers. And its open tools lower the barriers to entry into this community of people and organizations dedicated to solving shared problems together.

Key Takeaways

- Translation is key, and interoperability is essential. Because the future of education and employment relies on information that is dynamic and free flowing, tools that are static, inaccessible, or untransferable are not worth investing in.

- Constant research and ongoing conversations are essential. We cannot make decisions based on old information or without consulting with those we seek to align. Participating in actual dialogue is important. Bottom line? Find partners who can open the doors to engaged working groups.

- HR teams have a big role to play in the transition to a skills-centered ecosystem, but they need to be properly supported. The days of tiny teams of HR generalists wearing ten hats are over; their roles must be clearly defined, and they must be equipped with the right data and tools, so they can better protect and grow the most important asset any company has: its people.

Now let's examine an organization that focuses on the technology for connecting data and alternative learning solutions.

Case Study 2: Credly

Learner's Experience

I signed up for six online courses during the first weeks of the pandemic. I hadn't stuck with any of them. As much as it seemed like a good idea to spend my time productively when there were so few other things to do, I couldn't work up the energy. By the end of my workdays, I had some serious Zoom fatigue.

I felt lucky to still have a job, though. My company was doing things to boost morale—Zoom coffee breaks and happy hours, little public celebrations when someone did something cool. One of those celebrations was for a digital badge that someone earned for completing an Adobe Illustrator course. Everyone on our team has Illustrator, but few of us really know how to use it. My coworker got about twenty "likes" on that post just from our team, and I noticed that when she shared the badge on LinkedIn she had about sixty more.

That was the motivation I needed to finally finish one of the courses I had registered for—a course on instructional design. I work in sales, but I taught abroad for a year after college, and I still belong to a bunch of shared-interest teacher groups on Facebook and LinkedIn. I was pretty proud when my digital badge got its time in the spotlight; between my team, LinkedIn, and those teacher groups, I got more than a hundred likes and comments.

I was surprised when a member of one of the Facebook groups reached out and asked me for advice on his online course. And surprised again when my company's customer success team asked me to help them put together an online learning module for our clients. Suddenly, I could see myself taking on more of a teaching role at work. The first months of the pandemic are just a big blur in my mind, but I clearly remember the moment when my life started to get interesting again.

About Credly

"It is a movement. It's the kind of thing where it has to be bigger than just 'hey, use our software.' The kind of change we're talking about comes from people making cultural and behavioral changes. Whether they do that on our platform or not is not the ultimate point, quite frankly. It is all about changing minds and moving minds."
—Jonathan Finkelstein, CEO, Credly

Emsi has been framed as a translator, a player in the ecosystem that gets all the other players speaking the same language of skills. But once everyone understands what skills are, you still need a way to create a marketplace around them. That is what Credly does. It turns learned skills into a currency that can be spent in the pursuit of career opportunities. That currency is the badges that Credly offers via its platform Acclaim—digital credentials that verify that their holder has completed a program or gained a skill from a recognized provider.

Credly's mission, says Credly CEO Jonathan Finkelstein, is to bridge the "gap between those who have skills and those looking to employ them." It does this by working with "employers, certifying bodies, associations, training providers, and academic institutions."[5] Crucially, Credly does not control the learning content nor the assessments that must be completed in order to earn the credentials. Issuing organizations control those raw materials—which, in the credentialing world, are presented as skill-rich "metadata." By verifying, standardizing, and coining that data into a tamper-proof badge, Credly makes it fungible.

Given the diversity of experiences that could result in a "credential worthy" achievement, it seems self-evident that, in Finkelstein's words, "multiple learning theories and frameworks apply"—for example, Self-Determination Theory, "which speaks to motivation through the lens of autonomy, competence, and relatedness." This helps explain why the perceived value of credentials that are "animated by one's self-determination, mastery of skills, and connectedness to a broader ecosystem," in Finkelstein's words, is steadily expanding, rivaling that of the traditional degree, once considered the *sine qua non* denomination of employee value. Surveys reveal that "62 percent of American workers now strongly prefer nondegree and skills-based training over degree programs," according to Finkelstein. "To take that one step further," he continues, "49 percent of U.S. workers with only a high school degree and a skills-based professional certification say they are in good jobs, second only to those with PhDs."

No wonder the education market is paying attention and getting on board. "There isn't one path to success or one path to happiness," asserts Finkelstein. "The call to action is, 'Let's shine the light on pathways that actually lead people to good-paying jobs, and let's not be elitist about what those pathways are.'"

Problems Addressed

Establish the Source of Truth About Skills Data

Human resources typically constitute the biggest expense of doing business, yet far too many companies simply don't know what they are buying. Businesses have practical and effective ways to measure data on outcomes, on inventory control, on sales and customer relationship management. They know how to listen to data when managing their factories and their operations. But they struggle when it comes to quantifying the qualities, abilities, and resources that people bring to the table. We need "good data for making people decisions," says Finkelstein, "data that you can trust." Digital credentials fill that need. But for those credentials to be negotiable, they must be widely trusted. That requires transparency—which is what Finkelstein calls "the price of admission on our network." Credly works closely with organizations to unpack what "resumé worthy" means to them, and to help them understand and make the best use of the data that informs its badges. Credly also offers training and publishes research to help clients and nonclients alike create their own robust credentialing programs.

In the early days of what Finkelstein calls "the digital credentialing movement," the approach was more "gameified" than "resumé worthy"—credentials were more like the stars and badges that the addictive games on your smartphone or your health app awards you. With gamification, Finkelstein explains, "the credential is . . . not about communicating something to some future or current third party. It's the thermometer moving up, trying to encourage you to take the next step and complete your learning, but it may not have transferability or portability because it may lack the context or the meaning or the rigor that would mean something beyond feeling good in that moment. Where Credly can provide value is by reducing noise in the ecosystem"—in other words, "by focusing on 'resumé worthy' things that speak to the outside world."

"Having certain admission standards," Finkelstein explains, "requiring people to at least pay some price, even if it's nominal—and requiring them to adhere to a certain set of data standards—raises the quality of the network, and hence the reliability and the trust in the network." The aim is that "the credentials should have strategic value to the organizations issuing it. That's how we've created a sustainable model."

Promoting the credentials online benefits everyone in the ecosystem. Learning providers gain brand visibility as their graduates proudly share their achievements on LinkedIn and other platforms. They increase engagement, as learners are motivated to complete or enroll in programs; the cost of administering paper certificates and tracking learners' data is reduced; and the "gray market" of lesser or fake credentials is eliminated. Says Finkelstein, "If you are a group that believes that the outcomes that live on a network are going to help the people you serve connect to some next opportunity, regardless of what you do, you're in. You're aligned with what we're trying to do." So long as the credentialing adheres to a recognized standard, Credly withholds judgment as to its appropriateness. It doesn't tell people what credentials they should put on their resumés, in other words; it simply ensures that the credentials that they do include have credibility. "People can create their own resumé," says Finkelstein. "There are things that may seem unimportant one day that become more important in a different context, and it's not for us to ultimately decide what they choose to put there. The market is where the value gets determined. Our job is transparency and trust in the identity and a common set of standards about reporting outcomes"—in other words, the achievement or skill set represented in the credential, based on standards set within the structure of the data.

Similarly, Credly is not the arbiter of what makes a quality assessment of skill. "I think there is a sense that there's a Holy Grail, that there is one single assessment that's perfect for all project managers or for everyone who does DevOps or cybersecurity," Finkelstein says. "I actually don't think that there is a Holy Grail. I think learning and skills are so dynamic, and the context is everything. What makes good collaboration skills in a boardroom may be different than what makes it on a customer success team or in an effort to improve diversity and inclusion efforts. There are so many different permutations and types of learning, and I think every group that is in this space believes they have something to offer and they can set a standard or can create an assessment or a curriculum. This should be a rich and vibrant place for learning and for skill development."

By providing "a common way of looking at all those outcomes" and a digital currency for them that is widely trusted, Credly builds bridges between silos, enabling better human capital management decisions. A key plank in that bridge is "remaining agnostic," in Finkelstein's phrase, eschewing "opportunities . . . to either tie ourselves to exclusive relationships with one assessment provider or one content provider or to ourselves introduce an assessment within the platform." Instead, Credly sticks to what it sees as its unique role, which is "to organize that world and improve access to opportunity . . . to help magnify or amplify the work that [its members] do by putting them on a platform where they can coexist with others who are also doing quality assessments."

Ultimately, Finkelstein says, "I think of what we do as providing infrastructure for decision making." By upholding data standards and providing best practices, Credly enables a rich ecosystem of data that decision makers and learners can understand and use to make better and fairer decisions.

Make Skills Data Portable

When learners earn digital credentials, they own that data. They can share their achievements in social media to make their skills known across their networks or include it with a job application, and they won't have to pay a fee or jump through bureaucratic hoops to get it. Credentials are learner-centered and empowering. "Traditionally, there has been an all or nothing mentality about college degrees," says Finkelstein. "You can complete two-thirds of a program, do two-thirds of the work, and take on two-thirds of the cost, but you walk away with nothing to show for it. Digital credentials help institutions provide value to learners by providing useful credentials and recognition for skills gained along the way to earning a certificate or degree. Learners can take what they are learning in real time and make use of those skills in real time, thanks to a verified digital credential that provides context and proof of their abilities."

Finkelstein's words take on some of the cadences of poetry, as he describes the credential as "a living, breathing, dynamic, data-rich artifact that . . . doesn't get trapped in all the places where the learning is happening. . . . individuals should be able to be empowered to take that evidence with them. Those were Credly's founding principles." When they are, he continues, the ecosystem becomes a network, in which no one company can "cordon off what they do from the rest of the world." When silos come down, you see "business-to-business relationships that wouldn't have been possible. We're seeing groups that say, hey, I want to syndicate my tech curriculum from Facebook Blueprint or from Tableau or from Google into community colleges. And community colleges are using a common approach on the network to port outcomes."

Something as seemingly simple as a digital badge is capable of inspiring collaborations among groups that had not been able to connect in "a scalable way," according to Finkelstein. One such example is Credly's partnership with the American Council on Education's CREDIT program. An academic transcript provided through Acclaim that includes a learner's digital credentials can facilitate credit transfers, shortening the time to the completion of a traditional degree and drastically reducing its cost.

Connect People to Opportunities According to Their Skills

We've come full circle: connecting individuals to opportunities according to their skills. Says Finkelstein, "The most important part of learning is being able to connect the learning to an authentic next step in somebody's career and helping organizations find people based on the right skills." The historical reliance on what Finkelstein dubs "opaque proxies like degree completion" is waning. "More context and granular information about skills . . . level[s] the playing field for job applicants, creating greater opportunity for a more diverse and inclusive workforce."

Another aim, Finkelstein asserts, is to reduce—and eventually eliminate—"traditional and systemic biases in how decisions about people were getting made . . . implicit biases, like, 'Can I pronounce your last name? Otherwise, you move to the bottom of the pile.'" To that end, Credly "works closely with credential issuers to track how digital credentials impact individuals' ability to connect to jobs, get promotions, and experience other positive career outcomes." According to a case study Credly published in 2019, Autodesk found that after earning Autodesk credentials, 32 percent of individuals got a new job, 15 percent earned a promotion, 13 percent won new business, 19 percent earned a raise, 19 percent experienced job security, and 29 percent experienced other job-related benefits.[6] In short, credentials are making an impact on people's lives.

Credly provides resources for credential earners too—numerous ways to discover next steps. Individuals can find a host of labor market insights through Talent Neuron (at https://www.gartner.com/en/human-resources/research/talentneuron), which is plugged into "the rich and verified data within earned certifications and credentials, including constituent skills and competencies, and including top employers hiring for related positions, additional related skills, top job titles that require a skill or certification, and expected salary ranges for those jobs," according to Finkelstein. Learning opportunities based on a specific certification or credential are also listed, all of it accessible via the Credly platform.

"I might not be the one setting the price," summarizes Finkelstein, "but I can show you the jobs that are available to you. I can show you what organizations value the credential that you've earned, and I can help those organizations compare apples to apples and get smarter about widening their view on where to look for talent."

Solutions Pursued

CHANGE THE WAY ORGANIZATIONS SOURCE TALENT

Credly makes it possible for organizations to base its people decisions on real-time data for verified skills. "Self-reported information is often out-of-date, inconsistent, or outright inaccurate," says Finkelstein. "We're on the cusp of a massive shift in hiring and promotion practices. . . . Now that we have this critical mass of credential issuing in a common network in a common way . . . there's finally a chance at making some lasting change when it comes to removing systemic problems in our overall society. When "two people with the same skills to have equal access to the same opportunity," Finkelstein says, "we are finally doing more than saying, 'hey, we hired our chief diversity officer, we're done here,' [and are] actually delivering on metrics, delivering on results. I think there's going to be a level of accountability to those results that we haven't seen before."

Credly's Connect tool (https://info.credly.com/connect) allows third parties to sync skills data with talent job boards, recruiters, and HR systems. "You'll see a lot more of those kinds of things," Finkelstein promises. "It is a movement. It's the kind of thing where it has to be bigger than just 'hey, use our software.' The kind of change we're talking about comes from people making cultural and behavioral changes. Whether they do that on our platform or not is not is not the ultimate point, quite frankly. It is all about changing minds and moving minds."

Provide Organizations Visibility into Verified Skills

In addition to advocating for and building tools for companies to hire talent more equitably, Credly has developed tools to help them better understand, engage, and retain existing employees. Businesses are increasingly recognizing that engaging and retaining talent isn't an option, Finkelstein asserts. "It's mission-critical." Credly 360 (https://info.credly.com/360) allows employers to tap into the dynamic data within their own workforces to make better human capital investments and management decisions. According to Finkelstein, upskilling is self-guided up to 75 percent of the time, which means that employers aren't tracking it. "You have all these people earning credentials every minute of the day," says Finkelstein, "and even when employers are paying for it, virtually no employer has any kind of real-time view into what their people are learning." Credly 360 allows learners to share that information, so their employers can make better decisions about opportunities they may be qualified for.

He offers an analogy: "Every two weeks you get a paycheck. Every day, [you] should also be depositing something into your human capital account. And what's different about those two things is, generally speaking, the money in your paycheck you get to spend once, whereas your human capital you get to spend over and over again. And the company gets to reap the benefit of it over and over again."

Increase the Liquidity of Credential Currency

Credly is also pursuing solutions that can bring greater liquidity to earned credentials so that it is easier for people to use their human capital as they advance in their careers. "We have partnerships with organizations that are focused on shaping the higher education and employer communities to support the needs of individuals and the labor market at large," according to Finkelstein, "such as the American Council on Education, Lumina Foundation, Strada Education Network, City & Guilds, IMS Global, and Credential Engine." Credly's vision is of human capital accounts filled with skill currency, which people spend to achieve their full potential. As a mission-oriented organization, Credly is deeply aware of the responsibility it shoulders. "It's tricky when you're in charge of printing the currency," Finkelstein concludes. "You know, what role do you play in choosing the denominations? What role do we play in choosing what it's worth versus just being there to empower people? It seems like a simple business from the outside, but there are all sorts of existential and really deep societal questions that we wrestle with on a regular basis. We don't take that lightly."

Key Takeaways

- Digital credentials turn skills into currency. But unlike actual money, skill currency can be spent again and again. Creating a shared data structure, a shared network, and a shared marketplace means that we can all properly evaluate and use that skill currency in each of our own contexts.

- Trust—in general, and about self-reported abilities—is at an all-time low. To build trust, we need full transparency. Having reliable, consistent data means we don't need to fall back on what we *intrinsically* trust—someone who looks like us, who went to a school we admire, or who knows someone in our network. Having a source of truth means that we can focus on how we use that verified information to make fairer decisions.

- Real change at an ecosystem level starts with change at the individual level. People need to understand why the new approach benefits them, and they need data and tools to use it. In attempting to drive change, we need to meet people where they live and to speak in a language that will resonate with them.

So far in this chapter, our emphasis has been on technical infrastructure. For the final two case studies, we'll look to more human bridge-building efforts—those designed to bring the right people together to solve the ecosystem's hardest problems.

Case Study 3: Jobs for the Future

Learner's Experience

I lost both my parents when I was sixteen. My eighteen-year-old brother and I had enough support from extended family and our neighbors to stay in our home, but we both needed to work to afford food and the mortgage. My brother managed to complete high school before he started working full time, but I was so devastated I dropped out.

As we got close to paying off the mortgage, I started looking into ways to go back to school. I heard about my neighborhood's E3 Center, a drop-in center coordinated by my city's youth network and supported by something called Opportunity Works, a program run by Jobs for the Future. I joined the E3 Center's college success program as soon as the last mortgage payment cleared.

I continued working, but I studied hard and did well, and I encouraged my peers to do the same. After years of working just to pay the bills, it was energizing to be aiming for something I was really proud of and to be a part of a community working toward the same thing. In the second part of the program, I started taking credit-bearing courses at the community college.

By the time I earned my GED, I was already halfway to an associate's degree, and although I still needed to be bringing in an income, I wanted to keep going. The counselors at the E3 Center pointed me to an apprenticeship program where I could get hands-on work experience in IT while continuing to make a paycheck. Over the course of completing that pathway, I earned CompTIA and Apple certifications, created a cover letter, resumé, and business cards, and worked up the courage to network with the manager of a nearby Apple store. My story and skills impressed her, and I was offered a job making a living hourly wage.

It seems to have taken a village to get me here, but I finally feel secure. I know my parents would be proud.

About JFF

"Sometimes in history, quantitative capacities build up over an extended period of time until they reach a tipping point that ushers in a qualitative paradigm revolution. We are on the cusp of such a moment. . . . The work of Jobs for the Future has never been more important. We are scaling our work, we are scaling our organization, we are taking our work to the next level so that we can help more young people and adults fulfill their American dream."
—Maria Flynn, CEO, Jobs for the Future

Jobs for the Future (JFF) is a national nonprofit that drives transformation in the American workforce and education systems. Working at the national, state, and local levels, JFF facilitates collaboration among leading educators, employers, workforce development specialists, philanthropists, and policymakers who share the goal of expanding economic opportunity.

JFF is inspired by five guiding values:

- "Mission-Driven: We are fueled by the desire to create a world where everyone has equal opportunity for economic advancement.

- Bold: We lead with innovative ideas and actions that push the boundaries of what is possible.

- Transformative: We bring about meaningful and lasting system-level change.

- Rigorous: We work diligently to design, test, and scale evidence-based solutions.

- Passionate: We believe our efforts have the power to strengthen the nation's economy and improve people's lives."[7]

Since its founding in 1983, JFF has been at the forefront of innovation, advocacy, research, and practice in education and workforce development, developing powerful partnerships and networks that help scale its impact nationwide. Among them are the Bill & Melinda Gates Foundation, the U.S. Department of Labor, the Nellie Mae Education Foundation, Salesforce.org, Year Up, The James Irvine Foundation, and many more.

JFF focuses on change at a systems level. How does that work? As Elizabeth González, portfolio director of the James Irvine Foundation, explains in the JFF video "Building a Future that Works," "[Systems] are programs. They're also policies. They're the way people work together. They're the way money flows. So, when I think about system change, I think about how all of those pieces come together in service of families' lives."[8] To give just one example of what systems change looks like in practice, consider the Great Lakes College and Career Pathways Partnership (GLCCPP). In 2016, the Joyce Foundation launched the partnership in order to create and expand "high-quality college and career pathways to advance equity and economic mobility for the next generation in the Great Lakes region." Specifically, the partnership supports four communities: "the northwest suburbs of Chicago; Rockford, Illinois; Madison, Wisconsin; and Central Ohio." But the common goal is to "create sustainable systems of college and career pathways that increase the number of young people—especially students of color and from low-income households—who successfully transition from high school into college and career." To do so, all four community partners "draw upon national best practices and strategies to inform how they establish strong leadership and governance structures, seamlessly align students' academic and career preparation across high school and college experiences, and develop systems to provide equitable access to work-based learning that connect youth to the world of work."[9]

Each of the four communities' approaches is driven by local needs. In Chicago's northwest suburbs, for example, education and industry leaders partnered to create pathways geared to local opportunities. The result has been a significant increase in the number of high school students—especially students of color—taking college credit courses. That means work-based learning at scale.

In Madison, Wisconsin, the aim is a system of personalized pathways in health services fueled by a partnership among leaders at the school district, city, county, higher education, and industry levels. Early results included the enrollment of some 25 percent of ninth graders. The academic outcomes have been promising, especially among Black students.

In Rockford, Illinois, where a career academy infrastructure already existed at the high school level, the approach was to align pathways to industry demand, college and credential requirements, and students' interests. The local community college and Rockford Public Schools partnered to expand college credit course opportunities for high school students, enabling a framework for work-centered learning.

In central Ohio, a partnership among industry, educators, and state policymakers narrowed the racial and socioeconomic gaps in the numbers of students earning college degrees and credentials.

Collectively, the GLCCPP communities show early positive gains for students, including

- Greater representation of students of color, students from low-income households, students with special needs, and English language learners enrolled in college and career pathways compared to the overall student population;

- Increases in students earning college credits during high school;

- More students on track for graduation compared to non-Pathway peers;

- Narrowing of racial gaps in students' academic achievement.

The efforts hold key lessons for leaders in other regions who aim to improve outcomes and expand opportunities for young people through equitable pathways systems, among them the following:

- College and career pathways must be anchored in equity to ensure that all students, especially students of color and students from low-income households, benefit from them.

- Employers need to be strategically engaged to scale high-quality, work-based learning experiences.

- High schools and college partners need to develop policies jointly to reduce remedial education needs and expand dual enrollment options for students, while explicitly defining their respective roles in providing student supports.

- Communities need to build the capacity of local data systems so they can continuously collect, report on, and use student data to improve the programs.

The bottom line is that the needle can be moved—systematically—to ensure that all young people have the tools they need to realize their best possible futures. GLCCPP is just one of JFF's success stories. Others can be reviewed on its website: https://www.jff.org/what-we-do/impact-stories/page/1/.

In the midst of the COVID-19 emergency in 2020, JFF's work was recognized by a $6 million grant from the Walmart Foundation. Kathleen McLaughlin, president of the Walmart Foundation, noted at the time that "the pandemic has magnified social challenges yet also stimulated fresh thinking about solutions. This grant reflects our confidence in JFF as a bold, creative facilitator of the system-wide collaboration needed to create a more equitable economic recovery."[10]

The Walmart grant was aimed at enhancing the organization's operational capacity as it built out its plan, announced in 2018, to undertake a bold internal transformation and expansion plan, with significant investments in new talent and systems, and the launch of such initiatives as JFFLabs, a team within JFF that designs and scales technology-enabled approaches to economic advancement.

Problems Addressed

ENSURING EQUITY IN ADVANCEMENT

Even as the global economy has expanded, millions are trapped in multigenerational poverty. JFF believes that education and dignified work can break that cycle. To that end, it created the Student Success Center Network, which benefits half the community colleges in the United States. As state-level organizations, the centers create networks that allow those colleges to share resources, exchange ideas, and support one another as they make fuller use of existing programs to create guided pathways to opportunity—programs of study aligned to specific goals, including detailed academic plans—and assiduously track their progress. While the Student Success Center Network is geared to the community college experience, it is not limited to it. Pathways can be implemented at a high school level to open pathways to high-value jobs. This evokes the secondary education innovation we referenced in the Apprenti case study back in Chapter 6, in which vocational exposure would become a core part of the high school education experience.

Meeting Employer Needs

It is by now a cliché that employers are struggling to find people with the right skills to fill their jobs. JFF creates strategies to better match the supply of skilled workers to the demands of the market. Its Center for Apprenticeship & Work-Based Learning exemplifies this effort. Neither apprenticeships nor work-based learning are new concepts; we have seen both in the case studies on Apprenti in Chapter 6 and Practera in Chapter 4. The point is that they work. JFF aims to make them transformative by partnering with businesses, government agencies, secondary and post-secondary educational institutions, training providers, workforce boards, and more to develop, scale, and promote effective apprenticeship and work-based learning programs that work for a range of participants. Founded in 2017, the center provides a central hub of resources and expertise. Its team of experts develops program designs and reaches out to new sectors and new businesses to undertake the programs, supporting them as they do so.

Preparing for the Future of Work

Acting on the same understanding that launched this book—that the way work "works" is changing by the second—JFF created JFFLabs. Launched in 2018, its aim is to accelerate that transformation in order to create better opportunities. As its name implies, JFFLabs is a laboratory for strategy creation. Looking to "big thinkers with smart ideas," JFFLabs seeks to connect initiatives and models and the people who create them to ensure that the new world of work is more equitable. It operates in five areas, defined on its website (https://www.jff.org/what-we-do/impact-stories/jfflabs): impact acceleration, identifying and scaling workforce and educational technology that can drive transformation; incubation, or building and supporting early-stage products and services in partnership with mission-aligned entrepreneurs; investment in startups and solutions in the training-to-employment continuum; innovation networks, or developing and leading networks of education and workforce partners eager to modernize practices and systems; and corporate leadership, partnering with companies to solve workforce challenges while advancing bottom lines. An early acceleration partner of JFFLabs was SVAcademy, a bootcamp focusing on roles in tech that don't require coding.

Solutions Pursued

Lobby for Disruptions in Education Funding

Many of the organizations featured so far have mentioned their collaborations with policymakers or their lobbying efforts to generate public-sector support for their solutions. JFF has earned significant clout with policymakers—as seen in its partnership with the U.S. Department of Labor—and it uses that clout to advocate for changes in funding education. One recent example is CEO Maria Flynn' response to the problem of student loan debt during the COVID-19 pandemic. In an April 2020 opinion piece in *The Hill*, the influential Washington-based news website, Flynn made the point that many newly displaced workers "lack the startup capital to invest in themselves. What's worse, millions of Americans are heading into the crisis bearing the weight of student loan debt." Federal financial aid and traditional loans can help, but only up to a point. What Flynn proposed instead was a suite of "new financing tools" that, in her words, "aim to mitigate the risk for students." She noted the income-share programs San Diego, California, has implemented; the "performance-based approaches to funding higher education, where the cost of tuition is based on an individual's earnings after completion," an approach used by Purdue University, and "merit-based financing startups and . . . skills as collateral" initiatives that "de-risk training investments for learners . . . income-share agreements, alt-finance and performance-based pricing"—and more.

Admitting that there are risks inherent in many of these, Flynn reminded her readers that there are also "the risks of workers missing out on much-needed training, or of students taking on debt for education programs that don't lead to a job," concluding, "Our calculus must evolve."[11]

Clearly, JFF is advancing that task.

Support Technological Innovation for More Personalized Learning

Technological advancement is central to many of JFF's goals, including scale, collaboration, and the improvement of outcomes through more personalized learning. Though wary of the potential for bias inherent in big-data sets, JFF is confident that new tech can overcome it, provided that, in Flynn's words, "these capacities are applied with a commitment to individual empowerment and equitable access and outcomes."[12]

CONTINUE TO HELP ALIGN AND SCALE WORKFORCE AND EDUCATION INITIATIVES

JFF's approach to driving transformation in the American workforce and education systems requires ongoing innovation, evaluation, and iteration. The key goal is keeping up with what learners need, while expanding access and ensuring equity. To do so, JFF keeps its eye on both the present and the future.

Key Takeaways

- JFF drives change by turning a wheel whose spokes touch every aspect of the model we have been exploring, advancing the development of the interoperable language and currency that is needed to power the alternative learning model.

- Turning the wheel requires the fuel of funding and the power of human collaboration. The latter can be supported through technological innovations that speed processes and practices that decrease friction.

- Although the scale of the efforts needed is massive, their impacts are personal. Different approaches work for different communities, which is why there is so much need for strategic guidance. Similarly, each individual learner may take a different path, so we need to personalize individual journeys in ways that are also scalable. In practice, systems change occurs when individuals are supported locally, and local efforts are supported nationally.

Our final case study looks at another system-level bridge-builder, this time an initiative that is open to any organization aligned with its mission to create a more equitable labor market.

Case Study 4: The Open Skills Network

Learner's Experience

My name is Ram Vittal. When I was growing up I was fascinated by my father's ability to fix his scooter and car. I wanted to be a mechanical engineer like him so I too could make engines vroom. After I earned my master's degree, I realized that while I could solve many complex equations and had even successfully filed a few patents, I couldn't get a stalled car to start. While formal education provides a framework for intellectual curiosity and exploration, learning, I realized, is not just about course work completed and degrees earned. It is conditioned by actual experiences. The new products I was trying to launch at the multinational I work for were technically sound but thwarted by pesky financial considerations epitomized by letter clusters like NPV, IRR, and ROE. To understand them better, I enrolled in finance and accounting classes at the community college near my home in rural Ohio. My classmates ranged from high school graduates to grandmothers and were not "my type." But as I collaborated with them, I was impressed by their caliber and encountered my most valuable lesson yet: one can—and ought to— learn from everyone.

The classes I took inspired me to enroll in an MBA program, leading to a career change from engineering to finance. While my initial focus was on M&A and capital markets transactions, I was drawn by a variety of opportunities. I helped set up a support program for junior bankers that taught me the importance of factoring people's motivations into the design of organization structures. I led the acquisition and integration of an international company, leveraging our firm's global expertise and local acumen to change regulations and launch trendsetting new products—something that had not even been contemplated when the deal was first struck. Then I was tasked with enhancing the operating framework of a new line of business. I did so in a way that optimized both risk management and the ease of doing business, which are often thought to be contradictory. I am currently heading the growth of a commodities firm in North America as its CEO, leveraging the lessons I learned at large institutions to effect the nimble, controlled growth of a much smaller firm.

I entered all my roles, including my current one, without the requisite technical knowledge—as often happens when enrolling for courses at universities. Every step I took brought me to a place that was unexpected, but that in retrospect shaped my perspective in ways that allowed me to continue my explorations with greater confidence. Learning, whether at universities or in the workplace, is never a solitary pursuit and the outcome is always exhilarating. When you are curious to learn, there are many willing teachers. Just like you, Reader, I am a lifelong learner.

I recognize that my role in shaping the future of education is to harness the many channels and platforms (including OSN) now available for learning new things, undaunted by the technical rigor. What is yours?

About the OSN

"The OSN envisions a world where learners and workers are empowered to use their skills as currency—with the ability to understand the value of their achievements—within the employment and education marketplace."
—OSN founding members

"We believe that skills-based education and employment practices will bring greater opportunity to learners and workers across the nation who seek to understand the skills they need to succeed and find jobs that match their skill sets."
—Andy Trainor, vice president of learning, Walmart

This sixteenth and final case study explores an initiative that ties together organizations like the ones we have featured while pressing the continuing evolution of the alternative model of education. The Open Skills Network (OSN), established in 2020, is an initiative that calls upon any and all players within the alternative education model to represent those they serve, while pledging to adopt tools, standards, and practices that will allow not only their own stakeholders but all learners to thrive.

As of this writing, the OSN is made up of more than forty employers, educational organizations, and technology providers. Coordinated by BrightHive, with support from Walmart, Western Governors University, and the U.S. Chamber of Commerce Foundation, and building on the work of Concentric Sky, Credential Engine, Emsi, and others, the OSN is developing common standards and practices to serve as the infrastructure for skills-based education and hiring practices that advance equity, efficiency, and efficacy in job searches and hiring practices.[13] As the list of partner participants continues to grow, it is worth exploring why these players are joining forces, and why their eagerness to do so has continued to grow.

As we've seen throughout all the case studies, much of the data needed to support skills-based education and hiring already exists but is siloed, not easily accessible, and not machine-readable. All of this makes the switch to skills-based practices an expensive and manual effort for most employers and educational institutions. The OSN seeks to solve this problem by creating a decentralized network of open, accessible, machine-actionable skills libraries. The aim is to empower workers and learners to move rapidly and seamlessly between education and work along skills-based pathways. The higher goal is to reduce historical inequities in hiring and ensure that more and more people will be hired for what they can do and not for where they got their degrees.

The shared goals of the OSN partners, as stated on the website at https://www.openskillsnetwork.org, are as follows:

1. Create the foundations for a more equitable labor market.

2. Empower learner-workers to understand and communicate the value of their skills, talent, and experiences.

3. Eliminate barriers to implementing skill-based education and hiring practices across industry sectors at scale.

Partners can choose the ways they support the network's efforts by enlisting in any of a range of work groups, including the Governance Work Group, which manages the organization's charter and the organization's major tools, toolsets, and libraries; the Market Leadership Group, which acts as a thought leadership generator and fundraiser; the Policy Work Group, which identifies public policy gaps and barriers that may be preventing skills-based practices from flourishing, and develops actionable solutions; and the Technical Work Group, which supports the development of tools that further the OSN's mission, including the OSMT and Rich Skills Descriptors we read about in Chapter 4.

"By breaking down skill silos," the Open Skills Network Introductory Brief declares, "we enable a nimble work-and-learn ecosystem where individuals, employers, and educators are able to keep up with the speed of skilling, reskilling, and upskilling that the future of work requires." As more and more organizations that share the OSN's mission come together, they will use their own platforms to broadcast the importance of the work and rally others to the cause. We have seen the impact that these partners can have in isolation—JFF and WGU, for example. Imagine their power if they act together.

Problems Addressed

EXPANDING COMMITMENT TO OPEN SKILLS

The OSN mission is to accelerate the development and use of open skills data in order to effectuate the adoption of skills-based education and hiring as standard practices. Let's break this down. Each skill is defined in terms of knowledge, abilities, and learned behaviors, and described concisely. Open skills are datasets that use harmonized open standards and that are available on the open web. Skills-based *education*, in turn, focuses on building a learner's skills and making those skills evident across learning experiences and programs. It helps students capitalize on the skills they have earned no matter where they earned them, and it allows them to home in on further learning opportunities that will help them achieve their career goals.

Skills-based *hiring* focuses on a candidate's verified skills rather than on subjective criteria. Through skills-based hiring, employers can access talent who are often overlooked or screened out by traditional hiring methods—people of color, women, people with disabilities, people with criminal records, people who have paused their careers to care for family members, and people who lack four-year degrees.

None of these concepts is new; this book has explored all of them in its case studies. The importance of the OSN is that it mobilizes those who share a commitment to this idea to align on best practices and work in the same direction.

Developing Open Toolsets

The OSN is dedicated to making shared technology and open toolsets available to accelerate the adoption of skills-based practices. As we've seen, a great number and variety of tools are used by educators (as shown in Chapter 4), employers (consider Chapter 5), and independently by learners (Chapter 6). If the technology supporting those tools is built to be interoperable, learners can tap into all of these resources in a seamless way as they move through their lifelong learning journeys. That would be a tremendous asset for both learners and employers.

An example of the power of open toolsets is the Learning and Employment Record we explored in the WGU case study: "comprehensive, exchangeable digital records of achievements learned in school, on the job, through volunteer experiences, or in the military which may be represented as skills, competencies, courses, certifications, degrees, validated work history, and portfolio artifacts/evidence," according to the FAQs section of the OSN website.

Open tools are inherently learner-serving; in the case of the LER, for example, learners own their data and control that data's privacy, discovery, and sharing. Because the LER is something that learners carry with them throughout their lives, it is important that the systems they encounter are compatible. Ideally, their data "can be bundled and transferred across various data systems, potentially improving transitions, increasing mobility, and enabling matching to opportunities."[14]

Championing Open Standards

The OSN champions the adoption and evolution of existing open standards for meaningful and actionable skills data. This means that more perspectives will be heard as the standards governing the ecosystem evolve. Every partner represents the voices of the populations they serve. Imagine the people whose personal stories you read at the beginning of each case study actively participating in a conversation that is more typically held behind closed doors.

Solutions Pursued

The OSN's website puts it well: "The scale and urgency needed for this transformation necessitates a collective force dedicated to accelerating the adoption of skills-based education and hiring practices."[15] There is only one way to move forward: *grow the network.*

Key Takeaways

- The onus of figuring out how to plug-and-play in siloed systems should not be placed on the learner; it should be our collective aim to make the learner's journey as smooth and seamless as possible.

- Amazing work is being done to advance alternative models of learning. We have showcased only a handful of the organizations that are innovating in that space. Their successes are cause for optimism about the future of education and employment but must not lead to complacency; the work is ongoing and ever-changing.

- There are no obstacles to joining in the conversation. A good first step is to join a network and connect directly with the diverse array of organizations that are already doing so much work. The work is urgent, and everyone has a role to play in advancing it.

Concluding Thoughts

We've heard time and again about the importance of collaboration, partnerships, and interoperability. This chapter explored the bridge-builders who break down silos and tie the ecosystem together. As a translator, Emsi doesn't sit *within* any particular phase of our alternative model or learning. Rather, it represents the pipes connecting the various players that do sit within the model and thus enables the free flow of data throughout the system. As a digital credentialing platform, Credly mints the currency that is used in the alternative model's marketplace. Although the product itself sits firmly in the "Credential" element of the model, it can be earned and cashed in across all phases. Jobs for the Future is a driver of systems change across all phases. And the Open Skills Network is an initiative that brings any and all players within the alternative education model together to adopt the tools, standards, and practices that will allow not only their own stakeholders but all learners to thrive.

This chapter probed some of the challenges facing human resources teams, who are often blamed for making the "wrong" hiring decisions, and showed how work done across other layers of the ecosystem enables better hiring decisions that are made on the basis of skills. Yes, translating skills is challenging, but it is not impossible; mostly, it requires collaboration and alignment to get everyone speaking the same language.

Networks of shared practices, tools, and standards are the building-blocks of a marketplace of skills. While large-scale collaboration is needed to put them all together and scale them, efforts need to be driven at a local level. While change must happen at a systems level, systems rely on the minds and hearts of the individuals making decisions at every moment. That means that everyone—every reader of this book—has a role to play.

In this book's next and last section, we will explore the implications of all this for various stakeholders. Place yourself in whatever category you think you fit; it is our hope that you will find actionable steps to take, regardless of where you sit or where your own journey takes you.

PART III

DEMYSTIFYING GAP TRENDS AND
PROMOTING A CALL TO ACTION

EMERGENT THEMES IN ALTERNATIVE LEARNING

The case studies of the previous four chapters arm us with a significant reservoir of lessons and data. In this chapter, we analyze the research, focusing on the "top ten" themes crucial to today's educational and business concerns. Figure 8.1 provides a summary of the results.

What follows are, first, an "explanation" of each theme within the context of what we know from both the case studies and research into documented best practices, and second, a recommended call to action for learners, employers, and providers, as is relevant.

Learning Theory-Based Design

The education pathways in the preceding case studies are all based on best practices in learning theory—contextual, experiential, and constructivist—aimed at maximizing how adults retain information and develop skills. This contrasts with many traditional colleges, which still follow centuries-old traditions that, in a sense, prescribe and "hand out" learning through lectures, written assignments, and written assessments—methodologies that have simply not adapted to what we now know about adult learning theory. Colleges are being left behind as alternative models provide more relevant and more effective learning opportunities for adults.

Over the course of the fifty-year period circa 1970 to 2020, research on the

1	Learning-Theory-Based Design	Best practice alternative education pathways are deeply rooted in adult learning theory.
2	Corporate Culture of Learning	Employees optimize performance in work environments that support continuous improvement.
3	Cost and Access Solutions	The price of admission is the dominant obstacle or barrier to education, and alternative approaches promise broader inclusion.
4	Navigating the Learning Landscape	The alternative education environment is new, multifaceted, and complicated; learners need support navigating options.
5	Adaptive Certification	Documented validation of achieved competency is only relevant if it evolves in alignment with the changing demands of the market.
6	Transparent Skill Exchange	Both job seekers and employers need up-to-date information on the skills required by in-demand positions.
7	Colleges + Partnerships = Survival	The outcome of marketable, relevant, and impactful skills requires collaboration between schools and industry.
8	Platform Outsourcing	Education providers benefit from contracting out the development and management of technology tools that facilitate new innovation in learning design and delivery.
9	Soft Skills Gap	Although most providers focus on technical skills, surveys suggest that employers note a lack of such "soft" skills as collaboration, communication, and building relationships.
10	Credential Requires Brand	New industry credentials become respected when offered by trusted brands (such as Google) or in partnership with a well-known institution of higher education (such as Columbia).

Figure 8.1. Case Study Themes.

differentiated learning needs of adults has markedly increased. Starting in 1968, Malcom Knowles, considered the originator of adult learning theory, posited that adults have internal motivation both to learn and to understand why and how learning can benefit them. Particularly relevant to adults are task-oriented learning activities that enable them to apply their prior knowledge and skills while building new understanding and competencies.[1]

Over the decades, our understanding of learning strategies for adults has been further refined. For example, George Siemens's theory of connectivism outlines how much learning can proceed across peer networks when the instructor poses questions that act as a guide to self-directed learning activities. Further, connectivist learning theory stresses the role of internet technology to facilitate this type of learning.[2] As noted earlier in this book, David Kolb's work in the 1980s stresses the importance of *experiential* learning, developed in a learning cycle Kolb created that includes four stages: concrete learning, reflective observation, abstract conceptualization, and active experimentation.[3] More recently, Elaine Cox incorporated coaching, defined as direct support by an expert to an individual learner to expand skills and knowledge, into adult learning theory.[4]

These learning strategies are evident in many of the innovative programs put forward by the education providers discussed in our case studies. Western Governors University (WGU), for example, is explicit about how its programs are guided by principles of adult learning, as evidenced both in our interview and on the WGU website. The latter proclaims that "colleges like WGU are focused on helping adult learners . . . find success as they continue their learning and growth. Discover the theories behind adult learning and how they can help you with your higher education goals."[5]

In fact, all aspects of WGU's programs are threaded through with a deep understanding of adult learning theory. The university's advising system, to take just one example, assigns a coach to each learner to guide him or her in getting through the course of study completely and successfully. Similarly, Guild, another of our case studies, also has implemented a personalized coaching process to ensure that once learners enroll in a Guild program, they complete the program and meet their goals.

Practera offers real-world learning experiences by connecting students with companies. Universities and employers contract with Practera to provide students with real-world projects in which they can apply knowledge in practical situations. Practera specifically cites the work of Kolb as an influence on its experiential learning activities. Similarly, such providers as Jobs for the Future and Apprenti offer experiential learning opportunities in the form of apprenticeships.

Noodle provides a platform for education providers to offer learning opportunities on a wide scale. Its EPIIC framework, rooted in adult learning theory, was specifically developed to guide Noodle Partners in curriculum development. As the name suggests, the framework helps universities design online learning that is Engaging, Personalized, Interactive, Intuitive, and Collaborative.

Call to Action #1

Traditional education providers can become relevant by redesigning their programs to align with adult learning theories. In particular, they should *invest in, engage, and prioritize instructional design teams at the department level* who are

- Experienced professionals skilled in the theory and best practices of adult learning;

- Empowered to plan, develop, monitor, and evaluate (via the tenure and promotion process) all curricula and teaching on a semester-by-semester basis;

- Focused on and authorized to limit traditional "chalk and talk," rote instruction in favor of experiential, multimodal, and project-based designs.

Corporate Culture of Learning

In the rapidly changing environment of the twenty-first century, employers cannot leave learning to external education providers. Instead, they need to support ongoing learning and skills development rather than focus on specific degrees. To do so, they need first to create a culture that supports learning, and to do that, employers need to establish an environment that offers incentives for learners and that embeds knowledge development in its goals and objectives.

Research on effective organizations has long suggested that developing such a culture of learning—becoming a learning organization—is connected to enhanced performance.[6] Indeed, companies that have evolved into learning organizations can expect a 10 percent improvement in financial performance.[7] According to the *Harvard Business Review*, to create such a culture, employers should reward ongoing learning, provide constructive feedback, lead by example, and hire curious people.[8]

That these strategic goals are being embraced by education providers is evident in our case studies. Ernst and Young (EY) fosters a companywide culture of learning by making employee learning a cornerstone of business objectives and by providing incentives that encourage employees to participate in and celebrate their own learning. Degreed supports corporations creating a culture of learning by suppling data and analytic tools that enable employers to gain the insights they need to be effective coaches for their employees. Guild helps companies align best-in-class education benefits programs with each of their company's corporate strategies.

Call to Action #2

Employers need to create a culture of learning if they want to adapt to future work trends, support continuous upskilling, and optimize productivity of their employees. Specifically, employers need to *institutionalize a "real" culture of learning to maximize performance* by

- Aligning strategy and learning at the board and C-suite level—ensuring top-down buy-in, messaging, and alignment across the enterprise regarding fiscal goals;

- Providing employees and teams with real-time learning and management in the workflow, making it personalized and flexible for individuals;

- Aligning with the performance management system such that it complements stretch goals and tethers effective utilization to managerial evaluation and compensation.

Cost and Access Solutions

A significant barrier to gaining a college education is access to resources. Costs of college have spiraled exponentially, and many families cannot justify the debt required to help their children complete a college degree. If the spiraling cost of a formal degree is a major barrier, alternative programs need to be cheaper to remain accessible to a wide variety of learners.

Since the 1980s, in fact, financial and other resources and connections tied to socioeconomic status have been the major barrier to college access.[9] Surveys indicate that the American public is increasingly convinced that a degree is not worth the cost.[10] Data suggest that this has led to a reduction in college enrollment[11] and that an increasing number of individuals is looking for other opportunities to develop the skills required for the workforce.[12]

The organizations described in our case studies offer learning opportunities at a much more affordable price. Google Career Certificates, for example, are free and hosted on the learning platform Coursera, which charges $39 per month. Google offers scholarships to defray the cost. WGU charges a flat tuition of about $6,500 per semester. Students can take as many courses as they like for that one fee. Guild manages corporate educational benefits, brokers relationships with universities, and negotiates rates for large cohorts. For example, the programs Guild provides for Walmart cost employees about one dollar a day.

Call to Action #3

A college degree no longer provides the return on investment it once did, while costs have continued to increase exponentially. Both colleges and other education providers need to reduce costs to remain a valuable and viable option for learners. Alternative education providers, in particular, should capitalize on their agility to *aggressively compete for, and capture, share in the postsecondary education marketplace* by

- Leveraging a business model that markets and provides access to desperately needed, cheaper service, at scale, for a wider and more diverse segment of learners;

- Validating the value of that cheaper service by utilizing the proven efficacy of the alternative education model versus the traditional model;

- Engaging in public-private partnerships to further create funding subsidies and solutions for learners.

Navigating the Learning Landscape

In the twenty-first century, with the continuing-education environment changing rapidly, learners increasingly need support navigating novel options. They need counseling to understand what their continuous-education needs are. Adult learners, looking for new career opportunities, may not know which skills are in demand, the programs available to develop those skills, or even if they already possess some of the in-demand skills.

Adult learners face a bewildering landscape of higher education, certificate programs, and course completion requirements—plus confusing financial aid options.[13] The research documents how they can be supported effectively through learning management systems and specific web-based tools for collaboration and content sharing.[14] In addition, individuals benefit from personalized counseling around program options, prerequisites, or preentry skills assessments.[15]

These case studies reflect the various ways in which alternative education providers support adult learning. Noodle provides a platform to help individuals determine their interests and goals and to provide information on the programs available to help them meet their goals. This includes free phone consultation, in which a counselor can lead perspective students through the admissions process and financial aid options. In contrast, Google has recognized existing organizations that, in recent decades, have pioneered success strategies to support adult learning. Google partners with such organizations as community colleges and trade schools that have systems to support nontraditional students.

Call to Action #4

In addition to seeking out and taking advantage of supports offered by their education providers, learners should *develop and maintain a personal, dynamic lifelong education plan* that

- Identifies and tracks strengths and gaps in personal skills and competencies;

- Maintains access to sources that preview specific skill needs or demands and related job opportunities from employers;

- Leverages resources (advisory services, technology tools and platforms, and so on), to provide professional, just-in-time guidance and organized, tagged, and "stackable" pathway support toward skill-based and credential targets.

Adaptive Certification

Industry certifications have increasingly become a common alternative education pathway. These certifications adapt to changing market conditions and are updated to provide information about which skills match current jobs. Such certification helps not just employers but also job seekers who need a way to document their existing skills and develop new ones. It also assists effective employees by providing opportunities for continuous reskilling.

Industry standards are a way for "professionals themselves [to] set standards since they have the knowledge necessary to do so."[16] Many certificates are assessed by professional organizations, but increasingly, well-respected corporations (for example, Microsoft, Google) are developing their own certifications.[17] These credentials have been shown to be effective in documenting marketable skills.[18] Not only is this important for job seekers, but it supports upskilling, which is an essential part of work in the twenty-first century.[19]

Our case studies illustrate the importance of dynamic, adaptive credentialing. ZipRecruiter links job seekers with opportunities to complete certification programs that document skills relevant to the jobs for which they have applied. Google Career Certificates offers training to provide and document marketable skills to entry-level job seekers in IT. And Credly provides verified, digital credentials for in-demand skills and capabilities.

Call to Action #5

Alternative education providers should align with peer providers and employers to establish an industry clearinghouse for credentialing that

- Provides a standardized, global framework for assessing and documenting employee skills data;

- Provides a standardized, global credential that is universally recognized and accepted;

- Launches an inaugural network of employers who demonstrate the effective cohesive utility of the clearinghouse and advocate for widespread adoption.

Transparent Skill Exchange

The job market benefits from transparent data about current skills. Employees need awareness of what employers are looking for. This information helps employees assess their own skill profile so they can make informed career decisions. Employers also need better insight on available employees who possess targeted skill areas.

It is important, therefore, to assess the skills of job seekers, both to document their existing skills and to place them in appropriate skills training.[20] Skills mapping can help both employers and job seekers understand the skill required to be effective in a position.[21]

Our case studies emphasize the need to share data about jobs and required skills. Emsi collects labor market data to help employers, job seekers, and universities understand the in-demand skills. Universities, in turn, share the data with their students to help them shape their job search. Credly's skills badges help close the gap between those who have skills and those looking to employ them.

Authess, an in-demand skills-tracking organization, recognizes that there are not enough tools to measure the skills of job seekers. "It's not just a skills gap," Authess CEO Paul Crockett asserted in our interview with him, "it's a skills assessment gap. . . . We just didn't have a great way of measuring skills the same way we did for measuring knowledge."[22]

Call to Action #6

Alternative providers need to *build and introduce a new universal model that currently does not exist to assess and measure people skills* (both hard, technical skills and soft skills) to

- Support job seekers who seek to demonstrate mastery across a skills continuum;

- Support employers who seek both an objective assessment of job seeker qualifications and a tool for determining existing employee gaps, competence, and potential;

- Support colleges that seek to continuously redesign curricula based on the skill assessments of their students and skill needs of would-be partner employees.

Colleges + Partnerships = Survival

Since the Great Recession, organizations in all sectors find themselves dealing with a scarcity of resources. This has inspired them to seek collaboration with partners who can complement or reinforce their products and services. To stay relevant and keep pace with labor market demands, colleges have partnered with employers or third-party companies that provide a bridge across which students might walk to the colleges themselves. Otherwise, college graduates are increasingly unlikely to enter the workforce with practical, marketable skills.

There is increasing evidence that organizations can maximize scarce resources to address such important societal challenges as education and workforce development.[23] Across sectors, organizations with common goals and principles are combining resources to provide services.[24]

WGU stays close to employer expectations by convening an industry council that works with the company to set standards for its programs. Credly works closely with employers, certifying bodies, associations, training providers, and academic institutions to create standards that measure mastery of in-demand skills. Guild works closely with employers and universities to provide high-quality education opportunities to employees, tailored to the needs of their companies.

Call to Action #7

Traditional education providers need to *establish partnerships with employers and companies that provide bridge services to students* to

- Ensure that a curriculum stays directly relevant to labor market demands;

- Incubate collaboration opportunities to support the instructional design process, identify and engage professional mentors, and create supplemental on-the-job work experiences;

- Cultivate a pipeline between students with targeted profiles and managers with specific job needs.

Platform Outsourcing

Both universities and employers have benefited from partnerships with companies with technical skills. Education providers are increasingly finding it more efficient to outsource technical platforms—learning management systems, online classrooms, online skills assessment—and focus on content development.

IT outsourcing can be a cost-saving measure but is also leveraged as a strategic tool for acquiring cutting-edge innovation.[25] Outsourcing technology allows a company to hire expertise while focusing on its own core business.[26]

Many of the organizations highlighted in this book have filled a market niche by providing technology solutions to educational providers. Coursera provides a platform where other institutions can offer educational content. Practera provides online access to project-based learning. As noted earlier, Guild provides online services to help employers manage education benefits. Noodle's WorkforceEdge is another employee education management platform that streamlines administration of tuition assistance benefits.

Call to Action #8

Traditional education providers should *implement a strategy for a campuswide learning platform solution* that

- Allows focus on instructional design and delivery versus management of a team of staff and proprietary interface and on cost reductions (that can, in turn, reduce tuition burdens for students) by lessening the need for site-based classrooms;

- Captures and tracks learning objectives and outcomes more efficiently and effectively, and allows for expansive innovation in instructional design and learner-centric offerings;

- Expands access to wider and more diverse student populations on the basis of geography and time of offering.

Soft Skills Gap

Most alternative programs included in our case studies focus on technical skills. With rapidly changing technology, there is a need for regular upskillling of such skills. At the same time, employers emphasize that effective employees also need the "soft skills," also often called "human skills" because they concern human interaction—communication, collaboration, and the ability to be adaptable—or "power skills" because of their importance in the new world of work. Along with such skills, employees also need a willingness to learn new, evolving skills to meet new, evolving challenges. Despite the need for soft skills, few of these alternative models provide them. Programs that develop such twenty-first-century skills as collaboration and communication *and* that equip graduates with skills that will support lifelong learning will be the programs that graduate effective employees.

Best practices suggest that, rather than traditional skills of reading, writing, and arithmetic, the important skills for success in the twenty-first century are communication, collaboration, creativity, and critical thinking.[27] Indeed, many employers report a lack of these skills among employees,[28] while at the same time noting employee lack of adaptability and orientation toward lifelong learning.[29] These skills are vital in today's rapidly evolving environment.

Call to Action #9

Alternative providers need to *balance the heavy focus on technical with soft skills offerings* to

- Satisfy employers who are increasingly dissatisfied with employee competence in this area—that is, by responding and providing access to a wider population of potential customers (learners) who have largely developed their careers by enhancing their technical skills or serving as individual contributors and now need development in the soft areas;

- Increase revenue by broadening market penetration and, therefore, enhancing the opportunity to survive and to reallocate the profit pool to support quality improvement initiatives and partnerships;

- Innovate and advance instructional design techniques for such teaching skills as collaboration, communication, negotiation, motivation, and leadership via alternative modalities usually best applied to technical content.

Credential Requires Brand

Many of the alternative providers in this book are startups just establishing their reputations as we write. Many of these new, alternative education providers have partnered with organizations with trusted names. Having that trusted name—or brand—can be important to establishing or expanding market share.

Research suggests that trusted brands are important to build market share.[30] This takes time, but there is evidence that brand extension can be effective in building the trust of partners or subsidiaries that have a relevant connection to the company.[31] Brand alliances seem to offer two benefits: reputation endorsement and collaboration on core competencies.[32] Startup companies benefit from allying with established brands.

We see this in a couple of instances. Practera's website touts that the organization is "trusted by top-tier institutions"—by such well-respected universities as MIT and Boston University and by companies like Deloitte and Ernst & Young. EY, itself a trusted name, has partnered with the Hult MBA program to provide established education and training opportunities leading to a tech MBA. Finally, Google Career Certificates are accepted because of the company's reputation as a premier technology firm.

Call to Action #10

Education provider organizations can benefit from joining with companies or other education providers with established, trusted reputations. While this can benefit startup companies, colleges can *leverage competitive advantage of brand recognition and value* by

- Fixing the devalued deficiencies in the traditional model and by matching competitive advantages of the alternative model;

- Partnering with employer organizations that also have legacy brand awareness and extending the collective value;

- Engaging in a marketing campaign to eliminate lingering perceptions of outdated curricula and teaching practices and promote the new trifecta: top brand, alternative model career impact, and broad accessibility.

Concluding Thoughts

These ten themes, derived from research into the activities of more than twenty alternative education providers—and the calls to action they suggest—represent a rich palette of alternative education objectives and methods. Although there is some overlap among them, foreshadowing some sort of shakeout in the future, support for the alternative model is clearly strong and varied.

The ten calls to action are all aimed at improving the value proposition of the alternative model of learning. Again, that there is some overlap in the calls to action suggests that collective action may produce benefits faster, but clearly, the opportunities also exist for each participant to make changes that may advance the value of their separate efforts.

A key question remains: Who is responsible for leading the change to an alternative model of learning? Colleges and universities clearly failed to heed the call until forced to by competition. Alternative providers, meanwhile, remain segmented on distinct parts of the model—versus the whole—and are inherently limited by branding, credentialing, and instructional deficiencies. Leadership thus remains an open question, and it will be interesting to observe the horse race.

EVOLVING TRENDS IN THE
FUTURE OF LEARNING

The research and analysis in the preceding chapters focused on four subjects that proceeded in order: first, the historical evolution of the college degree, including contextual factors that influenced its rise and impending fall; second, the structural challenge the traditional model of learning presents and a proposition for an alternative model to replace it; third, the would-be "heirs apparent" to the higher education throne—key players in the alternative education movement; and fourth, the key lessons the research and analysis have taught us, to date, along with recommendations for how key stakeholders in the educational ecosystem should proceed. All four subjects are about what has already happened—what data and expert opinion tell us has already occurred, or is occurring now, and how we might proceed to deal with the new realities.

But what about the future? What trends emerge that may help us predict further disruptions and stir yet another season of destabilizing adaptation—hopefully, for the better?

In this final chapter, we offer our top five predictions—poised to dramatically affect the future of learning and work.

Of course, these are predictions, not recommendations. They constitute informed opinions and projected conjecture based on experience and research, and they are intended solely to inspire further discussion and study. Moreover, each prediction derives from evolving and already noticeable trends; indeed, the expectation is that we will see these predictions come to light in the United States within a period of some five years or so starting from approximately mid-2022, the time of the publication of this book.

1. Recalibrating ROI

> Colleges and universities will collectively reduce tuition expense by 50 percent.

- Starting in the last decade of the twentieth century and continuing aggressively in the twenty-first, college and university tuition has increased dramatically—by 250 percent in the first twenty years of this century.[1]
- At the same time, public funding has been decreasing, resulting in an unprecedented crisis of student debt.[2] U.S. students are carrying a collective debt of $1.41 trillion in education loans.[3]
- Meanwhile, the offered curricula, often derided as outdated or, at best, misaligned with employer expectations, have stagnated—leaving graduates less well prepared in the competencies associated with the needs of the future of work and therefore unable to get or keep jobs without supplemental training that needs to be paid for by the employee or employer.[4]
- To make matters worse, the global pandemic that started in 2020 shifted most learning to remote modalities—accelerating the spotlight on return on investment—ROI—and prompting the question, Is the degree worth all of this money? In the face of these developments, the answer is "no." The pandemic accelerated changes already under way. There is no more elasticity of demand in the market. Students and their parents have maxed out at the level they are willing to pay. Long-held, bullish employer perceptions of the value of the college degree are waning fast as their workforces struggle to remain competitive.
- In addition to the actions proposed in this book for innovative offerings that align with market needs, it will be imperative for colleges and universities to drop their prices significantly if they are to remain competitive. New reports suggest some schools have begun to do so.[5] Others have started to close shop for good.[6] Of course, the top-tier schools such as those from the Ivy League may resist price decreases thanks to their premium brands and hefty endowments. Ultimately, however, market forces will prevail.

2. Policy Change and Subsidization

For the first time in U.S. history, government-backed loans will be available to all students for reskilling and/or upskilling and for industry certification.

• As noted earlier in this book, the "golden age" of the college degree was supported by large-scale public investment from both the federal and state governments, which, in turn, stimulated massive enrollment through financial accessibility.

• Federal government supports for students began with work-study grants during the Great Depression.[7] Student loans backed by the federal government originated with the National Defense Education Act of 1958 for students of science, engineering, or education.[8] The Higher Education Act of 1965 extended loans to students in any discipline.[9]

• For alternative education, on the other hand, public support is currently not available. Although alternative education pathways are less expensive than traditional degree programs, most still charge students for the courses. And Pell Grants, for example, cannot be used for nondegree or noncredit programs that might otherwise be attractive to working adults who want to improve specific job-related skills.[10]

• Today, government workforce development programs and higher education programs remain largely siloed: workforce development and job training are the province of the Department of Labor while postsecondary education services are the domain of the Department of Education. Funding for additional career preparation programs reside in yet other, related federal agencies—for example, the Department of Energy or Department of Health and Human Services.[11]

Given the urgent call from industry for a better-skilled workforce, the failure of colleges and universities to respond with satisfactory solutions, and the recession conditions caused by the global pandemic, the U.S. government needs to consolidate these program areas as is done in Britain[12] and Switzerland,[13] to coordinate education and workforce development, and to prioritize an economic development agenda that is inclusive of alternative education and available to all citizens as a free public service.

3. Tenure Revisited

> The current model for college and university faculty hiring, review, and promotion will be disbanded and restructured.

- Tenure is an indefinite academic appointment that can only be terminated for cause or under extraordinary circumstances. The careers and responsibilities of college and university faculty are shaped by a tenure system, as are academic policy and governance, curricula and instruction, student services and support, and budgeting.

- Twenty-one percent of faculty are tenured, and only 10 percent are tenure track. Nearly 50 percent of schools' faculty members are part time. The reasons for this vary, from the cost savings gained by hiring part-time employees to tenured faculty refusing—or unable—to teach remedial or applied courses.[14] The percentage of part-time faculty is likely to increase as schools begin to drop tuition prices, as recommended above. In any event, the tenure structure governs the strategy and operations of the college or university, while most of the teaching faculty responsible for the transfer of knowledge to students are neither tenured nor eligible to become tenured.

- Proponents of tenure argue that it is needed to provide faculty the freedom to pursue long-term research agendas and challenge conventional wisdom without fear of losing their positions.[15] Detractors argue that tenure wrongly incentivizes a focus on narrow, theoretical thought leadership that is disconnected from the actual needs of students.

- Current criteria for tenure include teaching, research, and service (within the school). A new system may utilize the same criteria but embed in them additional metrics that satisfy the elements of the alternative education model by amplified focus on applied outcomes. Examples include adding such student outcomes as job placement to the "teaching" criteria, and categorizing relevant industry connections (for student mentorship and support) among the "service" criteria.

- Moving forward, both full-time, tenure-track faculty and part-time adjuncts may be evaluated under the same revised criteria, although with different weights. If more than half of all faculty are part time, it will be imperative for colleges and universities to more formally and to an equal degree embrace, include, and value the "lower tier" profile to ensure applied expertise in fields related to courses of study.

4. Benefits Disrupted

As the gig economy swells to become 40 percent of the workforce, paid benefits for reskilling and upskilling will be available to all full-time contractors.

- In 2018, over one-third of U.S. workers were engaged in or employed by the gig economy.[16] Many of these mostly short-term jobs exist because of new technologies and programs that make it feasible to organize and manage work on a project-specific basis.

- Gig work appeals to organizations because it allows them to continually hire a changing cast of diverse workers—with a mix of current skills appropriate and relevant for specific projects.[17] In many cases, this strategy yields a greater return than does investing in full-time employees—FTEs—who require repeated and ongoing training to remain relevant and productive. Gig work appeals to individuals, on the other hand, because of the flexibility it affords.[18] Millennials and Generation Z members, in particular, are drawn to this contract economy. Given that these two generations will constitute 70 percent of the workforce by 2025,[19] it's reasonable to assume that gig work will expand correspondingly.

- There are, however, downsides to gig work. One is that gig workers have few or none of the legal rights and protections afforded under the unemployment insurance system, the workers' compensation system, the Fair Labor Standards Act, and other laws and regulations written with more traditional employment arrangements in mind.[20] More specifically, gig work does not provide such benefits to employees as health insurance, retirement pensions, paid leave, and education assistance. Historically, these benefits were negotiated by the labor unions of the early 1900s and have evolved to support full-time workers—both unionized and non-unionized.

- As the prevalence of gig workers continues to surge, their collective power in the economic system will also surge—providing a platform for demands that rival or exceed those of FTEs. This power will also give rise to a new market to support gig work—for example, shared workspace, pooled insurance, community networking, and the like. Included in this market response will surely be the business of providing reskilling and upskilling opportunities— essential education to keep gig workers prepared for their livelihood, training them to do the work as the needs of the work change.

- Companies will pay for gig worker training for the privilege of accessing specialist workers. The government, as noted earlier, will pay for gig worker training as an outcome of realigned policies in support of a nondegree workforce agenda. Both companies and the government will benefit from a labor economy that ignores more productivity and a renewed period of advanced innovation and growth for the country.

5. VC Bullish on EdTech

> Educational technology (EdTech) will rise to become one of the top-three overall investment sectors in venture capital.

- Starting toward the end of the twentieth century and well into the twenty-first, venture capital (VC) has emerged as a leading and essential resource for startup and early-stage companies.[21]
- In the United States, in 2019, software, pharma and biotech, healthtech, and cybertech topped the list of VC investment sectors.[22] The amounts spent in these sectors range from $5 billion to $43.5 billion, a good demonstration of the tremendous influence VC has on the development and growth of new enterprises.[23] In Europe, the top five VC investment sectors are cybersecurity, artificial intelligence, EdTech, health care, and cannabis.[24] Given Europe's comparative advances over the U.S. in the education sector overall, the position of EdTech as number three on their list is reason to predict a similar ascension in the U.S.
- Still a relatively small segment of the VC market in the United States, EdTech in 2018 and 2019 has seen investors pour $12.5 billion into 1,656 deals. With educational institutions moving instruction online during and after the pandemic, incentive to invest in EdTech appeared to rise. Three fiscal quarters into 2020, for example, venture capital had already spread $10.3 billion across 505 deals—more than in all of 2019 combined.[25]
- Each of the alternative providers featured in this book has received venture capital investment. In 2020, Coursera received an influx of $120 million, Udemy received $50 million, Degreed $32 million, and Noodle investments of $16 million.[26]
- Each of the programs described in the cases is still evolving. As noted, none of them offer all elements to complete the alternative model cycle; to do that, they all need to scale up and out. Their expansion and, ultimately, their

ability to optimize impact, will be accelerated by increased venture capital investment to spur organic growth, mergers and acquisitions, and intensive research and development.

Concluding Thoughts

Trends in the future of learning suggest the need for supportive action—first, to disrupt the traditional learning model, second, to endorse the amplification of the alternative learning model on the basis of the market's response to the emerging skills gap, thus affecting productivity and competitiveness. Support is needed, in short, to clarify that change is needed and to amplify the change as it happens.

Essential to building a foundation for future solutions are (1) significant structural changes in colleges and universities and (2) funding both to support students and to broaden access and entrepreneurial investments that seek to incubate alternative ventures.

As noted in the beginning of the book, in a capitalist society, when money is at stake, failure to meet expectations is not tolerated; the result, as in the case of the skills gap, is that weaker forces will be eradicated and new replacements will be fortified. The U.S. economy has spoken, and colleges and universities will continue to rebuke the calls for transformation at their peril. Throughout history, people have learned skills and adapted to changing conditions and contexts, and, at the same time, learning providers have evolved from master craftsman to digital credentials. Trends indicate a revolution in learning not dissimilar to other dynamic movements that pepper our history.

The thesis of this book—that college, as structured, isn't cutting it and that alternative models are emerging to both support and replace the college education and the college degree—presents an opportunity to realize value, for value *will* be realized.

NOTES

Chapter 1

1. Zachary Karabell, *What's College For? The Struggle to Define American Higher Education* (New York: Basic Books, 1999), 1–22.

2. David Breneman, "US Higher Education and the Current Recession," *International Higher Education*, no. 55 (March 2009), https://doi.org/10.6017/ihe.2009.55.8431.

3. Ling Li, "Education Supply Chain in the Era of Industry 4.0," *Systems Research and Behavioral Science* 37, no. 4 (2020), https://doi.org/10.1002/sres.2702.

4. Stephen Rose, "The Value of a College Degree," *Change: The Magazine of Higher Learning* 45, no. 6 (2013): 24–33, https://doi.org/10.1080/00091383.2013.842101.

5. Paul Dimaggio, John P. Robinson, and Eszter Hargittai, "New Social Survey Perspectives on the Digital Divide," *IT & Society* 1, no. 5 (2003), http://citeseerx.ist.psu.edu/viewdoc/download?doi=10.1.1.177.1586&rep=rep1&type=pdf.

6. U.S. Bureau of Labor Statistics, *Economic News Release: Employment Situation Summary* (Washington, DC: US Department of Labor, November 6, 2020), https://www.bls.gov/news.release/empsit.nro.htm.

7. Mary C. Daly, Shelby R. Buckman, and Lily M. Seitelman, "The Unequal Impact of COVID-19: Why Education Matters," Economic Letter, Federal Reserve Bank of San Franciso, June 29, 2020, https://www.frbsf.org/economic-research/publications/economic-letter/2020/june/unequal-impact-covid-19-why-education-matters/.

8. Matthew A. Andersson, "Higher Education, Bigger Networks? Differences by Family Socioeconomic Background and Network Measures," *Socius* (January 2018), https://doi.org/10.1177/2378023118797217.

9. Hart Research Associates, *Falling Short? College Learning and Career Success* (Washington, DC: Association of American Colleges and Universities, 2015), https://www.aacu.org/leap/public-opinion-research/2015-survey-results.

10. Anthony M. Baird and Satyanarayana Parayitam, "Are Employers Dissatisfied with College Graduates? An Empirical Examination," *International Journal of Arts & Sciences* 10, no. 1 (2017): 151–168.

11. Raghu Krishnamoorthy and Keith Keating, "Education Crisis, Workforce Preparedness, and COVID-19: Reflections and Recommendations," *American Journal of Economics and Sociology*, 80, no. 1 (2021): 253–274, doi:10.1111/ajes.12376.

12. Jonathan Horowitz, "Relative Education and the Advantage of a College De-

gree," *American Sociological Review* 83, no. 4 (August 2018): 771–801, https://doi.org/10.1177/0003122418785371.

13. John R. Thelin, Jason R. Edwards, and Eric Moyen, "Higher Education in the United States—Historical Development, System," StateUniversity, 2013, http://education.stateuniversity.com/pages/2044/Higher-Education-in-UnitedStates.html.

14. Kate Purmal, Lisa Goldman, and Anne Janzer, *The Moonshot Effect: Disrupting Business as Usual.* (n.c.: Wynnefield Business Press, 2016).

Chapter 2

1. According to data released by the Department of Commerce's Bureau of Economic Analysis in 2020, 28 percent of jobs were professional services that would expect a university degree.

2. Michelle LaPointe and Jason Wingard, "How Did We Get Here? A History of Education and Training in the United States," In *Learning for Life: How Continuous Education Will Keep Us Competitive in the Global Knowledge Economy*, 3–9 (New York: AMACOM, 2016).

3. Eugène J. F. M. Custers and Olle Ten Cate, "The History of Medical Education in Europe and the United States, with Respect to Time and Proficiency," *Academic Medicine* 93 (March 2018): S49–S54.

4. In colonial times, a few colleges offered scholarships to young Native American men, according to Thelin and Gasman (2010). William & Mary was one such, but it discontinued its program because tribal elders were not impressed with the European-style education offered.

5. Oscar Handlin and Mary F. Handlin, *The American College and American Culture: Socialization as a Function of Higher Education* (New York: McGraw-Hill, 1970).

6. Farley Grubb, "Growth of Literacy in Colonial America: Longitudinal Patterns, Economic Models, and the Direction of Future Research," *Social Science History* 14, No. 4 (Winter 1990): 451–482.

7. Nicholas Lemann, *The Promised Land: The Great Black Migration and How It Changed America* (New York: Alfred A. Knopf, 1991).

8. James S. Olsen, *Encyclopedia of the Industrial Revolution in America* (Santa Barbara, CA: Greenwood, 2002).

9. Ibid.

10. Ross Thomson. "The Continuity of Innovation: The Civil War Experience," *Enterprise and Society* 11, no. 1 (2012): 128–165, *Project MUSE*, Oxford University Press.

11. LaPointe and Wingard, "How Did We Get Here?"

12. John Thelin, *A History of American Higher Education* (Baltimore: Johns Hopkins University Press, 2019).

13. Ibid.

14. Patricia Graham, *Community and Class in American Education, 1865 to 1918* (New York: Wiley, 1974); Edward Krug, *The Shaping of the American High School, 1880–1920* (New York: Harper & Row, 1964).

15. Thomas Snyder, *120 Years of American Education: A Statistical Portrait* (Washington, DC: National Center for Education Statistics, 1993).

16. David Labaree, "Learning to Love the Bomb: The Cold War Brings the Best of Times to American Higher Education," in *Educational Research: Discourses of Change and Changes in Discourse*, ed. Paul Smeyers and Marc Depaepe, 101–117 (Dordrecht: Springer, 2016).

17. Although the 10th Amendment to the Constitution in 1791 gave states the right to regulate health, education, and safety, it was almost a hundred years before this right was formally recognized. In 1889, the U.S. Supreme Court, in the *Dent v. West Virginia* decision, affirmed the right of states to license medical doctors. See https://www.loc.gov/item/usrep129114/.

18. Thelin, *A History of American Higher Education.*

19. Richard Axt, *The Federal Government and Financing Higher Education* (New York: Columbia University Press, for the Commission on Financing Higher Education, 1952).

20. Thelin, *A History of American Higher Education.*

21. Labaree, "Learning to Love the Bomb," 101–117.

22. Ibid.

23. Danielle Douglas-Gabriel, "Students Now Pay More of Their Public University Tuition Than State Governments," *Washington Post*, May 1, 2015, https://www.washingtonpost.com/news/get-there/wp/2015/01/05/students-cover-more-of-their-public-university-tuition-now-than-state-governments/.

24. John Thelin and Marybeth Gasman, "Historical Overview of American Higher Education," in *Student Services: A Handbook for the Profession* (Hoboken, NJ: Wiley, 2010).

25. Labree, "Learning to Love the Bomb," 101–117.

26. Ibid.

27. U.S. Department of Education, National Center for Education Statistics, *Biennial Survey of Education in the United States: Opening Fall Enrollment in Higher Education, 1963 Through 1965*; Higher Education General Information Survey (HEGIS), "Fall Enrollment in Colleges and Universities" Surveys, 1966 Through 1985"; Integrated Postsecondary Education Data System (IPEDS), "Fall Enrollment Survey" (IPEDS-EF:86–99); "IPEDS Spring 2001 Through Spring 2019, Fall Enrollment Component"; and "Enrollment in Degree-Granting Institutions Projection Model, 2000 through 2029."

28. Ibid.

29. Labaree, "Learning to Love the Bomb," 101–117.

30. Yohanes A. K. Honu, "United States' Higher Education Cost and Value: Opposing Views," *The Academy of Educational Leadership Journal* 23 (2019): 1–12.

31. Ibid.

32. Sophia Laderman and Andrew Carlson, *SHEF: 2017 State Higher Education Finance* (Boulder, CO: State Higher Education Executive Officers Association, 2017), http://www.sheeo.org/sites/default/files/SHEF_FY2017.pdf.

33. Ibid.

34. Honu, "United States' Higher Education Cost and Value."

35. Experian Research, "Student Loan Debt Climbs," July 24, 2019, http://www.experian.com.

36. U.S. Secretary of Education Betsy DeVos, prepared remarks to Federal Student Aid's Training Conference, November 27, 2018.

37. Investopedia, LLC, "Student Loans in 2019: A Snapshot," November 15, 2019, https://www.investopedia.com/student-loan-debt-2019-statistics-and-outlook-4772007#:~:text=The%20total%20amount%20of%20outstanding,total%20debt%20was%20%241.06%20trillion.

38. Experian Research, "Student Loan Debt Climbs."

39. Jason Wingard and Michelle LaPointe, *Learning for Life: How Continuous Education Will Keep Us Competitive in the Global Knowledge Economy* (New York: AMACOM, 2016).

40. Honu, "United States' Higher Education Cost and Value."

41. Strada Education Network, "Public Viewpoint," September 16, 2020.

42. Stephen McMurray, Matthew Dutton, Ronald McQuaid, and Alec Richard, "Employer Demands from Business Graduates," *Education and Training* 58, no. 1 (2016): 112–132, https://doi.org/10.1108/ET-02-2014-0017.

43. Tomas Chamorro-Premuzic and Becky Frankiewicz, "Does Higher Education Still Prepare People for Jobs?" *Harvard Business Review*, January 7, 2019.

44. Jon Marcus, "Some Colleges Seek Radical Solutions to Survive," The Hechinger Report, October 10, 2019, downloaded November 13, 2020, https://hechingerreport.org/some-colleges-seek-radical-solutions-to-survive/.

45. Paul LeBlanc, "Unveiling SNHU's 201802023 Strategic Plan," President's Corner, posted October 16, 2018, http://www.blogging.snhu.edu.

Chapter 3

1. Joy Blanchard, *Controversies on Campus: Debating the Issues Confronting American Universities in the 21st Century* (Santa Barbara, CA: Praeger, 2018).

2. Jason Wingard and Michelle LaPointe, *Learning for Life: How Continuous Education Will Keep Us Competitive in the Global Knowledge Economy* (New York: AMACON, 2016), 7.

3. Carole J. Gallagher, "Reconciling a Tradition of Testing with a New Learning Paradigm," *Educational Psychology Review* 15, No. 1 (March 2003): 83–99, https://www.jstor.org/stable/23361535 (accessed October 14, 2021).

4. Thomas J. Espenshade and Chang Young Chung, *Standardized Admission Tests, College Performance, and Campus Diversity* (Princeton: Princeton University, Office of Population Research, 2010), http://citeseerx.ist.psu.edu/viewdoc/download?doi=10.1.1.1052.2264&rep=rep1&type=pdf (accessed October 14, 2021).

5. Meredith Kolodner, "Why Are Low-Income Students not Showing Up to College, Even Though They Have Been Accepted?" The Hechinger Report, August 14, 2015, http://hechingerreport.org.

6. John Robst, "Education and Job Match: The Relatedness of College Major and Work," *Economics of Education Review* 26, no. 4 (August 2007): 397–407, https://doi.org/10.1016/j.econedurev.2006.08.003 (accessed October 14, 2021).

7. Madeline St. Amour. "As Times and Students Change, Can Faculty Change, Too?" *Inside Higher Ed*, April 3, 2020, https://www.insidehighered.com/news/2020/04/03/faculty-face-uphill-battle-adapting-needs-todays-students.

8. Since the writing of this book, Emsi has merged with Burning Glass and has been renamed to Emsi Burning Glass.

Chapter 4

1. businesswire.com, "Strategic Education, Inc. and Noodle Partners Unite to Provide Employers with Access to a Variety of Education and Upskilling Programs from the Nation's Leading Universities," September 21, 2020, https://www.businesswire.com/news/home/20200921005210/en/Strategic-Education-Inc.-and-Noodle-Partners-Unite-to-Provide-Employers-with-Access-to-a-Variety-of-Education-and-Upskilling-Programs-from-the-Nation%E2%80%99s-Leading-Universities.

2. John Katzman, founder and CEO, Noodle, interview by the author, October 27, 2021. All subsequent quotes are from the same interview.

3. Roger Schank, "Home Page," October 27, 2021, http://www.rogerschank.com/.

4. Noodle Partners, "Noodle Partners Raises Series B to Expand Its Network of Innovative, Resilient Universities," June 9, 2020, https://www.noodlepartners.com/noodle-partners-raises-series-b-to-expand-its-network-of-innovative-resilient-universities/.

5. Lindsay McKenzie, "A Long-Term Bet on Employer-Assisted Tuition Programs: Strategic Education and Noodle Partners Bet Big on Employer-Assisted Tuition Programs," *Inside Higher Ed*, September 22, 2020, https://www.insidehighered.com/news/2020/09/22/strategic-education-and-noodle-partners-bet-big-employer-assisted-tuition-programs.

6. Noodle Partners, "Noodle Partners Raises Series B."

7. Ibid.

8. Evelyn Ganzglass, "Scaling 'Stackable Credentials': Implications for Implementation and Policy," Center for Law and Social Policy (CLASP), Center for Postsecondary and Economic Success; Kentucky; Oregon; Virginia; Wisconsin, 2014, p. 5.

9. Wes Sonnenreich, co-CEO, Practera, interview by the author, October 26, 2020. All subsequent quotes are from the same interview.

10. David A. Kolb, *Experiential Learning: Experience as the Source of Learning and Development* (Saddle River, NJ: Prentice-Hall, 1984), p. 26.

11. Ibid., p. 28.

12. Ahmed Khaled Ahmed, "Teacher-Centered Versus Learner-Centered Teaching Style," *Journal of Global Business Management* 9, no. 1 (2013): 22.

13. Nikki James and Beau Leese, "Effective Experiential Learning: Practitioners Guide," www.practera.com, https://practera.com/wp-content/uploads/2020/12/Experiential-Learning-Practera-White-Paper.pdf (accessed March 4, 2022).

14. Ibid.

15. Marni Baker Stein, provost and chief academic officer, Western Governors University, interview by the author, November 1, 2020. All subsequent quotes are from the same interview.

16. Melinda Dorning, "Western Governors University: Helping Displaced Students Finish What They Started," October 5, 2020, https://impact.acbsp.org/2020/10/05/helping-displaced-students-finish-what-they-started/.

17. "WGU 2020 Annual Report," WGU.edu, https://www.wgu.edu/content/dam/western-governors/documents/annual-report/2020-annual-report-compressed.pdf (accessed December 1, 2021).

18. "WGU 2019 Annual Report," WGU.edu, https://www.wgu.edu/content/dam/western-governors/documents/annual-report/annual-report-2019.pdf (accessed December 1, 2021).

19. Ibid.

20. Western Governors University, wgu.edu/about/story/cbe.html (accessed December 1, 2021).

21. "WGU 2020 Annual Report."

22. Heidi Tyline King, "Reinventing Higher Education, Changing Lives: The Story of Western Governors University," Western Governors University, April 3, 2017.

23. Matt Walker, "Handshake Helps College Students and Recent Grads Get Hired and Avoid Tapping into Credit," Credit Care News, August 18, 2021, https://www.cardrates.com/news/handshake-helps-students-find-jobs-and-avoid-using-credit/.

24. Allyson Letteri, "A Bold New Image for Handshake," Handshake.com, https://joinhandshake.com/blog/our-team/a-bold-new-image-for-handshake/ (accessed November 23, 2021).

25. Chris Taylor, "How College Students Can Find Jobs—Without Much Work Experience," Reuters, April 9, 2019.

26. Ibid.

27. Ibid.

28. Garrett Lord, "Expanding Our Efforts to Help All Students Find Opportunity," Handshake.com, https://joinhandshake.com/blog/our-team/expanding-our-efforts-to-help-all-students-find-opportunity/ (accessed November 7, 2020).

29. Benjamin Laker, "The Surprising New Way to Connect Employers with Talent," Forbes, October 20, 2020, https://www.forbes.com/sites/benjaminlaker/2020/10/20/new-virtual-platform-helps-connect-employers-with-talent/?sh=3aab72785064.

30. Lord, " Expanding Our Efforts to Help All Students Find Opportunity."

31. Zach Guzman, "How This Startup Is Connecting Graduates to 'New Collar' Jobs Amid COVID-19," Yahoo Finance, October 20, 2020, https://www.yahoo.com/lifestyle/startup-connecting-graduates-collar-jobs-184725935.html.

Chapter 5

1. Julia Pollak, chief economist, ZipRecruiter, interview by the author, November 3, 2020. All subsequent quotes are from the same interview.

2. See, for example, KU Edwards Campus, "Investing in Professional Development Leads to Higher Employee Retention, Business Performance," PR Newswire, February 13, 2019, https://www.prnewswire.com/news-releases/investing-in-professional-development-leads-to-higher-employee-retention-business-performance-300794448.html; Derek Smith, "Investing in Employees: Why Training Is Important," Biz Library, January 2, 2020, https://www.bizlibrary.com/blog/employee-development/importance-of-investing-in-employees/; "The True Cost of Not Providing Employee Training," Shift eLearning, April 19, 2018, https://www.shiftelearning.com/blog/the-true-cost-of-not-providing-employee-training; Claire Brown, "How Training Your Staff Can Help You Retain Them," Coassemble, June 13, 2019, https://coassemble.com/blog/industry/how-training-your-staff-can-help-you-retain-them/; Meghan M. Biro, "Developing Your Employees Is the Key to Retention—Here Are 4 Smart Ways to Start," *Forbes*, July 23, 2018, https://www.forbes.com/sites/meghanbiro/2018/07/23/developing-your-employees-is-the-key-to-retention-here-are-4-smart-ways-to-start/?sh=1c397b443734.

3. Kelly Palmer and David Blake, *The Expertise Economy: How the Smartest Companies Use Learning to Engage, Compete, and Succeed, Illustrated Edition* (Boston: Nicholas Brealey, 2018), xv.

4. Pablo Illanes, Susan Lund, Mona Mourshed, Scott Rutherford, and Magnus Tyreman, "Retraining and Reskilling Workers in the Age of Automation," McKinsey & Company, January 2018, https://www.mckinsey.com/featured-insights/future-of-work/retraining-and-reskilling-workers-in-the-age-of-automation.

5. Kelly Palmer, chief learning and talent officer, Degreed, interview by the author, October 29, 2020. All subsequent quotes are from this interview.

6. Learn more about the Lumina Foundation's Connecting Credentials framework at this link: https://www.luminafoundation.org/resource/connecting-credentials/.

7. Palmer and Blake, *Expertise Economy*, 3.

8. George Siemens, *Connectivism: Learning as Network Creation* (Alexandria, VA: American Society for Training and Development, 2005).

9. Ibid.

10. Alexandra Wilson and Susan Adams, "Class Act: This 31-Year-Old's Company Rocketed to a $1 Billion Valuation Helping Workers Get Degrees," *Forbes*, December 19, 2019, https://www.forbes.com/sites/alexandrawilson1/2019/12/19/make-colleges-pay-the-31-year-old-whose-company-rocketed-to-a-1-billion-valuation-helping-workers-get-degrees/?sh=6527479c75f6.

11. "Our Story," https://www.guildeducation.com/about-us/our-story/ (accessed November 1, 2020).

12. Henry "C. J." Jackson, communications director, Guild Education, interview by the author, November 2, 2020. All subsequent quotes are from the same interview.

13. Lindsay McKenzie, "A Long-Term Bet on Employer-Assisted Tuition Programs: Strategic Education and Noodle Partners Bet Big on Employer-Assisted Tuition Programs," *Inside Higher Ed*, September 22, 2020, https://www.insidehighered.com/

news/2020/09/22strategic-educatio-and-noodle-partners-bet-big-employer-assisted-tuition-programs.

14. Guild Education, "Case Study: How Chipotle Improved Retention by Deepening Its Commitment to Mission," November 2020, https://resource.guildeducation.com/chipotle-case-study/ (direct: http://biz.guildeducation.com/rs/003-XMG-066/images/Chipotle-Case-Study-V2-11_11_20.pdf).

15. Ibid., pp. 3–4.

16. Ibid., p. 3.

17. Ibid., p. 4.

18. Trent Henry, vice chair of talent, EY, interview by author, November 2, 2020. All subsequent quotes are from the same interview.

19. McKenzie, "A Long-Term Bet."

20. Ibid.

Chapter 6

1. "Preparing the Next Generation of Tech Talent," Atlantic Re:think, https://www.theatlantic.com/sponsored/grow-google-2019/preparing-next-gen-tech-talent/3214/ (accessed November 1, 2021).

2. Ibid.

3. Ibid.

4. Natalie Van Kleef Conley, "From IT Certificate Completers to Googlers," Google: The Keyword, August 10, 2020, https://blog.google/outreach-initiatives/grow-with-google/it-certificate-completers-googlers/.

5. Justin Bariso, "How Google's New Career Certificates Could Disrupt the College Degree (Exclusive)," Inc., March 11, 2021, https://www.inc.com/justin-bariso/inside-googles-plan-to-disrupt-college-degree-exclusive.html.

6. Van Kleef Conley, "From IT Certificate Completers to Googlers."

7. "Preparing the Next Generation of Tech Talent."

8. Ibid.

9. Bariso, "How Google's New Career Certificates Could Disrupt the College Degree (Exclusive)."

10. Jeffrey L. Katz, "What You Need to Know About Google Career Certificates," U.S. News & World Report, May 3, 2021, https://www.usnews.com/education/google-career-certifications.

11. Coryanne Hicks, "What You Need to Know About Google Career Certificates," U.S. News & World Report, December 29, 2020, https://www.usnews.com/education/learn-google-it-guide.

12. "Build Your Future: Apprenticeships," Google, https://buildyourfuture.with-google.com/programs/apprenticeships/ (accessed November 1, 2021).

13. Lilah Burke, "Community College, with Google as Instructor," Inside Higher Ed, October 15, 2019, https://www.insidehighered.com/digital-learning/article/2019/10/15/google-expands-it-certificate-program-100-community-colleges.

14. "Fact Sheet: Investing $90 Million Through ApprenticeshipUSA to Expand Proven Pathways into the Middle Class," The White House: Office of the Press Secretary, April 21, 2016, https://obamawhitehouse.archives.gov/the-press-office/2016/04/21/fact-sheet-investing-90-million-through-apprenticeshipusa-expand-proven.

15. "Jump Start Your Career Through Apprenticeship," Career Seekers, Apprenticeship.gov, https://www.apprenticeship.gov/career-seekers (accessed November 1, 2021).

16. "Educational Attainment Statistics," Eurostat: Statistics Explained, June 2021, https://ec.europa.eu/eurostat/statistics-explained/index.php?title=Educational_attainment_statistics.

17. Paula Protsch and Heike Solga, "Going Across Europe for an Apprenticeship? A Factorial Survey Experiment on Employers' Hiring Preferences in Germany," *Journal of European Social Policy* 27, no. 4 (October 11, 2017): 387–399, http://dx.doi.org/10.1177/0958928717719200.

18. Jennifer Carlson, co-founder, Apprenti, interview by the author, October 26, 2020. All subsequent quotes are from the same interview.

19. "Know the Numbers," Apprenti, https://apprenticareers.org/hire/know-the-numbers/ (accessed November 1, 2021).

20. Ibid.

21. "New Grad Survey: Anxiety, Desperation and Salary Woes Revealed," Monster.com, https://hiring.monster.com/employer-resources/blog/labor-statistics/new-grad-survey/ (accessed November 1, 2021).

22. General Assembly. "General Assembly's Student Outcomes Report," General Assembly Blog, June 16, 2020. https://generalassemb.ly/blog/outcomes-report-2018-2019/?utm_source=twitter&utm_medium=social&utm_campaign=outcomes-report-2018-2019.

23. Josh Bersin, "Rethinking the Build vs. Buy Approach to Talent," JoshBersin.com, https://joshbersin.com/wp-content/uploads/2019/10/Build_vs_buy_Bersin_1.0.pdf.

24. "Student Financing Handbook," General Assembly, updated April 2021, https://ga-core.s3.amazonaws.com/cms/files/files/000/005/291/original/StudentFinancing-Handbook_21_US.pdf.

25. Tom Ogletree, Vice President of Social Impact & External Affairs, General Assembly, interview by the author, October 29, 2020. All subsequent quotes are from the same interview.

26. "General Assembly's Student Outcomes Report."

27. Ibid.

28. "Microsoft and General Assembly Launch Partnership to Close the Global AI Skills Gap," Microsoft News Center, May 17, 2019, https://news.microsoft.com/2019/05/17/microsoft-and-general-assembly-launch-partnership-to-close-the-global-ai-skills-gap/.

29. Shelley Osborne, vice president of learning, Udemy, interview by the author, November 3, 2020. All subsequent quotes are from the same interview.

30. Bill Pelster, Jennifer Stempel, and Bernard van der Vyver, "Careers and Learning: Real Time, All the Time: 2017 Global Human Capital Trends," Deloitte Insights,

February 28, 2017, https://www2.deloitte.com/us/en/insights/focus/human-capital-trends/2017/learning-in-the-digital-age.html.

31. Romina Ederle, "New Udemy Report Shows Surge in Global Online Education in Response to COVID-19," Udemy.com, April 30, 2020, https://about.udemy.com/press-releases/new-udemy-report-shows-surge-in-global-online-education-in-response-to-covid-19/.

32. Ibid.

Chapter 7

1. Andrew Crapuchettes, "CEO Address," Emsi20 Conference, https://www.economicmodeling.com/video/ceo-address/ (accessed November 24, 2021).

2. https://skills.emsidata.com/about (accessed November 24, 2021).

3. American Workforce Policy Advisory Board Digital Infrastructure Working Group, September 2020, https://commerce.gov.

4. https://skills.emsidata.com/faqs (accessed November 24, 2021).

5. Jonathan Finkelstein, CEO, Credly, interviewed by the author, October 23, 2020. Subsequent quotes are from the same interview.

6. Case Study: Credly and Autodesk, p. 8. https://resources.credly.com/hubfs/Credly_Autodesk_CaseStudy_2019.pdf?hsCtaTracking=2c279d29-ca5c-45d0-a901-eb8746fce8c8%7C0330d292-10ea-4a6b-9152-3acb3642948b

7. https://www.jff.org/about (accessed March 3, 2022).

8. "Building a Future That Works," JFF, November 5, 2018, https://youtu.be/9mkKWZVib4g.

9. Michael Grady and Kyle Hartung, "Case-Study: A Clearer Path to College and Career Success, jff.org, May 2019.

10. JFF.org, "JFF Receives $6M from Walmart" June 11, 2020, https://www.jff.org/points-of-view/jff-receives-6m-walmart-boost-economic-mobility.

11. Maria Flynn, "We Can't Let Student Debt Hold Pandemic-Displaced Workers Back," The Hill, April 2020.

12. Maria Flynn, "Moving Toward Precision Learning in Postsecondary and Workforce Education," Diplomatic Courier, August 15, 2020, https://www.diplomaticourier.com/posts/moving-toward-precision-learning-in-postsecondary-and-workforce-education.

13. Melissa Luke, "New Network to Accelerate Skills-Based Education and Hiring," OSN, September 16, 2020, https://www.openskillsnetwork.org/post/osn-announcement.

14. Ibid.

15. Open Skills Network, https://www.openskillsnetwork.org/about (accessed November 24, 2021).

Chapter 8

1. Malcolm Knowles. "Andragogy, not Pedagogy," *Adult Leadership* 16, no. 10 (1968): 350–352.

2. George Siemens, *Connectivism: Learning as Network Creation* (Alexandria, VA: American Society for Training and Development, 2005).

3. David Kolb, *Experiential Learning: Experience as the Source of Learning and Development* (Saddle River, NJ: Prentice-Hall, 1984).

4. Elaine Cox, "Coaching and Adult Learning: Theory and Practice," *New Directions for Adult and Continuing Education* 148 (2015): 27–38.

5. For more information, see https://www.wgu.edu/blog/adult-learning-theories-principles2004.html.

6. William Baker and James Sinkula, "The Synergistic Effect of Market Orientation and Learning Orientation on Organizational Performance," *Journal of the Academy of Marketing Science* 199, no. 27 (1999): 411–427.

7. Andrea Ellinger, Alexander Ellinger, Baiyin Yang, and Shelly Howton, "Making the Business Case for the Learning Organization Concept," *Advances in Developing Human Resources* 5, no. 2 (May 2003): 163–172, doi: 10.1177/1523422303251359.

8. Tomas Chamorro-Premuzic and Josh Bersin, "Four Ways to Create a Learning Culture on Your Team," *Harvard Business Review*, July 12, 2018.

9. Kristen De Vito, "Implementing Adult Learning Principles to Overcome Barriers of Learning in Continuing Higher Education," *Online Journal of Workforce Education and Development* III, no. 4 (2009); Kobena Osam, Matt Bergman, and Denise Cumberland, "An Integrative Literature Review on the Barriers Impacting Adult Learners' Return to College," *Adult Learning* 28, no. 2 (May 2017): 54–60.

10. Strada Education Network, "Public Viewpoint," September 16, 2020.

11. Integrated Postsecondary Education Data System (IPEDS), "Fall Enrollment Survey" (IPEDS-EF:86–99); IPEDS Spring 2001 Through Spring 2019, Fall Enrollment component; and Enrollment in Degree-Granting Institutions Projection Model, 2000 Through 2029.

12. Strada Education Network, "Public Viewpoint."

13. Osam, Bergman, and Cumberland, "An Integrative Literature Review."

14. Chi Zhang and Guangzhi Zheng, "Supporting Adult Learning: Enablers, Barriers, and Services," Proceedings of the 14th annual ACM SIGITE Conference on Information Technology Education, October 2013, 151–152, http://dx.doi.org/10.1145/2512276.2512323.

15. Ibid.; John Comings, "Persistence: Helping Adult Education Students Reach Their Goals," *Review of Adult Learning and Literacy* 7, no. 2 (2007): 23–46.

16. Thomas Bailey and Donna Merritt, *Making Sense of Industry Based Skill Standards* (Berkeley, CA: National Center for Research in Vocational Education, 1995).

17. Vincent Daniels, "Assessing the Value of Certification Preparation Programs in Higher Education," *American Journal of Business Education* 4, no. 6 (2011).

18. Lisa Davies, "Skills Recognition and Recognition of Prior Learning for Workforce Development: Challenges and Possibilities," in *Workforce Development*, ed. Roger Harris and Thomas Short (Singapore: Springer, 2014), https://doi.org/10.1007/978-981-4560-58-0_5.

19. Michelle LaPointe and Jason Wingard, "How Did We Get Here? A History of

Education and Training in the United States," In *Learning for Life: How Continuous Education Will Keep Us Competitive in the Global Knowledge Economy*, 3–9 (New York: AMACOM, 2016).

20. Davies, "Skills Recognition and Recognition of Prior Learning for Workforce Development."

21. Ambreen Ali, "Skill Maps and Skill Gaps: Improved Transparency for Workforce Talent," Smartbrief.com, April 27, 2020, https://www.smartbrief.com/original/2020/04/skill-maps-and-skill-gaps-improved-transparency-workforce-talent.

22. Sundar Subramaniam, founder and director, Authess, interview by the author, October 28, 2020.

23. John Bryson, Barbara Crosby, and Melissa Middleton Stone, "The Design and Implementation of Cross-Sector Collaborations: Propositions from the Literature," *Public Administration Review* 66 no. 1 (2006): 44–55.

24. Howard Buffett and Willima Eimicke, *Social Value Investing: A Management Framework for Effective Partnerships* (New York: Columbia University Press, 2018).

25. Ravi Aron, Jahyun Goo, Vijay Gurbaxani, Kunsoo Han, Rudy Hirschheim, Julia Kotlarsky, Mary C. Lacity, Natalia Levina, Ilan Oshri, Jeanne W. Ross, Ning Su, and Leslie P. Willcocks, "The Long-Tail Strategy of IT Outsourcing," *MIT Sloan Management Review*, 2016.

26. Young Bong Chang and Vijay Gurbaxani, "Information Technology Outsourcing, Knowledge Transfer, and Firm Productivity: An Empirical Analysis," *MIS Quarterly* 36, no. 4 (December 2012): 1043–1063, https://www.jstor.org/stable/41703497.

27. For more information, see www.p21.org.

28. Peter Cappelli, *Why Good People Can't Get Jobs: The Skills Gap and What Companies Can Do About It* (Philadelphia: Wharton Digital Press, June 2012); Deborah Stevenson and Jo Ann Starkweather, "PM Critical Competency Index: IT Execs Prefer Soft Skills," *International Journal of Project Management* 28, no. 7 (2010): 663–671, https://doi.org/10.1016/j.ijproman.2009.11.008.

29. Jessie Koen, Ute-Christine Klehe, and Annelies E. M. Van Vianen, "Training Career Adaptability to Facilitate a Successful School-to-Work Transition," *Journal of Vocational Behavior* 81, no. 3 (2012): 395–408, https://doi.org/10.1016/j.jvb.2012.10.003.

30. Sharmila Chatterjee and Arjun Chaudhuri, "Are Trusted Brands Important?" *The Marketing Management Journal* 15, no. 1 (Spring 2005): 1–16.

31. Susan Spiggle, Hang Nguyen, and Mary Caravella, "More Than Fit: Brand Extension Authenticity," *Journal of Marketing Research* XLIX (2012): 967–983.

32. Sinead Cooke and Paul Ryan, "Brand Alliances: From Reputation Endorsement to Collaboration on Core Competencies," *Irish Marketing Review* 2 (2000): 36–41, http://search.proquest.com.ezp-prod1.hul.harvard.edu/docview/204581366?accountid=11311.

Chapter 9

1. Scott Galloway, *Post Corona: From Crisis to Opportunity* (New York: Penguin, 2020).

2. Yohanes Honu, "United States' Higher Education Cost and Value: Opposing Views," *Academy of Educational Leadership Journal* 23 (2019): 1–12.

3. Matt Tatham, "Student Loan Debt Climbs to $1.4 trillion in 2019," Experian Research, July 24, 2019, https://www.experian.com/blogs/ask-experian/state-of-student-loan-debt/.

4. Hart Research Associates, *Fulfilling the American Dream: Liberal Education and the Future of Work: Selected Findings from Online Surveys of Business Executives and Hiring Managers* (Washington, DC: Association of American Colleges and Universities, 2018.

5. Kirk Carapezza, "Some Private Colleges Slash Tuition Price Tags, Hoping to Stay Competitive During Pandemic," WGBH News, May 6, 2020, https://www.wgbh.org/news/education/2020/05/06/some-private-colleges-slash-tuition-price-tags-hoping-to-stay-competitive-during-pandemic; Scott Jaschik, "Grinnell Pulls Loans from Aid Packages," *Inside Higher Ed*, November 23, 2020, https://www.insidehighered.com/admissions/article/2020/11/23/grinnell-eliminates-loans-citing-coronavirus.

6. Honu, "United States' Higher Education Cost and Value."

7. Richard Axt, *The Federal Government and Financing Higher Education* (New York: Columbia University Press, for the Commission on Financing Higher Education, 1952).

8. U.S. Department of Education, "About Ed: The Federal Role in Education," last modified June 15, 2021, https://www2.ed.gov/about/overview/fed/role.html.

9. Michael Simkovic, "Risk-Based Student Loans," *Washington and Lee Law Review* 70, no. 1 (September 5, 2011): 527, http://dx.doi.org/10.2139/ssrn.1941070.

10. Kobena Osam, Matt Bergman, and Denise Cumberland, "An Integrative Literature Review on the Barriers Impacting Adult Learners' Return to College," *Adult Learning* 28, no. 2 (May 2017): 54–60; Richard Kazis, Abigail Callahan, Chris Davidson, Annie McLeod, Brian Bosworth, Vickie Choitzand, and John Hoops, *Adult Learners in Higher Education: Barriers to Success and Strategies to Improve Results. Employment and Training Administration* (Boston: Jobs for the Future, 2007).

11. Anthony Carnevale, *Postsecondary Education and Training as We Know It Is Not Enough: Why We Need to Leaven Postsecondary Strategy with More Attention to Employment Policy, Social Policy, and Career and Technical Education in High School*, paper prepared for the Georgetown University and Urban Institute Conference on Reducing Poverty and Economic Distress After ARRA, January 15, 2010, https://www.urban.org/sites/default/files/publication/28536/412071-Postsecondary-Education-and-Training-As-We-Know-It-Is-Not-Enough.PDF.

12. Matt Foster, "New Department for Business, Energy, and Industry," Civil Service World, July 14, 2016, https://www.civilserviceworld.com/professions/article/new-department-for-business-energy-and-industrial-strategy-swallows-up-decc-and-bis-full-details-and-reaction.

13. For more information, see https://www.admin.ch/gov/en/start/departments/department-of-economic-affairs-education-research-eaer.html.

14. Dan Clawson, "Tenure and the Future of the University," *Science* 324, no. 5931 (May 29, 2009): 1147–1148, doi: 10.1126/science.1172995.

15. Ibid.

16. T. J. McCue, "57 Million U.S. Workers Are Part of the Gig Economy," *Forbes Magazine*, August 31, 2018, https://www.forbes.com/sites/tjmccue/2018/08/31/57-million-u-s-workers-are-part-of-the-gig-economy/?sh=446c397f7118.

17. Alan Krueger and Seth Harris, *A Proposal for Modernizing Labor Laws for Twenty-First-Century Work: The "Independent Worker"* (Washington, DC: Hamilton Project, Brookings Institution, 2015).

18. McCue, "57 Million U.S. Workers Are Part of the Gig Economy."

19. Ernst & Young, *Global Generations: A Global Study on Work-Life Challenges Across Generations* (London: Ernst & Young, 2015).

20. Krueger and Harris, *A Proposal for Modernizing Labor Laws*.

21. Sampsa Samila and Olav Sorensen, "Venture Capital, Entrepreneurship, and Economic Growth," *Review of Economics and Statistics* 93, no. 1 (February 2011): 338–349, https://doi.org/10.1162/REST_a_00066.

22. National Venture Capital Association, "Q4 2019 NVCA VENTURE MONITOR," Pitchbook, 2020, https://files.pitchbook.com/website/files/pdf/Q4_2019_PitchBook_NVCA_Venture_Monitor.pdf.

23. Ibid.

24. Tim Bird, "Top 5 Sectors Attracting Venture Capital Finance in 2019," *Growth-Business*, March 12, 2019, https://www.growthbusiness.co.uk/top-5-sectors-venture-capital-2019-2556086/.

25. Josh Slayton, Joe Watt, Danica Nilsestuen, Joe Kirgues, and Troy Vosseller, "Education and Workforce Innovation: Investment Trends Report," PitchBook and On-Ramps Education and Workforce Innovation, 2020, https://sstatic1.squarespace.com/static/5e1cdd7f6e7236735f1d91a7/t/5fb6b852b8ec6e359e36c38f/1605810266235/Pitc hBook+x+OnRamp+Education+and+Workforce+Innovation+Investor+Report+2020. pdf?utm_medium=email&_hsmi=100880741&_hsenc=p2ANqtz-8uD4CEQM2M-NokWXFmWO_Iow2LWQs7pGBPXyIKl5K848-Gk_MFtySWcgDBm0_jP5q5imF-7FExeRpwtxB_cX7ZFU4t1duQ&utm_content=100880741&utm_source=hs_email.

26. Tony Wan, "US Edtech Raises $803M in First Half of 2020 as COVID-19 Forces Learning Online," EdSurge.com, July 29, 2020, https://www.edsurge.com/news/2020-07-29-us-edtech-raises-803m-in-first-half-of-2020-as-covid-19-forces-learning-online.

BIBLIOGRAPHY

Ali, Ambreen. *Skill Maps and Skill Gaps: Improved Transparency for Workforce Talent.* Smartbrief.com, April 27, 2020. https://www.smartbrief.com/original/2020/04/skill-maps-and-skill-gaps-improved-transparency-workforce-talent.

Aron, Ravi, Jahyun Goo, Vijay Gurbaxani, Kunsoo Han, Rudy Hirschheim, Julia Kotlarsky, Mary C. Lacity, Natalia Levina, Ilan Oshri, Jeanne W. Ross, Ning Su, and Leslie P. Willcocks. "The Long-Tail Strategy of IT Outsourcing," *MIT Sloan Management Review,* 2016.

AWPAB Data Transparency Working Group. *White Paper on Interoperable Learning Records.* Washington, DC: American Workforce Policy Advisory Board, September 2019. https://www.imsglobal.org/sites/default/files/articles/ILR_White_Paper_FINAL_EBOOK.pdf.

Axt, Richard. *The Federal Government and Financing Higher Education.* New York: Columbia University Press, for the Commission on Financing Higher Education, 1952.

Bailey, Thomas, and Donna Merritt. *Making Sense of Industry Based Skill Standards.* Berkeley, CA: National Center for Research in Vocational Education, 1995.

Baker, William, and James Sinkula. "The Synergistic Effect of Market Orientation and Learning Orientation on Organizational Performance." *Journal of the Academy of Marketing Science* 199, no. 27 (1999): 411–427.

Bakhshi, Hasan, Jonathan Downing, Michael Osborne, and Phillipe Schneider. *The Future of Skills: Employment in 2030.* London: Pearson and Nesta. 2017. media.nesta.org.uk.

Bariso, Justin. "Google Has a Plan to Disrupt the College Degree." *Inc.,* August 19, 2020.

Bauer-Wolf, Jeremy. "Survey: Employers Want 'Soft Skills' From Graduates." *Inside Higher Ed* (January 17, 2019). https://www.insidehighered.com/quicktakes/2019/01/17/survey-employers-want-soft-skills-graduates.

Belkin, Douglas. "Is This the End of College as We Know It?" *Wall Street Journal,* November 12, 2020. https://www.wsj.com/articles/is-this-the-end-of-college-as-we-know-it-11605196909.

Bersin, Josh. *Rethinking the Build vs. Buy Approach to Talent: How Savvy Employers are*

Building Tech Skills from Within. Whiteboard Advisors, October 2019, https://josh-bersin.com./wp-content/uploads/2019/10_Build_vs_buy_Bersin_1.0.pdf.

Bird, Tim. "Top 5 Sectors Attracting Venture Capital Finance in 2019." *GrowthBusiness*, March 12, 2019. https://www.growthbusiness.co.uk/top-5-sectors-venture-capital-2019-2556086/.

Boston Globe Editorial Staff. "Vocational School Admissions Need a Fix." *Boston Globe*, October 26, 2020. https://www.bostonglobe.com/2020/10/26/opinion/vocational-school-admissions-need-fix/.

Bryson, John, Barbara Crosby, and Melissa Middleton Stone. "The Design and Implementation of Cross-Sector Collaborations: Propositions from the Literature." *Public Administration Review* 66, no. 1 (2006): 44–55.

Buffett, Howard, and Willima Eimicke. *Social Value Investing: A Management Framework for Effective Partnerships*. New York: Columbia University Press, 2018.

Businesswire. *Strategic Education, Inc. and Noodle Partners Unite to Provide Employers with Access to a Variety of Education and Upskilling Programs from the Nation's Leading Universities*. Sept. 21, 2020. https://www.businesswire.com/news/home/20200921005210/en/Strategic-Education-Inc.-and-Noodle-Partners-Unite-to-Provide-Employers-with-Access-to-a-Variety-of-Education-and-Upskilling-Programs-from-the-Nation%E2%80%99s-Leading-Universities.

Cappelli, Peter. *Why Good People Can't Get Jobs: The Skills Gap and What Companies Can Do About It*. Philadelphia: Wharton Digital Press, June 2012.

Carapezza, Kirk. "Some Private Colleges Slash Tuition Price Tags, Hoping to Stay Competitive During Pandemic." WGBH News, May 6, 2020. https://www.wgbh.org/news/education/2020/05/06/some-private-colleges-slash-tuition-price-tags-hoping-to-stay-competitive-during-pandemic.

Carnevale, Anthony. *Postsecondary Education and Training as We Know It Is Not Enough: Why We Need to Leaven Postsecondary Strategy with More Attention to Employment Policy, Social Policy, and Career and Technical Education in High School*. Paper prepared for the Georgetown University and Urban Institute Conference on Reducing Poverty and Economic Distress After ARRA, January 15, 2010. https://www.urban.org/sites/default/files/publication/28536/412071-Postsecondary-Education-and-Training-As-We-Know-It-Is-Not-Enough.PDF.

Chamorro-Premuzic, Tomas, and Josh Bersin. "Four Ways to Create a Learning Culture on Your Team." *Harvard Business Review*, July 12, 2018.

Chamorro-Premuzic, Tomas, and Becky Frankiewicz. "Does Higher Education Still Prepare People for Jobs?" *Harvard Business Review*, January 7, 2019.

Chang, Young Bong, and Vijay Gurbaxani. "Information Technology Outsourcing, Knowledge Transfer, and Firm Productivity: An Empirical Analysis" *MIS Quarterly* 36, no. 44 (December 2012): 1043–1063. https://www.jstor.org/stable/41703497.

Chatterjee, Sharmila, and Arjun Chaudhuri. "Are Trusted Brands Important?" *The Marketing Management Journal* 15, no. 1 (Spring 2005): 1–16.

Cheng, Michelle. "A Popular Job Site for the College Set Is Now Open to Students at Any US Four-Year School." *Quartz*, August 20, 2019. https://qz.com/work/1690572/handshake-opens-to-all-students-attending-four-year-colleges-in-the-us/.

Clawson, Dan. "Tenure and the Future of the University." *Science* 324, no. 5931 (May 29, 2009): 1147–1148. doi: 10.1126/science.1172995.

Comings, John. "Persistence: Helping Adult Education Students Reach Their Goals." *Review of Adult Learning and Literacy* 7, no. 2 (2007): 23–46.

Consumer Technology Association. *Future of Work: 2020 CTA Member Survey*. Arlington, VA: Consumer Technology Association, October 2020. https://shop.cta.tech/collections/research/products/future-of-work-2020-cta-member-survey.

Cooke, Sinead, and Paul Ryan. "Brand Alliances: From Reputation Endorsement to Collaboration on Core Competencies." *Irish Marketing Review* 2 (2000): 36–41. http://search.proquest.com.ezp-prod1.hul.harvard.edu/docview/204581366?accountid=11311.

Cox, Elaine. "Coaching and Adult Learning: Theory and Practice." *New Directions for Adult and Continuing Education* no. 148 (2015): 27–38.

Crapuchettes, Andrew. "CEO Address." Emsi20 Conference, 2020. https://www.economicmodeling.com/video/ceo-address/.

Custers, Eugène J. F. M., and Olle Ten Cate. "The History of Medical Education in Europe and the United States, with Respect to Time and Proficiency." *Academic Medicine* 93 (March 2018): S49–S54. doi:10.1097/ACM.0000000000002079

Daly, Mary C., Shelby R. Buckman, and Lily M. Seitelman. "The Unequal Impact of COVID-19: Why Education Matters." Economic Letter, Federal Reserve Bank of San Francisco, June 29, 2020. https://www.frbsf.org/economic-research/publications/economic-letter/2020/june/unequal-impact-covid-19-why-education-matters.

Daniels, Vincent. "Assessing the Value of Certification Preparation Programs in Higher Education." *American Journal of Business Education* 4, no. 6 (2011).

Davies, Lisa. "Skills Recognition and Recognition of Prior Learning for Workforce Development: Challenges and Possibilities." In *Workforce Development*, ed. Roger Harris and Thomas Short. Singapore: Springer, 2014. https://doi.org/10.1007/978-981-4560-58-0_5.

De Vito, Kristen. "Implementing Adult Learning Principles to Overcome Barriers of Learning in Continuing Higher Education." *Online Journal of Workforce Education and Development* III, no. 4 (2009).

Douglas-Gabriel, Danielle. "Students Now Pay More of Their Public University Tuition Than State Governments." *Washington Post*, May 1, 2015. https://www.washingtonpost.com/news/get-there/wp/2015/01/05/students-cover-more-of-their-public-university-tuition-now-than-state-governments/.

Ellinger, Andrea, Alexander Ellinger, Baiyin Yang, and Shelly Howton. "Making the Business Case for the Learning Organization Concept." *Advances in Developing Human Resources* 5, no. 2 (May 2003): 163–172. doi: 10.1177/1523422303251359.

Emsi. *The New Geography of Skills*. Indianapolis: Strada Education Network, December 10, 2019. https://www.stradaeducation.org/report/the-new-geography-of-skills/.

Ernst & Young. *Global Generations: A Global Study on Work-Life Challenges Across Generations*. London: Ernst & Young, 2015.

Experian Research. "Student Loan Debt Climbs." July 24, 2019. https://www.experian.com/blogs/ask-experian/state-of-student-loan-debt/.

Foster, Matt. "New Department for Business, Energy, and Industry." Civil Service World, July 14, 2016. https://www.civilserviceworld.com/professions/article/new-department-for-business-energy-and-industrial-strategy-swallows-up-decc-and-bis-full-details-and-reaction.

Friedman, Thomas. "After the Pandemic, a Revolution in Education and Work Awaits." *New York Times*, October 20, 2020. https://www.nytimes.com/2020/10/20/opinion/covid-education-work.html?referringSource=articleShare.

Friedman, Zack. "Student Loan Debt Statistics in 2019: A $1.5 Trillion Crisis." *Forbes*, February 25, 2019.

Galloway, Scott. *Post Corona: From Crisis to Opportunity*. New York: Penguin, 2020.

General Assembly. "General Assembly's Student Outcomes Report," General Assembly Blog, June 16, 2020. https://generalassemb.ly/blog/outcomes-report-2018-2019/?utm_source=twitter&utm_medium=social&utm_campaign=outcomes-report-2018-2019.

Gordon, Scott. *Gaps in the "Skills Gap" Debate Over Wisconsin Jobs*. WisContext, August 29, 2016. https://www.wiscontext.org/gaps-skills-gap-debate-over-wisconsin-jobs.

Graham, Patricia. *Community and Class in American Education, 1865 to 1918*. New York: Wiley, 1974.

Grubb, Farley. "Growth of Literacy in Colonial America: Longitudinal Patterns, Economic Models, and the Direction of Future Research." *Social Science History* 14, no. 4 (Winter 1990): 451–482. doi:10.1017/S0145553200020897.

Guild Education. "Case Study: How Chipotle Improved Retention by Deepening Its Commitment to Mission." November 2020. http://biz.guildeducation.com/rs/003-XMG-066/images/Chipotle-Case-Study-V2-11_11_20.pdf.

Guzman, Zack. "How This Startup Is Connecting Graduates to 'New Collar' Jobs Amid COVID-19." Yahoo Finance, October 20, 2020. https://finance.yahoo.com/video/startup-connecting-graduates-collar-jobs-184725935.html.

Handlin, Oscar, and Mary F. Handlin. *The American College and American Culture: Socialization as a Function of Higher Education*. New York: McGraw-Hill, 1970.

Handshake. "Virtual Career Fairs Are Here! Next Stop: Getting Hired." https://learn.joinhandshake.com/students/virtual-career-fairs-are-here-next-stop-getting-hired/.

Hart Research Associates. *Falling Short? College Learning and Career Success.* Washington, DC: Association of American Colleges and Universities, 2015.

——. *Fulfilling the American Dream: Liberal Education and the Future of Work: Selected Findings from Online Surveys of Business Executives and Hiring Managers.* Washington, DC: Association of American Colleges and Universities, 2018.

Honu, Yohanes A. K.. "United States' Higher Education Cost and Value: Opposing Views." *The Academy of Educational Leadership Journal* 23 (2019): 1–12.

Hubler, Shawn. "Colleges Slash Budgets in the Pandemic, with 'Nothing Off-Limits.'" *New York Times,* November 2, 2020.

Humez, Andrea, and Nikki James. "Practera: An Online Platform to Support and Scaffold Experiential Learning." 2019 Connected Learning Summit, 2019.

——. "Using Technology to Scaffold Experiential Learning Programs Based on Student Skill Level." 48th Annual Conference of the National Society for Experiential Learning, 2019. https://par.nsf.gov/biblio/10173801.

Illanes, Pablo, Susan Lund, Mona Mourshed, Scott Rutherford, and Magnus Tyreman. *Retraining and Reskilling Workers in the Age of Automation.* McKinsey & Company, January 2018. https://www.mckinsey.com/featured-insights/future-of-work/retraining-and-reskilling-workers-in-the-age-of-automation.

Investopedia, LLC. "Student Loans in 2019: A Snapshot." November 15, 2019. https://www.investopedia.com/student-loan-debt-2019-statistics-and-outlook-4772007.

James, Nikki, Andrea Humez, and Philipp Laufenberg. "Using Technology to Structure and Scaffold Real World Experiential Learning in Distance Education." *TechTrends* v.64 (2020). doi:10.1007/s11528-020-00515-2.

Jaschik, Scott. "Grinnell Pulls Loans from Aid Packages." *Inside Higher Ed,* November 23, 2020. https://www.insidehighered.com/admissions/article/2020/11/23/grinnell-eliminates-loans-citing-coronavirus.

——. "Well-Prepared in Their Own Eyes." *Inside Higher Ed,* January 20, 2015. https://www.insidehighered.com/news/2015/01/20/study-finds-big-gaps-between-student-and-employer-perceptions.

Kazis, Richard, Abigail Callahan, Chris Davidson, Annie McLeod, Brian Bosworth, Vickie Choitzand, and John Hoops. *Adult Learners in Higher Education: Barriers to Success and Strategies to Improve Results: Employment and Training Administration.* Boston: Jobs for the Future, 2007.

Knowles, Malcom. "Andragogy, not Pedagogy." *Adult Leadership* 16, no. 10 (1968): 350–352.

Koen, Jessie, Ute-Christine Klehe, and Annelies E. M. Van Vianen. "Training Career Adaptability to Facilitate a Successful School-to-Work Transition." *Journal of Vocational Behavior* 81, no. 3 (2012): 395–408, https://doi.org/10.1016/j.jvb.2012.10.003.

Kolb, David A. *Experiential Learning: Experience as the Source of Learning and Development.* Saddle River, NJ: Prentice-Hall, 1984.

Kolodner, Meredith. "Why Are Low-Income Students not Showing Up to College, Even Though They Have Been Accepted?" The Hechinger Report, August 14, 2015. https://hechingerreport.org/why-are-low-income-students-not-showing-up-to-college-even-though-they-have-been-accepted/.

Krueger, Alan, and Seth Harris. *A Proposal for Modernizing Labor Laws for Twenty-First-Century Work: The "Independent Worker."* Washington, DC: Hamilton Project, Brookings Institution, 2015.

Krug, Edward. *The Shaping of the American High School, 1880–1920.* New York: Harper & Row, 1964.

Labaree, David F. "Learning to Love the Bomb: The Cold War Brings the Best of Times to American Higher Education." In *Educational Research: Discourses of Change and Changes in Discourse*, ed. Paul Smeyers and Marc Depaepe, 101–117. Dordrecht: Springer, 2016. doi: 10.1007/978-3-319-30456-4_9.

Laderman, Sophia, and Andrew Carlson. *SHEF: 2017 State Higher Education Finance.* Boulder, CO: State Higher Education Executive Officers Association, 2017. http://www.sheeo.org/sites/default/files/SHEF_FY2017.pdf.

LeBlanc, Paul. "Unveiling SNHU's 201802023 Strategic Plan." President's Corner. Posted October 16, 2018, http://www.blogging.snhu.edu.

Lemoie, Kerrie, and Louis Soares. *Connected Impact: Unlocking Education and Workforce Opportunity Through Blockchain.* Washington, DC: American Council on Education, 2020.

Lord, Garrett. "Expanding Our Efforts to Help All Students Find Opportunity." Handshake, accessed November 7, 2020. https://learn.joinhandshake.com/our-team/expanding-our-efforts-to-help-all-students-find-opportunity/.

———. "Expanding Our Impact to Further Our Mission." Handshake.com, accessed November 7, 2020. https://learn.joinhandshake.com/our-team/expanding-our-impact/.

McCue, T. J. "57 Million U.S. Workers Are Part of the Gig Economy." *Forbes Magazine*, August 31, 2018. https://www.forbes.com/sites/tjmccue/2018/08/31/57-million-u-s-workers-are-part-of-the-gig-economy/?sh=446c397f7118.

McGarry, Kaye. *The Skills Gap: Employers Expect More Than What College Grads Offer.* Raleigh, NC: The James G. Martin Center for Academic Renewal, April 3, 2018. https://www.jamesgmartin.center/2018/04/skills-gap-employers-expect-college-grads-offer/.

McKenzie, Lindsay. "A Long-Term Bet on Employer-Assisted Tuition Programs: Strategic Education and Noodle Partners Bet Big on Employer-Assisted Tuition Programs." *Inside Higher Ed*, September 22, 2020. https://www.insidehighered.com/news/2020/09/22strategic-educatio-and-noodle-partners-bet-big-employer-assisted-tuition-programs.

McMurray, Stephen, Matthew Dutton, Ronald McQuaid, and Alec Richard. "Employer

Demands from Business Graduates." *Education and Training* 58, no. 1 (2016): 112–132. https://doi.org/10.1108/ET-02-2014-0017.

Mulesoft. "What Is an API?" https://www.mulesoft.com/resources/api/what-is-an-api.

National Venture Capital Association. "Q4 2019 NVCA VENTURE MONITOR." Pitchbook, 2020. https://files.pitchbook.com/website/files/pdf/Q4_2019_PitchBook_NVCA_Venture_Monitor.pdf.

Nierenberg, Amelia, and Adam Pasick. "Coronavirus Briefing." *New York Times*, October 26, 2020.

Olsen, James S. *Encyclopedia of the Industrial Revolution in America*. Santa Barbara, CA: Greenwood, 2002.

Osam, Kobena, Matt Bergman, and Denise Cumberland. "An Integrative Literature Review on the Barriers Impacting Adult Learners' Return to College." *Adult Learning* 28, no. 2 (May 2017): 54–60.

Palmer, Kelly, and David Blake. *The Expertise Economy: How the Smartest Companies Use Learning to Engage, Compete, and Succeed, Illustrated Edition*. Boston: Nicholas Brealey, 2018.

Practera. *Effective Experiential Learning: Practitioners Guide*. Sydney: Practera, 2018.

Rhe, Nicholas, Janice Black, and Kay Keels. "Are We Teaching What Employers Want? Identifying and Remedying Gaps Between Employer Needs, Accreditor Prescriptions, and Undergraduate Curricular Priorities." *Industry and Higher Education* 33, no. 6 (2019): 362–369.

Samila, Sampsa, and Olav Sorensen. "Venture Capital, Entrepreneurship, and Economic Growth." *Review of Economics and Statistics* 93, no. 1 (February 2011): 338–349. https://doi.org/10.1162/REST_a_00066.

Siemens, George. *Connectivism: Learning as Network Creation*. Alexandria, VA: American Society for Training and Development, 2005.

Simkovic, Michael. "Risk-Based Student Loans." *Washington and Lee Law Review* 70, no. 1 (September 5, 2011): 527. http://dx.doi.org/10.2139/ssrn.1941070.

Slayton, Josh, Joe Watt, Danica Nilsestuen, Joe Kirgues, and Troy Vosseller. "Education and Workforce Innovation: Investment Trends Report." PitchBook and OnRamps Education and Workforce Innovation, 2020. https://static1.squarespace.com/static/5e1cdd7f6e7236735f1d91a7/t/5fb6b852b8ec6e359e36c38f/1605810266235/PitchBook+x+OnRamp+Education+and+Workforce+Innovation+Investor+Report+2020.pdf?utm_medium=email&_hsmi=100880741&_hsenc=p2ANqtz-8uD4CEQM2MNokWXFmWO_Iow2LWQs7pGBPXyIKl5K848-Gk_MFtySWcgDBmo_jP5q5imF7FExeRpwtxB_cX7ZFU4t1duQ&utm_content=100880741&utm_source=hs_email.

Snyder, Thomas. *120 Years of American Education: A Statistical Portrait*. Washington, DC: National Center for Education Statistics, 1993.

Society for Human Resource Management. *The New Talent Landscape: Recruiting Dif-*

ficulty and Skills Shortages. Alexandria, Virginia: SHRM, 2016. https://www.shrm. org/hr-today/trends-and-forecasting/research-and-surveys/pages/talent-landscape. aspx.

Spiggle, Susan, Hang Nguyen, and Mary Caravella. "More Than Fit: Brand Extension Authenticity." *Journal of Marketing Research* XLIX (2012): 967–983.

Stevenson, Deborah, and Jo Ann Starkweather. "PM Critical Competency Index: IT Execs Prefer Soft Skills." *International Journal of Project Management* 28, no. 7 (2010): 663–671. https://doi.org/10.1016/j.ijproman.2009.11.008.

Strada Education Network. "Public Viewpoint: COVID-19 Work and Education Survey." November 12, 2020. https://www.stradaeducation.org/publicviewpoint/?_hsmi=98291738&_ hsenc=p2ANqtz-9dSlSVKdehoFhcseDNEDvOA8eXllyBLZcyjD2gh-1Qm7Z4dSvoT15lKSs-TOGKsZ57b_phbmnh5AJWsGDTh4PwIKluP9Q&utm_medium=email&utm_ content=98291738&utm_source=hs_email.

Taylor, Chris. "How College Students Can Find Jobs—Without Much Work Experience." Reuters, April 9, 2019. https://www.reuters.com/article/us-world-work-firstjobs/how-college-students-can-find-jobs-without-much-work-experience-idUSKCN1RL15H.

Thelin, John. " 'Free College' in Historical Perspective." *History News Network*, February 16, 2020. https://historynewsnetwork.org/article/174324.

———. *A History of American Higher Education*. Baltimore: Johns Hopkins University Press, 2019.

Thelin, John, and Marybeth Gasman. "Historical Overview of American Higher Education." In *Student Services: A Handbook for the Profession*, ed. John H. Schuh, Susan R Jones, and Shaun R Harper. Hoboken, NJ: Wiley, 2010.

Thomson, Ross. "The Continuity of Innovation: The Civil War Experience." *Enterprise and Society* 11, no. 1 (2012): 128–165. *Project MUSE*. Oxford University Press.

Tudy, Randy. "Employers' Satisfaction on the Performance of New College Graduates." *Slongan* 3 (2017).

U.S. Bureau of Labor Statistics. *Economic News Release: Employment Situation Summary*. Washington, DC: U.S. Department of Labor, November 6, 2020. https://www.bls. gov/news.release/empsit.nro.htm.

U.S. Department of Education. "About Ed: The Federal Role in Education." Last modified June 15, 2021. https://www2.ed.gov/about/overview/fed/role.html.

———. "Enrollment in Degree-Granting Institutions Projection Model, 2000 Through 2029." *Integrated Postsecondary Education Data System*.Washington, DC: U.S. Department of Education.

———. "Fall Enrollment in Colleges and Universities Surveys, 1966 Through 1985." *Higher Education General Information Survey (HEGIS)*. Washington, DC: U.S. Department of Education.

———. "IPEDS Spring 2001 Through Spring 2019, Fall Enrollment Component." *Inte-*

*grated Postsecondary Education Data System.*Washington, DC: U.S. Department of Education.

U.S. Department of Labor. "What Is Apprenticeship?" *Jump Start Your Career Through Apprenticeship.* Washington, DC: Department of Labor. https://www.apprenticeship. gov/become-apprentice.

U.S. Secretary of Education Betsy DeVos, prepared remarks to Federal Student Aid's Training Conference, November 27, 2018, https://contractwithamerica2.com/De-Vos-speech_11-27-2018_PDF.pdf.

Verougstraete, Remie. "Using Skills to Build Interoperable Learning Records." Emsi, November 17, 2020. https://www.economicmodeling.com/2020/11/17/skills-interoperable-learner-records/.

Wan, Tony. "US Edtech Raises \$803M in First Half of 2020 as COVID-19 Forces Learning Online." EdSurge.com, July 29, 2020. https://www.edsurge.com/news/2020-07-29-us-edtech-raises-803m-in-first-half-of-2020-as-covid-19-forces-learning-online.

Wilkie, Dana. "Employers Say Students Aren't Learning Soft Skills in College." Society for Human Resource Management, October 21, 2019. https://www.shrm.org/resourcesandtools/hr-topics/employee-relations/pages/employers-say-students-arent-learning-soft-skills-in-college.aspx.

Wilson, Alexandra, and Susan Adams. "Class Act: This 31-Year-Old's Company Rocketed to a \$1 Billion Valuation Helping Workers Get Degrees." *Forbes Magazine,* December 19, 2019. https://www.forbes.com/sites/alexandrawilson1/2019/12/19/make-colleges-pay-the-31-year-old-whose-company-rocketed-to-a-1-billion-valuation-helping-workers-get-degrees/?sh=47307e1b75f6.

Wingard, Jason. *Learning to Succeed: Rethinking Corporate Education in a World of Unrelenting Change.* New York: AMACOM, 2015.

Wingard, Jason, and Christine Farrugia. *The Great Skills Gap: Optimizing Talent for the Future of Work.* Stanford, CA: Stanford University Press, 2021.

Wingard, Jason, and Michelle LaPointe. *Learning for Life: How Continuous Education Will Keep Us Competitive in the Global Knowledge Economy.* New York: AMACOM, 2016.

World Economic Forum. "The Future of Jobs Report 2018." *Centre for the New Economy and Society Insight Report.* Geneva: World Economic Forum, 2018. www3.weforum. org/WEF Future of Jobs 2018.

Zhang, Chi, and Guangzhi Zheng. "Supporting Adult Learning: Enablers, Barriers, and Services." Proceedings of the 14th annual ACM SIGITE Conference on Information Technology Education, October 2013, 151–152. http://dx.doi.org/10.1145/2512276.2512323.

INDEX

Lightning Source UK Ltd.
Milton Keynes UK
UKHW010232290622
405088UK00004B/100/J